ONE INCH ABOVE THE WATER

One Inch
above the
Water

Running away on America's rivers

Jim Payne

LYTTON PUBLISHING COMPANY
Established 1975
Sandpoint, Idaho

ISBN 9780915728190
LCCN 2008903264

Interior layout by Heather McElwain
Cover design by Heather McElwain, Doug Fluckiger
Front cover graphic created with photographs by John Gordy and
    Jens Olson
Back cover photographs by Jim Payne
Maps by Doug Fluckiger, Christine Barrett

For a photo album of Jim's adventures go to
www.oneinchabovethewater.com

Table of Contents

Maps

Introduction

AT AGE 57, I RAN AWAY FROM HOME. Despite what the calendar said about my years and despite the furrows on my brow, inside me was a boy that needed to come out. This latter-day youthful rebellion played itself out in long-distance solo kayak trips along the waterways of America.

When we are young, we are admonished to "Grow up!" The years pass and, gradually, we do. We become sober, mortgage-paying citizens with an image of responsibility to uphold, irritated when mud splashes our shoes, embarrassed when a spaghetti noodle flicks onto our nose. Caught up in this process of maturing like everyone else, I fathered children, paid the mortgage, and tried to vote Republican. I found myself inside a church more Sundays than not and stood in mortal danger of becoming a pillar of the community.

Still, a little voice kept telling me that I was losing a valuable part of myself. I don't object to the trappings of adulthood. Mortgages are fine. Churches are generally good things. My enemy was the adult mind, that rational, sensible part of the brain that says there should be an end to play and exploration. There's a far-off mountain peak towering in the sky, and the child in us says, "Wouldn't it be neat to climb it?" Then the grown-up replies, "But it's too far," or, "There might be an avalanche," or, "Don't we need a permit?" Maybe the job of the adult mind is to let the air out of the balloon of exuberance by thinking about what is safe and comfortable, but I didn't feel happy about it.

The youth that was bottled up inside of me expressed itself in petty ways, in the form of pranks and smart-aleck remarks. At my niece's wedding, my sisters and I joined Mom and Dad for a formal family photograph—probably, as we correctly suspected, the last picture of all five of us together. Just as the shutter was snapped, I made a "V" sign over Mom's head as she, poor dear, peered earnestly into the camera. For some reason my antic wasn't noticed at the time, and this proved to be the only useable image of the family together.

That picture stood in its gold frame on Mom's dresser in the nursing home, and I picked it up one day to inspect this droll but embarrassing portrait. She gave me a gentle shove. "You and your silliness!" she said, expressing exasperation mingled with maternal indulgence.

A few years later, family pictures were being taken for our church directory. As the photographer arranged my wife Judy and me in a dignified pose, I spotted some stuffed animals from the church nursery on the floor and picked one up. The directory was soon printed and distributed to all members of the congregation. Page after page showed photos of respectable adults striking decorous poses, and then there was ours: a guy with a cockeyed grin holding a skunk nibbling his wife's ear. The children of the church thought it was the funniest picture they'd ever seen. The adults didn't comment.

Reflections on my career also suggested it was time to indulge my youthful yearnings. By profession, I was an academic in the field of political science. My job was to research and analyze political institutions and write books about what I learned. When the first of these books was published, I held my breath, waiting for my ideas to be praised and adopted. Nothing happened. The world went on watching *Jeopardy!* and *Baywatch,* not an ounce wiser about the intricacies of political science I had just revealed. As the years passed, I was forced to conclude that practically no one read the books I wrote. Still, I consoled myself with the thought that some day they would. Maintaining this pale hope, I received a rude jolt when my first book was remaindered.

Aspiring writers dream of publishing a book, believing that once the hurdle of publication is cleared, they will have made a literary contribution of lasting value. Alas, books have a life cycle just like everything else. They are born, but they also die, and this death generally takes the form of a remainder letter. Yale University Press sent me a letter saying that my book was no longer selling and that instead of dumping the remaining copies in the landfill, they would sell them to me for 25 cents a copy.

I still have those two hundred copies in my attic, waiting to be shipped to anyone who will buy them. Over the years, I've steadily lowered my asking price. It now stands at 26 cents a copy.

The experience of seeing my books remaindered one after the other shook my sense of priorities. It suggested that the fruits of adult labors were by no means as important as adults profess. As the years of middle age accumulated, I keenly felt that I had only one life to live, that it was being used up at an alarming rate, and it would be cruel indeed to spend the rest of it cooped up in libraries looking things up to write down. And besides, my attic was full.

One thing that sets children apart is they are fascinated by unusual modes of travel, while adults endorse the fastest, easiest way. As a boy growing up in Leonia, New Jersey, I recall seldom using the sidewalk when there was an unorthodox way to get to my destination. My friends felt the same way. The map of town showed a grid of streets nicely laid out for the convenience of citizens, but they were largely wasted on us. We preferred footpaths and backyards—and vacant lots, swamps, alleys, driveways, and disused trolley lines. That these detours from prudent travel often made for muddy shoes was a point we overlooked—though perhaps our mothers did not. We were motivated by curiosity, by an inclination for risk, and perhaps also by a secret impulse to set ourselves apart from humdrum, rule-obeying humanity.

The travel deity we worship today is the motor vehicle, and streets and highways are its pantheon. We go to homes, stores, and jobs on roads; commerce flows on the same surfaces in vans, pickups, and semis. My instincts told me that to find an unexplored world I would have to leave motor vehicles and this web of asphalt and convenience behind.

In acting out my return to youth, then, it was fitting that I should gravitate toward watercraft. My original idea in buying a second-hand kayak, along with a helmet, life jacket, and Mitchell paddle for $100—what a deal!—wasn't to go anywhere in particular. I wanted something to putter with. The kayak was a means of transportation that, well, piqued my curiosity, appealed to a sense of risk, and put me a little apart from humdrum, rule-obeying humanity.

When the puttering blossomed into long-distance trips, I saw that I had reverted to the travel instincts of my youth, for as it happens, America's waterways are the nation's footpaths and backyards, the offbeat, inconvenient routes that provide novelty and adventure. America has a different and unusual appearance when experienced from its waterways. A house does its public business with the street. Its riverside is private space, places for sunbathing and barbecues, and for holding birthday parties—to which a kayaker may be invited. Factories and hydroelectric dams have high fences topped with barbed wire on their street sides to keep out curious children. From the water, the kayaker slips in unimpeded and unnoticed, free to poke about important and dangerous machinery.

Because people aren't expected there, waterways don't have the amenities people expect. I don't see Wal-Marts from a kayak, or Safeways or post offices. I see barges, container ships, and ducklings. And despite the disadvantage of sitting just an inch above the water, the kayaker has spectacular vistas of cities and countryside, because he is well clear of the trees, buildings, and hills that usually block the view.

The kayaker encounters a world bypassed by the ordinary tourist. He comes upon lonely islands where battles were fought or colonies founded, and paddles through long-forgotten locks that sustained commerce a century ago. Even visiting traditional tourist sites by water can turn into an unusual and challenging experience. To see these sites, the kayaker may have to climb a blackberry-choked cliff or sneak past uptight security guards.

So the vehicle for my youthful adventures became a kayak—a frail, quaint craft not far different from the raft of Huckleberry Finn and Tom Sawyer. Like them, I started out with a desire to see the world and with not much more than a crust of bread in my pocket.

The question was, *Could I have as much fun?* It's one thing to imagine youthful adventure in your mind's eye, seated comfortably in your study, but quite another to go out into the rain and live it. It might be that youth has a capacity to find joy in discovering new worlds that those of greater years lack. Is the exhilarating, coming-of-age odyssey to be experienced only by those with few birthdays?

That's what I was about to find out.

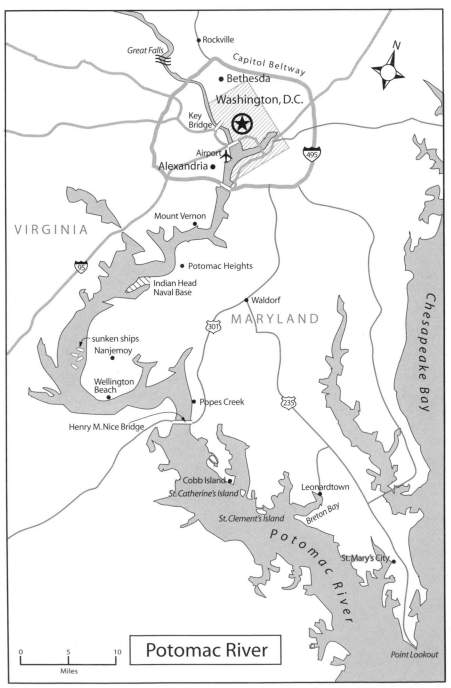

Rockville

Great Falls

Capitol Beltway

N

Bethesda

Washington, D.C.

Key
Bridge

Airport

495

Alexandria

Mount Vernon

VIRGINIA

95

Potomac Heights

Indian Head
Naval Base

Waldorf

MARYLAND

301

Chesapeake Bay

sunken ships
Nanjemoy

Wellington
Beach

Popes Creek

235

Henry M. Nice Bridge

Cobb Island

St. Catherine's Island

Leonardtown

St. Clement's Island

Breton Bay

P o t o m a c   R i v e r

St. Mary's City

Point Lookout

| 0 | 5 | 10 |

Miles

Potomac River

River width not to scale

1

Sneaking Around History

THE POTOMAC RIVER
Washington DC to Chesapeake Bay (August 1996)

I WANTED AN EARLY START to beat Washington DC's summer heat, but I didn't reckon with pitch-blackness at 5:30 a.m., and I'd neglected to bring along any kind of light for my kayak. Boat traffic was busy by the Key Bridge on the Potomac when I eased my boat into the water. The local rowing crews—doubles, fours, and eights from Georgetown and American University—were out in force on their training runs, paced by well-lighted chase boats carrying coaches.

Within minutes of leaving the dock, I earned a rebuke. I was hugging the north shore and a voice from one of the boats boomed out at me on a bullhorn. It was one of the coaches.

"I don't like to tell people what to do, but you're absolutely, totally black."

"Okay," I said.

"There're launches coming up in this direction and they're not going to expect you on this side."

"Okay."

I lowered my head like a scolded dog, and paddled closer to the bank. I was grateful my critic couldn't see my face in the darkness.

This was my first long-distance trip, and I was more than a little nervous. I was spending the year in Washington, far from my home in Sandpoint, Idaho, working at one of the city's many think tanks. Looking for a way to stay active, I bought a 12-foot fiberglass kayak, which I stored at Jack's boathouse under the Key Bridge (named after Francis Scott Key). In the summer afternoons, I lifted it off the rack and paddled around in the Potomac alongside the city, enjoying vistas of the Lincoln Memorial, the Kennedy Center, and other great monuments. An exhilarating place to paddle, but even so, I found it confining. Instead of paddling around in circles, I wanted adventure, to strike out for a far-off destination known only through the imagination. The Potomac is a river after all. *Why couldn't I go where it led? What could go wrong?* With thoughts no more complicated than this, I formed the idea of following the river to Chesapeake Bay, 110 miles away.

What could go wrong? Well, here I was 400 yards into the trip, and I was already discovering one of the answers. It didn't have to do with the more obvious problems of inconvenience, suffering, or danger—we shall get to those issues later. It was the psychological sting of humiliation. When you attempt something unusual, especially if you do it rather impulsively, it's likely that you won't know all the angles. You will make mistakes that reveal you to be, well, incompetent. Then you will hear the voices of spectators ringing in your ears, "There he goes, just like some dumb kid."

Adults typically avoid this kind of humiliation by spending lots of time planning and researching a journey, providing for all possibilities. Adults would prepare a checklist of needed equipment for a kayak trip, and on that long list would be a light for the boat. This kind of preparation goes against my makeup. Give me the unplanned adventure, or not at all. Well, now I was learning that one consequence of my approach was . . . looking like some dumb kid.

I tried to put the scolding behind me, and listened to the gurgle of my tiny bow wake cutting the water, enjoying the delicious August morning air wafting across my tank top. I headed down the river, aiming directly for the Washington Monument that loomed behind the Watergate complex. Then I changed course and dashed across the river to Theodore Roosevelt Island to get away from the crew traffic.

Skimming along the edge of the island was like being in a Louisiana bayou, as I dodged overhanging trees and startled brooding herons one after the other. On my left, across the river, stood the Washington Harbour complex, its lights reflecting on the river like a Monet painting. Suddenly, a scull—a single—drew out of the darkness and slid by me, quite close. We exchanged hellos as we passed. He seemed a serious rower, maybe an athlete who came out in predawn darkness year after year to train for Olympic events, *and he didn't have any lights!*

I felt ridiculously pleased. My embarrassment melted away. I was not inept after all, but one of those savvy paddlers too cool to be bound by petty conventions and the rules of nagging coaches.

My father had died earlier that summer, a peaceful death at the fulsome age of 93. Though his passing was not unexpected, it registered in my outlook on life, and played a role in motivating this trip that family and friends found so peculiar.

Any death closely experienced is a reminder of our own mortality, and to this extent Dad's passing refocused attention on the point that I wasn't getting any younger. If I had ambitions in mind, I'd better stop leaving them in the nebulous category of "one of these days" and make them happen. Dad's death was particularly tied to ambitions of boyhood adventure because, more than anyone, he supported and encouraged those adventures. My first childhood memory is an example.

An adult had told me about the pot of gold found at the end of a rainbow, and, being four years old, I accepted it as true. One day while playing in our backyard, I saw a rainbow, its end seemingly touching down on a creek at a golf course about six blocks from our house. I was seized with a desire to go there and get that potful. When Dad came home from work, I pleaded with him to take me. A smile played across his face, but he did not argue or try to disillusion me. The next morning we made an outing of it, taking the shovel and heading to the golf course.

When we got there, I was uncertain about exactly where the gold was buried. We walked along the creek, back and forth, and I pointed to a spot where I wanted my father to dig. Again that cheery, indulgent smile played over his face, and he began to dig. After the hole was a foot deep, he looked at me, as if to ask whether he should dig further: my wish was his command. I admitted to myself that I now had no clear idea where the gold was buried, and I agreed to give up the project—for the moment—and return home. I was by no means discouraged by the outcome. I realized I needed to know more about how to find gold, but I was exhilarated at being so close on my first try.

On every childhood adventure, it seemed, Dad was there, whether he was taking me fishing or looking for Indian arrowheads. Later adventures he endorsed and, if necessary, funded. After my senior year in high school, I made a hitchhiking trip all around Europe. My goal was to spend less than a dollar a day by eating bread and cheese, and sleeping in youth hostels, barns, and half-constructed houses. I figured I could do it on the money I'd saved up from working summers. At the last minute, Dad surprised me by giving me a check for $100 (equal to about $1,000 in today's purchasing power), "just in case," he said. I carried it in my wallet around Europe for two months. When I got home, I took it out for the first time and proudly gave it back to him. He opened it and we both laughed at what we saw: all the writing on the check had been completely worn off by the friction in my much-traveled wallet: it was worthless as a financial document.

Dad had a keen interest in sea adventures. He was too much a family man and responsible breadwinner to consider undertaking voyages of his own, but over the years he read and passed along to me many accounts, including R. H. Dana's *Two Years Before the Mast*, and Thor Heyerdahl's *Kon Tiki*. He was especially fascinated by Captain Joshua Slocum's book *Sailing Alone Around the World*, because, I think, he saw himself in Slocum's shoes, improvising his way around the world in a 37-foot yawl. Dad delighted in the way Slocum foiled the marauding natives of Tierra del Fuego by scattering carpet tacks on the deck. When the barefoot aggressors climbed aboard his boat at night, they were soon howling in agony and fleeing.

When, after moving to Sandpoint, Idaho, I bought a tiny sailboat to explore Lake Pend Oreille and other local waters, Dad encouraged my effort by sending a copy of Slocum's book. He inscribed it, "To another sailor—a lone sailor, Dad." As I saw it, in setting off down the Potomac to pursue the river over the horizon, I was following not just my own dream, but one Dad would have prized as well.

Half an hour after passing Roosevelt Island, I paddled under Arlington Memorial Bridge. The long, shallow stone arch made an echo chamber that begged to be tested, but it seemed irreverent to break the early morning stillness with any loud noise. The boy in me won out. "Hey!" I shouted. A gratifying cascade of echoes came back, "Heyhey-heyheyheyhey" in a decaying blur.

Four geese flew low overhead in a half-V. Sunrise began with a spectacular purple-red sky, which soon brightened to orange, giving the buildings of the city a soft glow. I took what might have been a stunning photo of the Washington Monument, an orange-tinted obelisk mirrored in the glassy water of the Potomac. Alas, it came out somewhat fuzzy—the price of snapping the shutter from a continually rocking kayak.

I was taking the peaceful morning for granted until I realized how unusual the quiet was. There were no jet planes!

On my afternoon excursions, I had found that one drawback of this stretch of the Potomac is that it lies under the approach path for National Airport. Yes, it's exciting to be just a few feet below the flying monsters as they hurtle overhead, but after a while their screaming and thundering become oppressive. I especially dreaded the older 707s, so poorly designed for noise control. When one came screeching by, I had to drop my paddle and clap my hands over my ears to preserve what was left of my hearing.

The noise wasn't the jets' only menace. One afternoon, paddling a mile from the airport, I saw a miniature tornado: air rotating violently in a tiny cone, whipping up water with leaves and bits of paper, making an angry hissing noise. It was a vortex created by the jet plane that had passed overhead a minute earlier. It began to drift toward me. I stopped being a curious scientist and became a scared rabbit, paddling away from it as hard as I could. I was so busy attending to the danger behind me that I ignored where I was going—until I heard that same hissing noise in front of me. It was another vortex! It made sense: one from each wing. It was drifting slowly and I easily escaped that one, too. Perhaps they weren't all that dangerous, but I didn't have the guts to offer myself as a Guinea pig by paddling into one.

At that early hour of the morning there were no screaming planes or vortices because National Airport has a policy of not allowing flights until 7:00 a.m. The world belonged to twittering birds and to human beings who now could hear themselves think.

A light breeze blew against my face as I paddled under the bridge that carries the Metro trains, a wind that foreshadowed a possible problem. Two weeks earlier, I had taken a day trip down the river, hoping to reach Mount Vernon. What had been a manageable breeze blowing against me in the narrow waters by the city became a stiff wind below Wilson Bridge where the Potomac broadens out. I was so intimidated by the high waves that I turned back. Turning back wasn't an option this time. When you run away from home, if you have any self-respect at all you can't come back the same day.

Friends and family were apprehensive about my making this trip, feeling that it was unseemly and unnecessary. If I wanted to see the Chesapeake Bay, for goodness sake, I could drive there in a few hours.

Most of the advice focused on the dangers. My wife Judy cautioned me to be careful because people are edgy about protecting their property. If I happened to stop in the wrong place, she warned, they might shoot me, or sic vicious dogs on me. Adam, my boss, thought my trip was ill advised. "People get murdered in parks around here," he said. "You can't be too careful. It's not like Idaho."

Such talk put me on edge and made me plenty nervous before I set out, but I questioned the logic behind it. There is some small risk in everything we do. For example, hundreds of people are killed every year falling on stairs. Yet when a loved one heads upstairs to bed we don't say, "Oh, by the way Ted, before you go, make sure your organ donor card is up to date."

We don't worry about the dangers of stairs—or driving a car or walking down the street—because these activities are habitual and familiar. Certainly there are dangers on a long-distance kayak journey, but there are dangers in everyday life, too. I think friends and family members who spooked me with their warnings were exaggerating the risks, confusing doing something *unusual* with doing something *dangerous.*

I hit the first rain shower as I came alongside National Airport and paused to rig my spray skirt, a neoprene garment that hugs the waist and fits snugly around the lip of the cockpit. Should I turn over, the spray skirt keeps water from entering the kayak, giving me a chance to roll back upright, if I can (a point I'll discuss later). And it keeps rain out of the boat and off my pants. Normally, I don't wear the spray skirt or life jacket, as textbook kayakers are supposed to do, because they're too confining, too hot, and offend my free spirit. I store them in the bow, out of reach but tied to a string, so when waves or rain threaten, I can draw them out and put them on in a few seconds.

The rain had stopped by the time I reached Alexandria, Virginia, where I paddled past the *Alexandria,* an old-fashioned, three-mast sailing vessel tied up alongside the dock, and saw the deliciously funky artwork at the Transpotomac Canal Center, a display of broken white marble stones and sculpture made to look like the ruins of an ancient civilization. Further down the river, a covered barge was unloading crates the size of refrigerators. Lettering on it said, "Irving Maple, St. Johns N. B.," which implied that it was originally from New Brunswick, Canada. I was now making a nodding acquaintance with oceangoing traffic!

At 8:30 a.m., I reached the Wilson Bridge, which carries the Capital Beltway, I-495, and flinched at the howling and clattering made by the trucks slamming across the metal grating of the drawbridge above my head. The Beltway marks the edge of the Washington metropolitan area, so I felt I'd made good my escape from the city.

My fears of wind and high waves in the bay beyond the bridge were unfounded: the air was nearly calm and the wavelets were just three inches high. The river became surprisingly rural, its banks choked with trees and shrubs, the wall of green broken only occasionally by man-made structures. I hugged the Virginia side, where Mount Vernon is, and which I planned to visit.

The water was muddy, the tips of my paddle invisible only two inches below the surface. Several dead fish floated belly-up—one was nearly 2 feet long—seemingly poisoned by the water. For years, the Potomac has been notorious for its pollution. It is said that on summer nights, President Lincoln used to retreat to the higher ground in Maryland to escape the river's smell. But if the Potomac is an unhealthy river, one fact didn't compute: the many herons. They were stationed several hundred yards apart all along the shore, and I was spooking them into flight, one after the other, as I came along. I also saw ospreys, one with a fish in its talons heading to a nest in a dead tree, where its mate sat squawking. Somehow, despite the pollution, fish were surviving, and somehow the birds were able to see through the opaque water to catch them.

I'd long wanted to visit Mount Vernon, George Washington's estate and one of the premier tourist attractions of the Washington area. Since it lies on the Potomac River, and has a wharf of its own, I thought I would be welcomed with open arms. What could be less complicated?

It was early afternoon when I reached the grounds of the estate, having paddled 15 miles from my starting point at Key Bridge. I came upon a sloping boat ramp at the upriver edge of the property, about a quarter-mile from the main wharf where tourists were milling about. It seemed a secluded place to leave the boat where no one would notice it or bother it, so I drew it up onto the concrete, turned it upside down to keep potential rain out, quickly ate a bagel and an apple, and went to play tourist.

I walked confidently along the riverfront path to the wharf and came to a chain blocking my way. A sign hung from the chain, facing the other way. I stepped over the chain and turned around to read it. It said, "No Entry." An alarm bell began to ring in my brain, softly at first, then louder as I grasped the implications.

Along the wharf, notices forbade the landing of boats, the idea being, I supposed, that everyone visiting Mount Vernon should do so by car and pay the whopping parking and admission fees. The authorities had stationed a security guard in a kiosk by the wharf. His function was to shoo away boats that tried to dock, and to report any visitor who stepped across the chain that said "No Entry." It was not a complicated job, so he had plenty of time to do it very thoroughly. The guard had not seen me jump the chain, but his unconscious told him something didn't compute, because I seemed to have materialized out of thin air. After staring at me for a long time, walkie-talkie in hand, he grudgingly concluded I was a legitimate, fee-paying visitor who had come by car.

For one making a completely innocent and unprovoked visit to the shrine of the Father of Our Country, I had stumbled into a ridiculous fix. I had enough sense to realize that jumping back over the chain while the guard was watching would be a mistake, so I decided to walk up to the mansion and think of a way around my predicament. I figured I might as well take in the sights, so that if I was arrested or kicked out trying to return to my kayak, I would at least have seen what I came for.

The bombing at the Atlanta Olympic Games had occurred just two weeks earlier, and it had put the entire country in a security-conscious mood. The Mount Vernon Ladies' Association, the voluntary group that owns the place, apparently believed its beloved mansion was the next target of terrorists, and they had hired busloads of security guards to patrol the grounds. They took an unusual interest in me since I was dressed like a kayaker, not a legitimate tourist. So there was no chance of slipping off into the forest to make my way back to the kayak. It occurred to me that these security types would be eager to do their job, especially with nothing to do hour after hour but watch docile tourists file past. How wonderful it would be to break the monotony and capture a real, live terrorist suspect! And what explanation could I give for sneaking onto the grounds by kayak? Isn't that just the way a terrorist would do it?

To top it off, I had left my driver's license at home with my wallet and other documents. I had money, but my theory was that ID documents would be ruined if I took a spill in the water. Judy disagreed, and she was right, of course, but I hadn't taken her advice. If I was stopped and questioned, the police would have no place to begin an inquiry. They would probably hold me for fingerprinting, and maybe even drive me home to have Judy identify me. What an absurd outcome of my attempt to run away from home, being taken back to mommy by the police!

In a distracted frame of mind, I went into the mansion and tried to listen to the docent's lecture. I feigned intense interest in the wallpaper, nodding vigorously as she explained its background, but of course I was much too preoccupied with the mess I was in to register a word. After a few minutes of glancing at mahogany tables and ormolu clocks, I decided that escaping from Mount Vernon was much more important than appreciating antiques. I slipped out of the mansion and made my way back to the riverside.

How was I to get back to the boat unobserved? If I just could get over the chain and 20 yards down the path without the guard in the kiosk noticing me, I would be out of his field of vision. I needed a diversion to distract the guard. The tourists tended to come down to the wharf in groups, a point I saw I could use to my advantage. I sauntered along the path and then sat quietly on the bench right next to the chain, a tourist serenely contemplating the many contributions George Washington made to his country. In this pose, I waited a few minutes until a throng of noisy, active children and their parents headed for the wharf. My unwitting accomplices distracted the guard's attention as they passed his kiosk. I stepped over the "No Entry" sign and walked swiftly down the path as though I had every right to be there. Nothing happened, no shout of alarm, no blast of a police whistle. Breathing hard, I reached the kayak, slid it quietly into the water, and paddled away, James Bond—but without a driver's license to prove it.

As the afternoon wore on, a blustery, downright chilly wind pushed aside the mild air of the morning, and I grew apprehensive about finding shelter for the night. I had not really given this issue much thought. I vaguely assumed I would find motels alongside the river, just as motels sit along highways. But I hadn't seen a single one all the way from Washington and a little thought revealed why. Except for mad, long-distance kayakers, no one needs motels along the water. The power boaters can make it back to their marinas and homes.

Assuming that I would be using motels, I brought neither tent nor sleeping bag. I did have a shrunken orange wool blanket Judy bought for me at the Montgomery County Thrift Shop. This could serve as a bedroll if I had to sleep in the open. But if it rained, I knew I'd be miserable, and the forecast that night was a 100-percent chance of rain.

My arms ached from paddling—I'd gone 28 miles—and I needed to stop. I pulled off the river in the area known as Potomac Heights and scrambled up a steep, grassy bank, hoping to ask directions to a nearby motel. The houses at the top were distinctly low-budget structures: small wooden boxes without porches or garages, plunked down in tall grass and weeds. I advanced toward them prepared for any kind of reception, from armed homeowners and mad dogs to desperate housewives. What I found was a complete absence of human beings! No one was taking out trash or walking a dog; no lights were on, and no laundry was on the line. It almost seemed like the place had been evacuated.

As I was to learn as the trip progressed, this emptiness was the rule in neighborhoods along the river. The overwhelming majority of houses and cottages all the way to Chesapeake Bay were unoccupied. It brought home just how common owning two residences is for Americans, the second home being a vacation place with some kind of claim to getaway status. It also suggested how little people use these getaways. I could have understood the empty houses if it had been January, but this was August.

Although the area seemed deserted, I was leery about using it as a campsite. Even empty houses have eyes, and you can never be sure who might be lurking inside. Furthermore, someone might return later in the evening and let his hungry and curious German shepherds out for a run. I went back to the boat and pushed off into the gathering darkness, under a lowering sky that was beginning to spit rain. I put on the spray skirt and paddled along, pitching and tossing, reproaching myself for having planned things so poorly, and wondering how on earth I was going to get through this stormy night.

Suddenly, a large boathouse loomed out of the dark. Signs said "Authorized Personnel Only," "Government Property," and "Don't come in or we'll electrocute you," or some such thing. I didn't take them too seriously: that's just the way grown-ups talk. I peered through the plastic strips hanging across the boathouse entrance and saw two bays for large boats, both empty. If they were empty now, at happy hour, it seemed reasonable to assume they would stay empty. I parted the plastic curtains and glided into one of the bays. All was quiet except for the hollow gurgling of the waves slapping inside the empty building.

The map indicated I had made it to the Indian Head Naval Base, and this apparently was a Navy boathouse. The naval base, established in 1890, specializes in "energetics," which is the bureaucrats' fancy language for blowing things up. They design and manufacture explosive warheads for torpedoes and mines. It occurred to me they could well be jumpy about strangers sneaking around in kayaks.

In that boathouse, I was about to try what kayak writer Ralph Diaz calls "commando camping," that is, camping where technically one doesn't have a right to be. After years of kayak travel, commando camping has become second nature to me. Most of the time when a kayaker needs to stop on a waterway he will be trespassing to some degree, and he wants to keep this innocent usage from turning into a federal case. The commando kayaker is using a spot of beach, or a dock, or a picnic table just as a seagull would, pausing to rest, and leaving after a few hours without a trace. If he were covered in feathers, the folks in the house on the hill would take no notice of him. But because he is a son of Adam, his presence triggers primitive instincts of fear and possessiveness, and other humans in the vicinity cannot rest until the intrusion is resisted or at least reported.

Even on that first day, my instincts told me that the key to successful commando camping was choosing places where no one would
notice me at any time throughout the night. That was why I rejected
camping around the cottages at Potomac Heights: there were too many
possibilities for an encounter. And that was why my first question
about this boathouse was, would anyone enter during the night? The
answer lay in the condition of the door that led to the land.

I climbed onto the walkway and tiptoed over to it. Quietly, I
turned the handle and tried to pull it open. It was locked: a good
sign. I inspected the door frame and saw cobwebs across it. I began to
breathe easier. If there were night watchmen on this military base, they
apparently didn't enter the building. And why should they? There was
nothing in the boathouse to watch. I became increasingly convinced
that the purpose of this boathouse was to provide an improvident
kayaker with shelter on a stormy night.

Though my stomach growled with hunger I delayed eating. I had
miscalculated my food supply, incorrectly assuming that I would be
able to buy food along the way. With only a bagel and an apple left to
last me for supper and breakfast, I needed to kill some time. By the
light of the naked bulb over the door, I worked on a crossword puzzle,
and read the book I'd brought along, Alfred Lansing's *Endurance*, an
account of explorer Ernest Shackleton's escape from Antarctica. He
was 400 miles into the Weddell Sea when ice crushed his ship, and
he and his crew made it back to civilization in a whaleboat. It put my
tame adventures into perspective.

I passed a surprisingly comfortable night in that boathouse, sleeping on the wooden walkway wrapped in my orange blanket. I felt
especially secure, even safer than at home, protected against all enemies,
foreign and domestic, by the military might of the United States government. I woke occasionally during the night to rain clattering on
the metal roof and the wind buffeting the plastic strips guarding the
entrance. When the gray dawn began to show, I saw the weather had
not improved, and stuck my nose back under the blanket.

An hour later it was time to move. After peeking out the window
to make sure my exit from the boathouse would be unobserved, I paddled out into the river and down to a boat basin, which was part of the

naval base. I had to get food before I continued my journey, so I left the kayak and walked toward the main gate. On the way, I asked a service-man about a place to eat. He directed me to a café on the base where they served a formidable three-egg omelet that boosted my spirits.

Next I faced the problem of getting out of the base to reach a market in town. I approached the guard's kiosk at the main gate with trepidation, knowing that a spit-and-polish guard could easily decide to throw me in the brig. As I explained my predicament, the marine's face registered the complexity of my case. Which higher-up would he have to roust out of bed to deal with me? What kind of paperwork would he have to fill out? I had in my favor that I was already on the base, so if he let me out and back in, nothing was changing. With some hesitation, he accepted my story and agreed to let me back onto the base when I returned from the supermarket.

An hour later, after stocking up, I returned to the gate only to find a different guard who hadn't been told anything about me! This seemed like a formula for a ridiculous snafu. All I could do was plead the truth, saying that I was going down the Potomac on a kayak, and had spent the night down by the shore. An improbable tale, but I must have looked the part because the guard bought it. After giving me a warning about not making this a usual practice, he let me go back to my kayak.

While I was deeply appreciative of the hospitable, laid-back secu-rity at the Indian Head Naval Base, it made me wonder. If a scruffy, unidentified stranger could talk his way into and out of the base, what was the point of having guards?

Back at the boat basin, a brisk wind kicked up waves nearly 2 feet high. I hesitated to go back on water so rough, but since it was a tail-wind, I decided to swallow my butterflies and take advantage of it. I figured I would have only 2 miles of high waves until a bend in the river would shelter me from the wind. Many years of kayaking on waterways have since revealed this thinking as flawed: on large rivers, the wind generally curves around the bends. I put my tape recorder and camera in Ziploc bags, then put on my spray skirt and life jacket, preparing for the worst.

The worst, when it comes to kayaking, is being tipped upside down. If I tipped, I would have to swim out of the boat and tow it to land, if I was able, or watch my feet rot off in the water if I couldn't. A proficient kayaker doesn't have to worry about this because he has an Eskimo roll. This is not a pastry served in the cafés of Anchorage, but the ability to right the kayak from an upside-down position with a flip of the paddle and continue on your way as if nothing had happened.

If the kayaker is upside down and can't roll upright, he pries the spray skirt from the rim of the cockpit and swims out of the kayak. Thus, while failing to accomplish an Eskimo roll is disagreeable with the modern spray skirt arrangement, it isn't fatal. In an authentic Eskimo kayak, a failure to roll upright *is* fatal. In this craft, the spray skirt is part of the kayak fabric and the paddler is laced into it. If he goes over and can't flip the boat, he remains imprisoned upside down in the water. Hence it is safe to say that all Eskimo kayakers know how to roll, because any lacking this skill are no longer with us.

Shortly after I bought my kayak, I took a three-session rolling class held at an indoor swimming pool in Rockville, Maryland. The first week, I had to be pulled upright by the instructor every time. The second week was the same, though perhaps I was making some slight progress. The third and last week, just before it was my turn to make one last try, I said to a fellow student, "I'm never going to learn this." Then I went out and did it!

When summer came, I occasionally practiced the roll in the Potomac in the flat water a mile upriver of Key Bridge. I positioned myself next to a rock outcrop in the middle of the river, so that if I failed to roll, I could dump out the kayak there and start again. In each session, the pattern was the same. On the first attempt, I failed— and had to "wet exit"—that is, pop the spray skirt, swim out of the kayak, and tow it to the island to start over. On almost every following attempt, I was successful. So, statistically, I had a 90-percent success rate doing the Eskimo roll. This average figure was of course worthless, because in a real emergency, it's the first roll attempt that matters.

You don't get a second chance. If you're going to have a dependable Eskimo roll, you have to practice it constantly—and I hadn't.

As I set out onto the waves from the Navy base that morning, I knew I had a poor chance of accomplishing an Eskimo roll if I went over. At first, the waves were manageable: invigorating little roller coasters. "Yahoo, I'm Nanu the Eskimo!" I shouted, raising my paddle over my head. Then I hit the stretch of water that opened to Occoquan Bay, where the waves had built up over a fetch of 5 miles. Suddenly the waves mounted 4 feet high, making cocky Nanu quite tense. It took all my grim attention to keep balance, heavy spray soaking me all the while.

An hour later, I made it to safety in a little cove, where I rested and enjoyed a Mars bar. I was gaining confidence. In fact, I was starting to believe, for the first time, that I would be able to make my objective of getting down the river. Up until then, the trip had been so much paper theory. The sun came out and chased the sense of danger away. I put on sunscreen and paddled back into the waves, no longer carefree Nanu, but not frightened, either.

At the beginning of my third day, I began to feel that I had viable systems for traveling and surviving. I slept on a bit of beach in an unpopulated area a mile upriver from Wellington Beach, Maryland. The night was clear and calm. For my money, sand makes the world's greatest mattress because you can wriggle around and make it conform to your body's bumps. The only problem was voracious mosquitoes that paid no attention to my insect repellent. Using my blanket propped up on sticks, I made a canopy to serve as a mosquito net over my head and arms, and stuck my feet in a large black plastic bag. Thus defended, I had a fine sleep.

In the morning, I took advantage of the privacy to shave and bathe in the river. As well rested, well fed, and well groomed as any Washington commuter, I got into my working clothes—a green tank top and khaki shorts—and steered onto the only empty thoroughfare in the metropolitan region. The sun hadn't yet risen and the cool air was perfectly calm. A delicate mist hung over the river and only my paddle blades disturbed the glassy surface of the water. When I tipped my head back to look at the sky, all I could see was crystal blue. It was a kayaker's dream moment.

An hour later, life's little struggles began. The rays of the rising sun touched me, and immediately I was attacked by sand flies, half a dozen pinpricks at once. Unlike mosquitoes, which prefer the darkness of dusk, sand flies come out in bright sunshine. Their bites are sharp, but only briefly painful, and they don't seem to leave visible marks afterward. I dropped the paddle, flailing and swatting with my hands and then paddled several hundred yards from shore to escape them.

The river's water was somewhat cleaner than it had been at the start of my journey; now my paddle tips were visible down to about a foot. On the previous afternoon, I discovered what really pure water looked like. I entered a bay where, for several hundred yards, underwater springs pumped out water that was crystal clear, ready to be bottled and sold at a premium at supermarkets. I could see every twig and leaf of vegetation on the bottom 10 feet down. I stayed there paddling around for some time just to enjoy the water's exhilarating clarity.

A few miles further down the river, west of the Maryland town of Nanjemoy, I encountered the environmental opposite of this pure spring water: a junkyard for oceangoing cargo ships. Numerous freighters were sunk in the mud, standing in rows, rusting away. Flowers, bushes, and even small trees grew in pockets of soil lodged in their iron crannies. One ship's hatch was open at the waterline, so I could paddle into its midsection. I didn't go far into the dark, unnatural space, however.

Recently, I viewed the place using high-resolution satellite photos on Windows Live Local, the Internet site. I was astonished to see how many ships there were. At the time, I had the impression that only about a dozen were grounded there, but the aerial photos revealed a multitude. I counted them over and over, getting a different result each time—it reminded me of trying to add up receipts at tax time—and settled on an official count of 78. I thought they might be Liberty ships, but these were around 200 feet long, half the size of Liberty ships. My guess is they were marooned there in the 1930s, when the Depression paralyzed the shipping industry, and scrap iron had no value.

At Wellington Beach, the Potomac makes a sweeping turn, inviting the paddler to save several miles by cutting across to the Virginia side. The river grows to a width of several miles at this point, and I was nervous about going too far from shore. But the water was like glass in windless conditions, so I took the shortcut.

One danger that goes with straying far from shore is the possibility of being hit by a powerboat whose driver fails to see you—or sees you but is a homicidal maniac! Thinking about this risk while making the long crossing, I devised a two-part strategy that has become part of my kayaking repertoire. Plan A applies when an approaching boat gets to within half a mile and is still heading dead at me. I turn broadside so the approaching boat can see me better, and splash the water with my paddles to create flashes that will attract attention. If that doesn't work, Plan B comes into action at the last minute: I swing around to head directly at the oncoming boat, holding my paddle parallel to the kayak. In that position, it would be almost impossible for an oncoming boat to hit me squarely. At worst, I'd be overturned.

I should note that, in all my years of kayaking and intersecting the courses of hundreds of powerboats, I've never come close to needing Plan B. On open water, everyone sees me and veers away; homicidal maniacs are obviously much more rare than television gives reason to believe.

On that sunny morning on the Potomac, I didn't even need Plan A. There were no boats on the river at all, just a double dose of sun, blazing down from the sky and glaring up from the water. I made good time cutting across to Virginia's Mathias Point, noticing the current pulling against the buoys of crab traps as the tide drained out.

In the stretch downriver of Washington, it is somewhat misleading to speak of the Potomac as a river. It's an estuary, an arm of the ocean. Washington itself is nearly at sea level. As is true with most estuaries, the tides are higher further up the estuary because the narrowing channel amplifies the surge of water. This means that while the tide at the mouth of the Potomac is only about 1.5 feet, Washington DC has a tide of 3 feet. This surge feeds the famous Tidal Basin, the body of water by the Jefferson Memorial and the famous cherry trees. There's a dam between the basin and the Potomac River (you can see it only from a kayak because it's under a road). When the tide rises higher than the dam, water spills into the Tidal Basin. When the water level in the Potomac drops, the dam holds the water in the Basin.

I had brought along a tide table for Washington DC, thinking it would apply to the whole area. Even that first night in the Navy boathouse, just 30 miles downriver of Washington, I saw it was way off. The water came up several hours earlier than the Washington time. A fishing guide I met at the marina told me that high tide at Washington is six hours later than at the mouth of the Potomac: it takes that long for the tidal push to travel up the river.

Though the tidal current was helping me down the river, my pace began to slacken as the midday August sun drained away my energy. It was all I could do to cross back to the Maryland side, arriving long past noon at a celebrated crab restaurant at Popes Creek that a local fisherman told me about. I ate too much in my exhausted condition. Added to sunburn, dehydration, and a general feeling of lassitude, I felt ill and tried to take a nap in the shade of a boathouse. But every time I started to doze off, sand flies attacked me. To flee their harassment, I forced myself back into the kayak and headed down the river in the blasting mid-afternoon heat. It was the lowest point of the journey.

I dragged myself along as far as the Henry M. Nice highway bridge, the last road crossing the Potomac as it widens out toward Chesapeake Bay, and ran out of gas at the Aqualand Marina. I asked if there was a motel nearby. There wasn't, but the owner offered to let me spend the night on the marina grounds, a blessing indeed. The marina had a restroom, drinking water, and covered picnic tables out of the sun. For sleeping, I dragged a rubber mat onto the concrete slab under a propane supply tank, where I would have some privacy. The location wasn't a nature preserve by any means, especially with the hammering of trucks on the nearby highway bridge, but I accepted the logic that beggars can't be choosers.

In the evening, after the marina closed and the staff had gone home, I was reading my Shackleton book at a picnic table when a late-model Cadillac drove up, driven by a black man. A young boy got out and asked me for a dollar to pay the toll on the bridge. He claimed they didn't have any money and were trying to get home. The story seemed inherently implausible. *How did they pay for gas for the Cadillac?* I wondered. *Indeed, how did they pay for the Cadillac?* Nevertheless, I gave the boy a dollar. The marina owner had helped me, and I was in a mood to pass it forward. In one way or another, it seemed to me at the time, we are all beggars in this world.

I had barely set out the next morning when I found myself in rapids! One minute I'm paddling along in glassy water, surrounded by a dreamlike early morning calm, then suddenly I'm buffeted by whirl-pools and boilers, struggling to stay upright. My brain couldn't grasp what was happening. Was it an earthquake, or just a nightmare in an unfinished sleep? In a second, the answer became clear. Just below the marina stood the Morgantown Generating Station, one of the big-gest power plants in the state. I had paddled into the violent outflow of heated water from its cooling system. It was a good example of how disaster, or at least danger, can strike when you least expect it. Of course I wasn't wearing my life jacket.

As my paddling took me down the broadening Potomac, I began to be aware of a hectic bird life. In addition to the herons that I had been seeing since Washington, I was now encountering a multitude of birds crisscrossing the sky, all busily seeking fish, including gulls, bald eagles, and sandpipers. I was rather repelled by the thuggish cor-morants, with their black feathers and hooked bills, and which reeked of rotten fish. At the other end of the scale, easy winners of the bird beauty contest, were the terns, sleek, delicate white birds with black caps and forked tails.

From time to time I came across algal blooms, iridescent green powder on the water's surface. At times, it collected into ugly-looking green clumps, like gunk from outer space that won't stop multiplying. The algae feed on excess nitrogen in the water, their growth spurred by the warm temperatures of late summer. The blooms of recent times are minor compared to the 1960s when the river was covered shore to shore with the stuff and President Lyndon Johnson called the Potomac "a national disgrace."

By mid-afternoon, I'd reached Cobb Island. I pulled the boat onto a sliver of parkland by the water where I didn't think anyone would bother it. That's the advantage of having a scruffy, nondescript kayak that says, "Don't bother to steal me." I walked around the friendly little town, got some film and new batteries for the camera, and crossed the bridge to look at the modest, mostly unoccupied, bungalows on Cobb Island proper. In the shade, I read my book, then fell asleep.

When I returned to the park, someone had used that one hour in all the week to mow the lawn, and moved my kayak to do it. In dragging the kayak, the worker scraped off my homemade keel. My kayak was a whitewater boat, built with a perfectly smooth bottom, so the paddler could twist and turn quickly in rapids. This design made it a poor sea kayak because it would not track in a straight line on flat water. The moment I stopped paddling, it would start rotating, and soon be heading backward while still coasting forward. To fix that I had found a piece of sheet metal in the street, bent a right angle in it, and fastened it to the bottom of the boat with duct tape. This homemade keel worked perfectly, keeping the boat straight between paddle strokes. Now it was torn off.

For once, I was prepared for an emergency. I had a roll of duct tape and simply taped it on again, doing even a better job than the first time.

The wind shifted to the southwest and gave me the job of bashing directly into it in order to cross three-mile wide Neale Sound that afternoon. I clawed my way across, spearing the waves, spray blowing back in my face, and late in the afternoon reached what the map called St. Catherine Island.

Some structures stood on the island that my mind wanted to call houses, but something wasn't quite right about this assumption. There was no sign of life, so I began to think the island was deserted and therefore a viable campsite. I landed as far away from the structures as possible and found some sand where I could perhaps sleep, but I wasn't looking forward to it. The sand was wet from the previous tide and the mosquitoes were pesky.

Then a man, a woman, and a young girl came across the channel separating the island from the mainland in a small outboard. *Just my luck,* I thought. *The rule that no one uses his vacation home in August is about to be broken just to inconvenience me.* I lurked behind a sandbank, so they didn't see me, and debated whether I should announce my presence or just sneakily spend the night on the beach out of sight. I decided the best strategy was to meet them and ask permission to camp on the beach. Colleen and Daryl turned out not to be vacationers but caretakers for the resort that owned the island, and they had come over from the mainland for an hour to mow the grass. (So the rule that people don't use their summer homes in the summer was not contradicted after all!)

When I asked about camping on the beach, Colleen pointed to the clubhouse, "Stay up there. Everything's unlocked."

"Do you mean it?"

"Sure. Everything's turned off—water, electricity, gas—because no one ever comes. We would turn it on for them if they did come. But they never do. The place is just going to waste." She seemed irritated with the absent owners.

"Well . . ." I said, not quite able to grasp the dimensions of my good fortune.

"Go ahead. Take any room you want. They're all open. Somebody might as well get some use out of it."

I thanked her profusely, paddled around to the dock in front of the lodge, and walked up to the building, consumed with curiosity about this resort that nobody ever came to. The building was not luxurious, but rather camp-like, right down to the worn linoleum and screen doors that didn't quite close. A trophy deer head jutted out over the mantle in the bar.

I learned from reading material on the bulletin board that I had stumbled into a political shrine. The name of the place was the Jefferson Islands Club. It was founded in 1931 by leaders of the Democratic Party to be, as the brochure put it, "a refuge from their hectic political lives." The idea that politicians could ever stop being politicians proved unrealistic however, and the club quickly became a venue for more hectic politics. President Roosevelt hosted a gala reception there for 450 senators and congressmen. President Harry Truman frequently held court at the club, along with other Democratic Party luminaries, including House Speaker Sam Rayburn and Justice Hugo Black. A picture of Bill Clinton hung in the lobby. The place was, as the literature put it, "a shrine for Democrats."

The founding politicos were pleased to take the name of Thomas Jefferson for their getaway resort. They pledged in their club *Objectives* "to support, defend, and advance the fundamental principles of government enunciated by Thomas Jefferson." One had to smile at that, since these New Dealers obviously weren't paying attention to his fundamental principles. Jefferson advocated small and decentralized government, just the opposite of the centralized welfare state they were establishing. In politics, as in religion, saints are more exploited than heeded.

Though the founders renamed the place Jefferson Island, all the maps show it as St. Catherine. Apparently, even the mapmakers haven't taken the claim of allegiance to Jefferson seriously.

While it was still daylight, I checked out the rooms to see which was the best. The standard rooms were surprisingly small, with almost no walking space around the beds. It was hard to believe that U. S. congressmen and senators found these airless cubicles an acceptable place to sleep. The "Presidential Suite" was larger, about the size of a normal motel room, with two double beds and large vanity with mirror. I decided I would sleep there when bedtime came.

Prowling around the reading room, I found a copy of an article from the July 14, 1994 *Washington Post*, headlined "Private Island

Club Granted Bailout." After the Democrats purchased the island, they discovered it was slowly washing away into the Potomac, so they got a $650,000 Maryland erosion control loan to put huge seawalls around the island. Later, they didn't have the money to pay off the loan. So—in a bit of a scandal—insiders in the Maryland state government arranged for the club to forego payment. I wondered what Thomas Jefferson would have thought about that!

What happened to turn this thriving political club into a mausoleum with the electricity shut off? I pondered the question all evening and finally decided the answer was that politicians became too sophisticated. In earlier days, lawmakers came from farm and rural settings and were used to roughing it. They were normal people who enjoyed wooden rocking chairs that creaked and didn't mind flies buzzing around the dinner table. Then the age of big money, television, and glitz overtook the political scene, and politicians' tastes changed. Now their lives require chrome, glass, valet service, and $2,000 suites at the Hyatt Regency. Modern politicians wouldn't have anything to do with a summer camp, however spotless Colleen kept it, any more than they would shine their own shoes.

Now in its days of decline, the club is open to anyone—of any political coloration—who will pay the $1,000 entry fee and another $1,000 a year. One might wonder who in his right mind would pay two grand for a $35 motel room he never intends to use. But you have to remember that Washington is the home of lobbyists, whose job it is to gush money in every plausible political direction.

The Jefferson Islands Club may not be good enough for modern-day politicians, but it was perfect for me. I had my supper of peanut butter and pumpernickel bread seated in a recliner on the veranda, enjoying the gentle breeze, looking out across the Potomac at the twinkling lights on the Virginia side.

When night came, I groped my way through the dark building to the "Presidential Suite." Not wanting to make extra work for Colleen by using the sheets, I pulled the spread aside and lay down on top of the covers. I closed my eyes, then opened them wide with a sudden question: *Who else had slept in this bed?* It was not new, and the mattress sagged dreadfully, evidence that it could well be over 60 years old. The more I thought about it, the more convinced I became that I was lying in the same bed Franklin Roosevelt used when he came down to Jefferson Island to make politics!

I suppose I should have been awed to be this close to history, lying on the same innersprings that supported Franklin—and possibly Eleanor as well—so many years ago. But I found myself in a skeptical mood. It was probably my political science background at work, my experience with how well-intentioned laws actually turn out. The New Deal is a case in point. At the time, the public assumed that Roosevelt's economic policies were combating the Great Depression, but economists have now concluded that they actually made it worse. Another example was his policy of family assistance, AFDC, which aimed to cure poverty. In the end, it subsidized the breakup of families and promoted unwed teen childbearing. In the summer of 1996 when I was making my trip, AFDC was condemned by everyone in Washington, and the program was abolished in that year's welfare reform.

Knowing this background, I wasn't impressed with the politicos' earnest plotting and coalition-building of yesteryear. It seemed to me that the achievements of politics are, in the long run, rather insubstantial. This view echoed, of course, my disenchantment with my own career, where with great industry and effort I wrote books of political science that nobody read. My answer to the futility of worldly accomplishment was to balance work with play, to paddle over the horizon in search of adventure. Each day I paddled, this formula was making more sense.

So as I wriggled into a comfortable position on that Jefferson Island mattress, my thought was not Wow! but that FDR would have been a happier person if he had done less politics and more kayaking.

After breakfast the next morning, I made my way to St. Clement's Island, a spot of land that deserves to be called the Catholics' Plymouth Rock. We are not taught much in school about the Catholics' arrival in the New World—American history has a Protestant bias—but these settlers deserve equal billing with the Pilgrims. Like the Pilgrims, the St. Clement's colonists sought to escape religious persecution in England, and, like the Pilgrims, they had a long, harrowing sea voyage—on two little ships, the *Ark* and the *Dove*. In 1634, under Lord Baltimore, the colony was established on the island to keep a safe distance from the numerous Piscataway Indians. Later, the colonists made friends with the Indians and relocated inland. Unlike the Pilgrims, who believed in violent persecution of other religions, the Catholics at St. Clement's adopted the principle of religious toleration. In this they were two years ahead of Roger Williams of Rhode Island, who is often credited with being the father of toleration.

The day was warming up, and there seemed to be no one about—the entire island is a state park—so I skinny-dipped, washing off the filth of two days. The water was now very salty, proving that I had, by the taste test at least, reached the Chesapeake.

I had just finished putting my clothes back on when a chunky man came jogging down a path from the other side of the island. This was Dave, who had come in a motorboat and was making a half-hearted attempt at a workout. He said he had just quit his construction job because of an angry misunderstanding with his boss. Reading between the lines, I guessed he had been fired. He was 29 years old, jittery and stressed. It gradually came out that he had a serious alcohol problem, and he had come to the island for some peace and quiet and, as he put it, "to get my head together."

We walked to the other side of the island to see the towering concrete cross that marks the site of the first Catholic mass performed in English in North America. A display board noted that the island was 400 acres when the settlers came, and had now shrunk to only 40. This is the result of a natural process of erosion affecting all Potomac estuary islands—except those protected by the powers of Thomas Jefferson.

I said goodbye to Dave and paddled south into the withering sun. I felt extremely stiff getting up that morning, and now my arms felt weak and creaky. My original theory was that I would get stronger as the trip progressed, but the reverse was happening. I polished off 30 miles on the first day, did 20 the second, 15 the third, and 13 the next. I was losing strength at an alarming rate. Maybe I wasn't eating well enough—this was before I learned the importance of protein in diet—or maybe it was the southern sun sucking the life out of me as I paddled, but I just wasn't bouncing back. My body was telling me it was time to end this trip.

My recovery arrangement was to call my brother-in-law Mike to pick me up wherever I landed. Examination of the map revealed that I could get home that night by going up Breton Bay to Leonardtown, 9 miles away. The idea was *very* attractive. So I paddled through the heat of the day on glaring, glassy water up the interminable length of Breton Bay, ran out of drinking water, and finally arrived, quite parched, at Leonardtown at three o'clock in the afternoon.

Walking up from the bay to the center of town to find a phone, I noticed a small handmade sign in front of a house: "Knives and Scissors Sharpened." It happened to be just what I needed for my cherished KA-BAR jackknife. I had bought this knife 30 years before in a pawnshop in Reno, Nevada, when I was a student hitchhiking from California to Idaho. I paid 25 cents for it; when I got to Idaho, savvy locals told me KA-BAR was the Cadillac of knives and it was worth 25 dollars. I always try to keep the blade razor-sharp, but on this trip it had suffered unpardonable abuse, being used to cut open a can of tuna fish, and this violation was weighing on my mind. I knocked on the door and met a retired Navy man who gave the knife its finest sharpening in years. He was impressed by the hardness of the blade. He charged me five dollars, which I was happy to pay, and also gave me a drink of water and let me use his phone to call Mike.

Officially, I didn't reach the Chesapeake. I covered 90 miles altogether, including 12 miles on the last day, leaving me 20 miles short of the Bay. But I was satisfied. It had been a grand adventure that proved that my own muscle fibers could take me to undiscovered realms over the horizon. It was a lesson I wouldn't forget.

On the way back to Bethesda with the kayak strapped on top of the car, we were hit by a thunderstorm triggered by a cold front that pushed across the region. It was a monster, flinging sheets of rain across the road and hammering our cars with a mortar barrage of thunderclaps.

"It looks like you got off the river just in time," Mike commented.

A sensible adult opinion, of course. I murmured assent, because I didn't want my brother-in-law to doubt my sanity, but I was being a hypocrite. *I regretted missing that storm on the river.* The reader needn't suppose I would have been out in the middle of the water, daring the lightning: I do have some common sense after all. The way I saw it, I would have found shelter in a boathouse, a clump of trees, or under a broken panel of plywood, cozily defying Nature's anger.

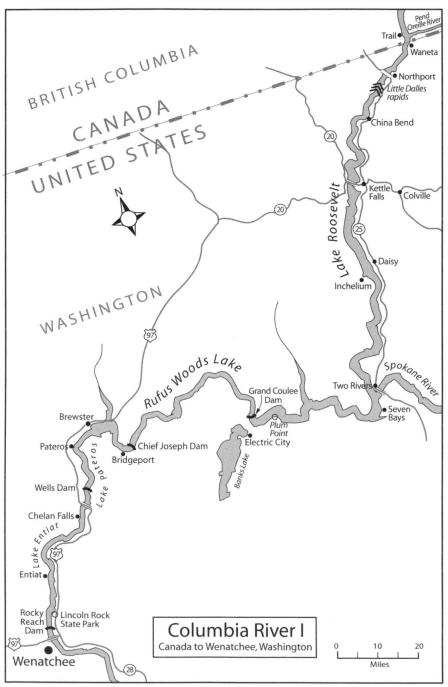

BRITISH COLUMBIA

CANADA

UNITED STATES

N

WASHINGTON

Pend Oreille River

Trail ●

● Waneta

● Northport

Little Dalles rapids

● China Bend

20

Kettle Falls ● Colville

25

● Daisy

Inchelium ●

Lake Roosevelt

Spokane River

Two Rivers ●

● Seven Bays

Grand Coulee Dam

Plum Point

● Electric City

Banks Lake

Rufus Woods Lake

97

Brewster ●

Pateros ●

● Chief Joseph Dam

Bridgeport

Lake Pateros

Wells Dam ●

Chelan Falls ●

Lake Entiat

97

Entiat ●

Rocky Reach Dam

○ Lincoln Rock State Park

97

Wenatchee

28

Columbia River I
Canada to Wenatchee, Washington

0   10   20

Miles

River width not to scale

2

Over My Head

THE COLUMBIA RIVER I
Trail, British Columbia to Wenatchee, Washington (June–July 2001)

KAYAKING WENT ON THE BACK BURNER after I moved back to Sandpoint from Washington DC, for my attention turned to another youthful fantasy: the search for gold. As I've mentioned, the desire to find gold in the dirt of creeks and rivers was my first real childhood yearning, and it has remained a fixation all my life. One reason I settled in Idaho was because it's the home of the Idaho batholith, a mass of hot granitic plutons that ages ago worked deep under the surface of the earth to separate gold from the magma of the earth's core. (Notice that my theories about how to find gold progressed beyond the pot at the end of the rainbow.)

Any time I had a few free days, and sometimes when I didn't, I threw my sleeping bag in the back of the station wagon and headed out for another river or creek, to exhaust myself digging and panning. When I found a minuscule flake of gold, I would transfer it to a tiny vial filled with water. When I tipped the vial sideways and looked down through the glass, the speck was magnified to the size of, well, a large speck. Sometimes the vial would contain 15 or 20 of these flakes. I would proudly show it to Judy the minute I returned from an expedition, and she would oh and ah exactly as she does for a grandchild's crayon drawing.

My gold-hunting expeditions took me to rivers all over the Northwest, including the Clark Fork, Kootenai, Snake, Salmon, and, of course, the Columbia. For most of its length, the Columbia is a string of lakes impounded behind hydroelectric dams, but where the river leaves Canada and enters Washington State near Northport, it runs free, and in that stretch one finds the bedrock formations that trap placer gold. The movement and energy of the free-flowing river fascinated me when I went there to pan. Its surface is never calm but roils with powerful whirlpools and boilers, forces capable of sucking entire trees below the surface. I never dared to enter its frigid water beyond knee depth to wash at the end of the day, but I gazed at the panorama of its endlessly rushing movement for hours.

Then one day I thought: *Wouldn't it be neat to follow this river all the way to the Pacific Ocean!* I could paddle down rapids, along lakes, around dams, through mountain ranges and finally wind up alongside oceangoing freighters in Astoria, Oregon. Once the germ of the idea was planted, my mind kept working on it, figuring out how such a trip could be accomplished.

To make the effort that a long-distance kayak trip demands, I needed meaningful starting and ending points. The mouth of the river at the Pacific Ocean was the obvious ending, but where should I start? The natural place would be the source of the river at Columbia Lake in British Columbia. This was the starting point for Robin Cody, who made a solo canoe trip down the Columbia in 1990, and who wrote up his adventure in *Voyage of a Summer Sun.* The Columbia runs 520 miles in Canada before crossing the border, and then flows another 680 miles in the United States before reaching the Pacific. Cody was Mr. Muscle, able to paddle an ungainly canoe 40 miles in a day. For me, 20 miles a day in a kayak is a major achievement. So I selected the U.S. border as a starting point, giving me a voyage with enough psychological meaning to fire up my engine.

Since the 680-mile trip translated into six weeks of paddling, longer than I felt I should be away from work and other obligations,

I decided to break the trip into three stages, and carry it out over a period of years.

The next issue was finding a craft I could carry on portages around the eleven dams that stood on the route. I settled on a folding kayak made by a German firm, Klepper, and purchased their lightest model, a Klepper Aerius 2000 that weighs 48 pounds.

Johann Klepper, a tailor by trade, designed his folding kayak in 1907, at a time when European adventurers had to rely on trains to get them where they wanted to paddle. That meant the kayak had to be turned into a compact piece of luggage. Klepper came up with a clever invention consisting of 22 wooden pieces that fit together into a frame that locks tight inside a canvas/Hypalon skin.

Even with the instructions spread out in front of me, I needed all evening and the next morning to put it together for the first time on my living room floor. Once I learned how, I could assemble it in 20 minutes.

The Klepper does not have the easy-release neoprene spray skirt that my fiberglass kayak had on the trip down the Potomac. The Klepper spray skirt, if installed, is fixed to the boat, and the kayaker is laced tight into it. If the kayaker capsizes, he simply has to execute a successful Eskimo roll or he breathes water. Since I didn't have a dependable Eskimo roll even when I regularly practiced it, and had long given up practicing, the spray skirt had to be left behind. I would go down the Columbia with an open cockpit.

In addition to being portable, the Klepper also handles rough water better than a hard-shell kayak. Its flexible structure enables it to "give" against waves, so it doesn't turn over easily. Facing the cold and turbulent Columbia, with no ability to perform an Eskimo roll to right myself, I saw this as a desirable feature indeed.

The protagonists of outdoor adventures are generally expected to be highly proficient in their sports, heroes of athletic accomplishment. Their great abilities give them confidence when facing challenges that would terrify the rest of us. Alas, this theory worked in reverse for me when it came to facing the rapids of the Columbia. I lacked the requisite ability, had no confidence, and therefore was terrified.

During my year in Washington DC, I learned that the Potomac River wasn't just the flat water by the Lincoln Memorial and the Tidal Basin where I had been calmly paddling. A few miles above the city, the Potomac goes over a mass of rapids and falls. On a summer weekend, the cars of whitewater fanatics are parked bumper to bumper for miles along the river. It seemed to me that a self-respecting kayaker ought to know how to negotiate rapids, so before leaving the area I signed up for two whitewater kayaking lessons.

I was a beginner in a class of intermediate paddlers, and quickly found I was in over my head in every possible way. Time and again, our instructor would lead across some turbulent water, the class would follow without any noticeable problem, and I would come last—and be instantly thrown upside down! I must have had a dozen spills. Fortunately, I had been assigned a guardian, a child kayaking prodigy who was half fish, and who took her assignment of keeping me alive as seriously as only an eleven-year-old with her first paying job would. I had total faith in her. Each time I spilled, I patiently waited upside down, holding my breath until she nosed the bow of her kayak against my hand. Then I would grab her bow and twist myself upright.

Almost every night during the following week I had nightmares involving fast-moving water: rapids, whirlpools, waterfalls. Even seeing water gushing out of the bathroom faucet alarmed me. With the greatest reluctance, I forced myself to get my money's worth and go back for the second lesson. Once on the water, a strange thing happened. I didn't go over once! Some unconscious part of my brain, some nerve center beyond my control or understanding, had acquired a sense of balance.

Psychologically, however, something was still wrong. The instructor paddled up to me and said, "Jim, you're doing fine, but would you do one thing for me?"

I nodded.

"Close your mouth."

I realized I had been wearing the rictus of fear all afternoon. I concluded that I wasn't cut out for whitewater kayaking. Unlike the youngsters in class, I got no thrill from being dangerously shaken up. They sought out the roughest rapids to "play" in, whereas I dreaded turbulent water and avoided it whenever possible.

It is a testimony to the power of my irrational need for a fitting beginning for this Columbia journey that I swallowed my fear and put myself through the rapids in that first stretch of the river. I could have started 15 miles south and missed them. But then I would not have been able to start *at* the U.S. border.

I originally planned to put the kayak in the water just inside the United States, a few yards south of the Waneta customs and immigration control point. A bureaucratic snafu put me on the wrong side of the border, and the wrong side of the law, to start my trip.

Judy and I spent the night at a B&B in Trail, British Columbia, and planned to recross the border early the next morning. The U.S. Customs Service told us that the border crossing at Waneta opened at 6 a.m.. Driving up at 8 a.m., we found it gated and locked with a sign announcing it did not open until 9 a.m.! Unwilling to waste an hour fuming, I drove back up the river and found a spot a mile north of the border where I could launch.

While Judy collected large rocks to take back for her garden in Sandpoint, I assembled the kayak, stowed my three bags of supplies and equipment, attached the paddle tether (so that if I did turn over in the rapids, the paddle would stay with the boat), and strapped my green plastic gold pan onto the deck. After a kiss, Judy got in the car and drove away—rather hastily, I thought. (She later said she didn't want her last memory to be me in my tiny kayak tossing forlornly in the fast-moving water.)

I lifted the boat into a calm backwater and climbed in. For a time I sat quietly watching the bouncing waves rush by on the other side of the sand bar. Then I took a deep breath and touched the water with my paddle tips. With just a few gentle strokes my boat left the glassy water of the eddy and was yanked into the swift current. It was like being born.

Almost immediately I faced a crisis. The mighty Pend Oreille River spurts from the east into the Columbia at a right angle just before the border, a collision of waters that creates a hash of steep, crazy waves.

Robin Cody made the mistake of steering to the east side, where the Pend Oreille comes in, and trying to fight those waves. His reason for this perverse behavior was that he wanted to stop and register with U.S. Customs at the border kiosk. He was a bureaucrat—he worked for the Bonneville Power Administration—and I guess he couldn't conceive of ignoring anybody's regulations. The violent waves overturned him and washed him and his canoe down into the United States. Still in thrall to the god of paperwork, he pulled himself from the river, scrawled out a declaration of entry with his name on a scrap of paper, and gave it to a nearby fisherman to deliver to the border guards if he got around to it. (He apparently didn't notice the fisherman's amused smile.)

I was less concerned about legality than Cody and much more keenly interested in self-preservation. *To heck with the border guards,* I thought, and paddled furiously to the far west side to avoid the turbulence from the Pend Oreille River, using my pedal-controlled rudder to give me additional steering power in the twisting currents. The river was a maelstrom of upwelling currents and whirlpools bigger than my boat sucking down. Anyone in the water there, even with a life jacket, would be in trouble. I had just about cleared the outflow of the Pend Oreille when I saw the steep Waneta rapids coming up on the west side. I reversed directions and paddled like mad back to the east side. In seconds, drenched with river water and perspiration in equal parts, I was deep into United States territory. I didn't give any fisherman memos about it and if the feds were disturbed about my passage, they never told me.

A few minutes later, my mouth dry and my arms trembling, I pulled to the bank to rest and celebrate my victory, exhilarated at having successfully passed what I assumed was the worst whitewater of my trip. According to the river guidebook, the rest of the rapids were Class I, the easiest, and were supposed to be avoidable. After catching my breath, I resumed my trip. A powerboat came up the river, hammering its way against the current, reminding me of another danger to worry about whenever my course took me to the middle of the river. In a slow section, I had a moment to slip the GPS out of its Ziploc bag. It showed the current was going at 6 miles an hour. The speed in the rapids was probably twice that.

My next landmark was Dead Man's Eddy, 9 miles below the border. I assumed it was named for the bodies of people drowned higher upriver that end up circling in this giant pool. Although the name of the place put me on edge, I figured it should be easy cruising.

I knew something was wrong a quarter mile away when I began to hear the characteristic roar of rapids. I tightened my grip on the paddle and peered into the distance with alarm. I hadn't realized it, but the flow of the river was much lower than normal, and this meant that Dead Man's Eddy was drained like a swimming pool in winter. Instead of driftwood and dead bodies lazily circulating in calm water, the spot had become a sweeping curve of rapids.

This seemed a cruel injustice to a novice who had already screwed his courage to the breaking point for one set of rapids. In panic, I searched for a route around the whitewater, but there was none. The rapids stretched from bank to bank. I could only grit my teeth, keep the bow pointed downstream, and entrust myself to Klepper's handiwork. It didn't let me down and I bounced helplessly but safely through the churning water.

Below these rapids, the current slowed as I entered Lake Roosevelt, the body of water impounded by the Grand Coulee Dam 130 miles away. I breathed easier knowing there was nothing but flat water to Wenatchee, Washington, 250 miles away, my destination for the first stage of my trip.

A few miles after crossing under the bridge at Northport, 15 miles below the border, I stopped for lunch and to pan for an hour. It proved to be a good spot, probably part of the old riverbed undisturbed by glacial action, leaving gold in place against the bedrock. I marked the place with my GPS to return some day. With my gold specks safely stored in a vial, I reentered the river, which was now without current.

Or was it? Heading into a narrow gorge—the Little Dalles—I saw the current picking up again. The Little Dalles used to be a major rapid, but the rising waters of Lake Roosevelt had drowned it, supposedly turning it into quiet water. The moving water said something was wrong with this theory. My heart sank. Was the promise of no more rapids to be betrayed yet again?

What I didn't know was that the level of Lake Roosevelt varies enormously, according to hydroelectric needs and plans for absorbing runoff. In the early summer when I came through, the rapids were partially exposed. The water looked smooth as I entered, but I began to hear rushing and sucking sounds as I paddled further into the gorge. Whirlpools spun out of nowhere, yanking my boat this way and that. Some of the whirlpool holes were over a foot deep, indicating very powerful currents below. Steep rock walls blocked the daylight, making it dark and difficult to see. The sound of cascading water reverberated off the walls, proving that danger lay somewhere about. Cautiously paddling down the gorge, I strained my eyes to inspect every inch of the dark water ahead for telltale signs of a hidden waterfall.

Nothing of the sort appeared. As so often happens on my journeys, the danger proved to be mostly in my head, not in the water. I sailed out into the sunshine and the current dropped away, leaving me once again on the smooth waters of Lake Roosevelt.

Paddling the rest of the afternoon was an idyll. I was completely alone on the glassy water. The cliffs and mountains glowed vivid amber in the setting sun, and there wasn't a cloud in the crystalline blue sky. I felt I had the energy to paddle on forever, a perpetual motion machine unhindered by human limitations. As evening came on it took a positive effort of will to make myself stop and call it a day. I pulled over to a secluded sandy beach to camp. After a supper of instant rice, dried plums, and hot tea, I curled up in my sleeping bag under the open sky and slept the sleep of the just.

I woke briefly in the night to see a sky splashed with stars. The Milky Way was laid out in such detail that I could see crisscrossing avenues and paths within it. Despite the chilly air, the sleeping bag was warm, untouched by dew because of the low humidity. I filled my lungs with a long, deep breath of the crisp air, and thanked my maker for the gift of life.

On the second day, I passed China Bend (named after the Chinese laborers who moiled for gold in the placer deposits there) and found the lake opening wider. With this openness came the wind, wind that scared me, trammeled me, and occasionally helped me for the rest of the span of Lake Roosevelt. For the most part it was a headwind, and it tended to follow a pattern: light in the morning, strong at noon and afternoon, then lighter toward evening. Its rhythms came to regulate my life, often forcing me off the water for the middle part of the day when it was strongest.

The pattern was set on that second day. The wind against me built up all morning, and finally got too strong and scary to allow me to continue. I stopped alongside an open forest of ponderosa pines, well sheltered from the wind, and busied myself with killing time. I panned for a while along the shore, but found no colors at all. I sat under a tree, ate a few nuts and figs, and read *Don Quixote,* the book I had brought along, enjoying the slapstick antics of Don Quixote and Sancho Panza.

While passing time under the trees, I spotted a most unusual sight out on the lake. It was another kayak! The paddler was a man of about my age and build. His green hard-shell kayak was extremely low in the water—the explanation for which I was, in due course, to learn. He was coming along the same route I had been following. I waved at him but he was too hunkered down against the wind and spitting rain to see me. He plodded right on past, secure and powerful against the waves. For the kayaker cowering among the trees, the lesson about courage was difficult to miss.

After three hours on the island, the wind seemed to slacken, and goaded by my mentor in the green kayak, I started again. I did well for a time, making reasonable progress against the wind. Then I rounded a bend in the lake and had to make a decision. I could waste miles following the shore of the bay on my side, or I could take a more direct route by making a two-mile crossing of the lake. In view of the moderate wind, I opted for the crossing.

Nature stage-managed the wind speed precisely. As soon as I was well out from shore and beyond the point of return, the wind doubled in strength. Soon I was in heavy seas and whitecaps. My bow cut waves that broke all the way back against the coaming of the cockpit. And rain was starting. It was white-knuckle time!

The real fear in these situations is not so much that I will turn over in the existing conditions, but uncertainty about how much more Mother Nature has in store for me. If the wind has increased once, one reasonably fears, it could easily increase again. Looking back over my shoulder to the downwind course where I would drift if I did turn over, I saw nothing but miles of cold, empty water. I was like a cliff climber dangerously high with no safety rope.

Fortunately, the wind did not increase, and I made it to a protected cove just as darkness fell. With gray clouds already spitting rain, I had to make some provision against a storm. I was able to make a pup tent out of my ground cloth, using my paddle as a ridgepole, and tying the sides to a long piece of plastic pipe I found on the beach. I dug some dry sand from under a log to make a dry floor inside the tent. Into this roomy shelter I brought all my bags to keep them dry, well pleased with my cozy defense against the rain.

I awoke the next morning to the delicious sound of rain splattering down on my tent. I'd had huge sleep, but was not about to leave my shelter. I could hear the wind roaring in the trees on the hill above me, so I knew the lake was not the place for me. I spent the entire morning lazing in bed, dozing, listening to rain, and dozing some more. Only when the sun came out at midday did I resume the journey.

When they made Grand Coulee Dam and Lake Roosevelt in the late 1930s, the government took over an extra band of land fringing the lake. As a result, no houses, docks, roads, or stairways touch the shoreline. This band of public land also has trees that block most houses and cabins from view. So from a boater's point of view, the entire 600 miles of lake perimeter is a secluded public park, and all the beaches are informal, free public campsites.

Despite its wonderful recreation opportunities, the lake was lightly used in early June when I traversed it. As I paddled along I never saw any human-powered craft, except the green kayak, and saw motorboats only occasionally, and almost always at a great distance. It was therefore highly unusual when, early in the morning crossing the middle of the lake on the stretch below Kettle Falls, a motorboat whizzed up behind me, slowed down, and stopped.

"You've got a perfect right to be here," said the burly driver, "but I should tell you that in about five minutes the boats for the fishing derby will be coming up this lake at 50, 60 miles an hour. I just wanted to warn you."

He was a judge in a contest sponsored by the Lake Roosevelt Walleye Club—the fish they're going after. It was a fairly serious undertaking, with entry fees of $350 and a first prize of $6,000. The previous day, motorboats had been scooting around the lake as fishermen tested likely fishing spots, using high-tech sonar and radar equipment.

It was to be a catch-and-release tournament and the judge was uptight about his upcoming responsibilities and not paying attention. After giving me his warning, he gunned his motor, creating a huge wake, a wave that came closer to swamping me than any Mother Nature had created. I had to smile at this example of small-minded authority at work, assuming that other people don't have enough sense to manage their affairs and causing more harm than good by interfering.

In due course, the contestants came roaring down the lake in their shiny fiberglass boats powered by chrome-plated 200-horsepower engines, racing for fishing spots identified by their electronic depth sounders. I wondered what Izaak Walton, the 17th-century English advocate of contemplative fishing, would have thought.

On my fourth day, nearly halfway along Lake Roosevelt, I was pinned down for most of the day by adverse wind. It had been calm in the early morning when I set out, but as the sun rose the wind picked up. By 8:00 a.m. I had all I could do to fight my way to small cove and take shelter. Above me stood a summer cabin where a group of local young people had come for a holiday. The owner of the cabin—Jono—was a local farmer with a 1-year-old baby boy he was quite proud of.

I did everything I could to pass time, even shaving in the cold water of the lake. I had a new razor, but nevertheless it dragged across my face most painfully. I exercised, as part of my regimen to keep my legs in shape for the hike around Grand Coulee Dam. I picked up a big rock and did two sets of 20 squats, as well as sit-ups and stretches. I read *Don Quixote*. At lunchtime, a teenage couple brought me a plate of scrambled eggs and hash browns, and a bottle of cold Evian water.

In the afternoon, more of Jono's friends arrived. Each visiting couple had an identical black lab, and these dogs—their numbers peaked at five—were tireless retrievers. One adopted me as his play-mate, and at first I enjoyed flinging his stick as far as I could into the water and watching him paddle to retrieve it. Eventually I tired of the game, but he did not, though he was panting with exhaustion. I tried to deceive him by throwing the stick in unexpected directions, but he smoked each move. Finally I did a Statue of Liberty play, pretending to throw the stick forward while flipping it backward into the trees. This confused and defeated him, but not for long. Soon he was back, dropping a saliva-covered ponderosa pine cone at my feet. I ignored him. He nudged it closer with his nose, pushing it against my shoe. He groveled low and twisted his head up at me, staring with plead-ing eyes. Not even a Pharaoh with the hardest heart could deny this entreaty. I picked up the gooey cone and tossed it into the water, then ran to lose myself in a group of partygoers seated on the beach.

One of the young men took his windsurfer out into the swirling, gusting winds, and even though he was experienced, he fell several times. On his last fall, he broke his fiberglass mast. Jono stood ready with his motorboat to rescue him, but he managed to paddle himself back in against the wind and waves.

Later in the afternoon, two pretty young women stripped down to bathing suits, and started what looked like a war dance at the edge of the water. Their purpose was not battle, but beauty. They knew that the fine glacial mud of the shoreline could be agitated into a liquid mud bath, a bath they said would cost hundreds of dollars in big-city spas. At first they sat sedately in their little mud puddle and delicately applied the goo to their bodies. Then they began to fling bits of it at each other, gently at first, then more vigorously as the audience egged them on. I had my camera out.

"I bet you don't see this on television, Kenny," said one of the girls teasing the husband of another.

"That's because he can't afford the porno channel," commented one of the men.

All this was not bad entertainment for a lonely sailor pinned down on a windy shore.

In an effort to beat the arrival of the wind on the next day, I resolved to get started as soon as I could. I got out of the sleeping bag at 4:20 a.m., when I could just make out the blue color of my sleeping bag, and went through my morning routine as quickly as possible. When finished, I got into the kayak, pleased with what I thought was a world-class early-bird effort, and was dismayed to see that the GPS said it was 6:00. My morning chores, even when promptly performed, consumed over an hour and a half.

My camping system, limited and primitive as it was, involved a vast number of operations. To set up and start my little stove, a 14-ounce Whisper Lite that runs on white gas, involved nine steps, and about the same number to shut it down and put it away. All told, it took over a hundred steps to cook a meal—oatmeal for breakfast, rice for supper—eat it, clean up, and get packed up.

All these steps were made difficult because I was cooking on the ground, with no good place to put things. A cup balanced on a rock wanted to tip over; a spoon rested on the ground transferred sand into the oatmeal. And if the wind was blowing, I needed to put a rock on top of each item. Hopping up and down as I prepared a meal, I often felt like Rumpelstiltskin doing some mad dance. I longed for a picnic table.

On that day, instead of having to fight the wind as I had feared, I was able to use it! A breeze sprang up in my favor, so I raised my double-wing sail. I had cursed buying and bringing the sail rig, because the cost ($290) and extra weight had seemed a waste. The winds in this part of the world are predominantly from the south and west, directly opposed to my direction of travel. Since this was a downwind sail rig I could only go in the direction of the wind, plus or minus about 30 degrees with the help of the rudder. But on this occasion, the sail paid off. It was a wonderful feeling to make progress just sitting on my fanny.

However, sailing has a nerve-racking aspect, too, and this downside finally led me to abandon the sail on later trips. With the sail rigged, there is no way to balance the boat. When paddling, the paddle can be braced in the water for leverage against tipping. However, the sail system uses half of the paddle as the top segment of the mast. So when sailing, the paddle's gone and I'm just dead meat, helplessly rocking back and forth in the waves.

Furthermore, the kayak has no keel, so an unexpected gust against the sails could easily tip it over. To guard against this danger, I had to hold both sheet ropes in my hands, so I could release them immediately if a gust struck. If I was even a second slow in letting go, I could be blown over. For these reasons, sailing proved to be an unsatisfactory catch-22. In light winds, it was safe to cleat the sails and relax, but I would make only 2 miles an hour, less than I could make by paddling. In stronger winds, I could make a respectable 4 miles an hour, but it turned me into a nervous wreck.

My sailing that morning brought me to the town of Two Rivers, where the Spokane River joins the Columbia. I had traveled 96 miles, and had only 40 to go before reaching Grand Coulee Dam.

I left the boat at the marina and went up to the Indian gambling casino that stands on the hill overlooking the water. I wasn't interested in gambling—I was having my fill of that on the water—but in getting some decent food. Sure enough, they served breakfast, a plateful of scrambled eggs and sausages for just $3.00 (they keep the price low to attract gamblers).

I wolfed this food down, even though I'd had a full breakfast—double serving of oatmeal—just four hours earlier. Obviously I was using a lot of calories. I also used the restroom at the casino to get that top-of-the-world feeling that comes with a hot water wash and shave.

The casino itself was a depressing place, an electronic hell of red, orange, and white lights flashing at random; mirrors multiplying this wild flashing, and incessant, phony electronic tunes dinning from the slot machines, each song clashing with its neighbor. Television sets blared daytime TV shows and news headlines, completing the setting of stressful mindlessness.

The customers were elderly, retired folk, so one can't say that gambling is subverting youth or undermining the work ethic of America. In the end, casino gambling may just be a cumbersome way of transferring funds from the Social Security bureaucracy to the Indian tribal bureaucracy—supplying much-appreciated below-cost breakfasts to kayakers as a by-product.

Later that afternoon, I pulled into Seven Bays, a marina and general store 6 miles down the lake from Two Rivers. I was walking off the dock when I saw a man in a bathing suit about to go in for a dip in the icy Columbia's waters. I overheard him say something about "kayak" to someone, and went to investigate. Did he have a green kayak? Yes! It turned out that he was the lone kayaker I had seen several days earlier, taking a quick swim before he headed home.

He lived in the Seattle area where he kayaked all the time, an experienced, savvy kayaker who had perfected an Eskimo roll because he practiced in a swimming pool every winter. Why was his boat so low in the water? He carried six gallons of drinking water because he didn't trust local water supplies, afraid of agricultural chemicals that might be in it.

I admired his energy and abilities, but we differed on a point of psychology. His trip was an 80-mile circuit in a segment of Lake Roosevelt, up one shore, then back down the other: a convenient, predictable way to enjoy fresh air, scenery, time alone for contemplation, and exercise. To my mind, this paddling in a circle has no appeal. The excitement of a kayak trip lies in not knowing what lies over the horizon, and in completing a trip to a place you have never been.

As I said, this man was the only other paddler I saw on the entire lake. A strong karma indeed must have been working in that vast universe of water to draw us together, not once but twice.

Just as happened on my Potomac trip, friends and acquaintances reacted with anxiety on hearing about my plan to kayak down the Columbia. "Of course you're taking a cell phone," they said in a tone that implied I would be violating a government regulation if I weren't. I shifted my weight from foot to foot, and tried to come up with sufficiently evasive responses to keep them from reporting me to the authorities, but finally admitted that no, I wasn't taking a cell phone.

To deal with their disbelief, I turned the question around and asked them why this device should be thought necessary. One answer was that it is needed to stay in touch, to keep up communications with friends, family, and the wider world.

But on a kayak trip I don't want to stay in touch. Much of my joy on these trips comes from taking on another life. Miles from home and away from anyone who knows me, I am reincarnated as a new person, capable of seeing the world with new eyes. Anything that connects me with the old life interferes with this feeling of freshness. I didn't want to hear about the leak in the dishwasher or what's happening with the Mideast peace process.

Robert Louis Stevenson made the same point about breaking contact with home on a trip. He took a kayak trip in the north of France with a friend in 1876, and wrote up his adventures in *An Inland Voyage*. He arranged to have mail sent and held for him at

Compiègne, a town near the end of the trip, but later regretted it. "Our journey may be said to end with this letter bag at Compiègne," he wrote. "The spell was broken."

Stevenson explained his theory of leaving aside the old life when traveling: "I wish to take a dive among new conditions for a while, as into another element. I have nothing to do with my friends or my affections for the time; when I came away I left my heart at home in a desk." His dictum: "No one should have any correspondence on a journey."

When friends insisted I should have a cell phone they were not mainly thinking about staying in touch, however. Their primary concern was danger. They thought that anyone who ventured defenseless into new places and travels by unusual means is likely to encounter disaster. It's probable this attitude comes from the media, whose stock in trade is terrifying people with tales of tornados, landslides, and savage killings. To a TV viewer, the world beyond his home and neighborhood is a frightening place, and he assumes that to deal with it one must have that modern security blanket, a cell phone.

But is the world all that dangerous? I'm not talking about deliberately taking risks like intentionally plunging over waterfalls, or swallowing fire, but going from A to B by natural, primitive means, and using what little common sense I may have to steer clear of obvious danger. As I did this, I found that strange rivers, strange towns, and strange people are not hostile, but accommodating. Nature's winds are almost always breezes, not tornados, and outstretched helping hands outnumber clenched fists by an enormous margin.

To be sure, one is often apprehensive. On a kayak trip, hardly a day goes by without a moment of fear, or at least anxiety. Take camping out, which often involves stressful nights of non-sleep. One lies with eyes wide open listening to each sound in the forest, imagining what threat it poses. One learns to distinguish between the rustling of leaves caused by tiny animals you need not fear—chipmunks, mice, and such—and the cracking of branches that portends an animal of greater weight.

On this Columbia journey, I was occasionally disturbed by nocturnal noises. Several days into the trip I was awakened shortly after falling asleep by noises of the branch-cracking kind. I decided I needed to be aggressive. If the creature was a nuisance animal like a raccoon, it needed to be chased away for good with a hair-raising holler. If it was a life-threatening animal like a cougar or grizzly bear, it must have scented me and was in an aggressive mood. Therefore, I reasoned, I needed to put on a bold front. I gathered myself into a crouching position in the mouth of my sleeping bag, leaped to my feet screaming bloody murder, and flashed my light at the animal.

I couldn't believe what I saw.

Instead of a looming monster with eyes fiercely glowing in the beam of my flashlight, it was a deer, but a kind I had never seen before. It was tiny, even smaller than an ordinary fawn, but with adult features and bearing. It did not seem wild, either, because my scream did not send it running away. It raised its head and gave me a look of dismay, as if to say, "Why are you, whom I trusted, shouting at me?" Then it moved away, glancing back as if in regret. I felt guilty at having distressed so inoffensive a creature. And I was thoroughly puzzled. Was it a miniature, domesticated deer? If so, what was it doing roaming about? Was it an exotic species that had escaped from a zoo? But I was hundreds of miles from any zoo. No explanation fit.

In any case, thank goodness I did not have a cell phone to call 911 in that first moment of panic when I heard those branches cracking in the forest. I never would have lived down the headlines: "Kayaker rescued from pet deer; billed $15,000 for bothering local sheriff."

Not all worrisome situations are merely harmless or funny, of course. Some are difficulties that the traveler must grapple with and surmount. But the grappling and the surmounting are part of the invigorating challenge of the trip. Imagine calling 911: "I'm about to be rained on and will end up cold and wet, and might eventually die of pneumonia if some kind of shelter isn't provided." I assume that anyone on the other end of the line would say what I'm already telling myself, namely, "Use your imagination. Figure something out. Take care of yourself!"

If you deliver pizzas, or leave your teenage daughter at coed slumber parties, by all means carry a cell phone. But on a long-distance kayak trip I really don't think you need one.

My seventh night was spent at a semideveloped campsite that had—*hurray!*—a picnic table. I also had a vista across the lake of a towering granite cliff turning ever-deeper shades of yellow in the setting sun.

My record keeping showed that I had traversed 105.5 miles since the trip began, and was only 32 miles from the Grand Coulee Dam. To pass the time on a long, slow afternoon, I measured my paddling efficiency. I found that 800 paddle strokes took me a mile in flat, windless conditions, so my 105 miles corresponded to 84,000 strokes. In retrospect, it certainly didn't feel like that much work.

When I reached for my shoes the next morning—I always put them near my head—I was amused to see that both laces on my right shoe had been chewed off at the eyelets and taken away. It stopped being funny when it occurred to me that if rodents on this beach were so bold and so dental as to chew my shoelaces right under my nose, they may well have destroyed everything of cloth that I owned, including the kayak!

An inspection revealed that nothing else had been touched, not even the food bag. It was just one of those strange pranks of nature—probably a mouse or pack rat looking for stuffing to line a nest.

While eating breakfast, I was treated to another natural curiosity. A deer walked out to the end of a little spit of land and kept right on walking into the water, deeper and deeper, until it was swimming, apparently attempting to swim across Lake Roosevelt, which was 2 miles wide at that point. It was making surprising speed, considering it had only thin hoofs to paddle with, about 300 yards in a few minutes. Then it abruptly turned around and came back. Was the deer out for a refreshing morning swim? Or did it intend a long-distance migration, but then thought better of it?

When I rounded Plum Point later that day, I saw the electric pylons of the Grand Coulee Dam complex. I had almost reached the first major destination on the trip!

The last 6 miles proved to be unexpectedly harrowing, however. At first, the wind blew in my favor, and I put up my sail and was soon cruising along, singing "Grand Coulee here we come, tra la, tra la." Then out of nowhere came a blast of wind, almost like a bomb exploding. The boat bucked and tipped, but fortunately I was holding sheet ropes and immediately let go of both sails or the boat probably would have been knocked over. Then the waves got crazy, because the wind shifted 90 degrees. Without a paddle—it's part of the mast in the sailing rig—all I could do was hunker down in the pitching boat and try to shut my ears to the wildly banging sails. Little by little, I inched forward in the boat and gathered in the sails and lashed them to the mast. Then, using my half paddle, I limped to a picnic area on the south shore.

The gust and violent change in wind conditions thoroughly unnerved me, and I did not want to go back on the water for several hours. It was the surprise factor that added to my fear, just as it did back at the Little Dalles. I assumed I would have smooth sailing, and didn't know—as locals told me later—that the area upstream of the dam has treacherous winds that even powerboat drivers fear.

I finally got my courage up, stowed the sail, and grimly took on the job of making the last few miles. The mountains ringing the lake funnel the winds in odd and changing patterns, and I was continually hit by gusts from all directions. I couldn't control the boat with the paddle alone and had to lower the rudder to keep myself on course. Rainstorms in the distance indicated an unstable atmosphere—and danger of lightning. I headed for the base of some cliffs to get out of the wind, but found it was blowing strongly along the cliffs, too. Head down, I clawed my way along the cliff face. After several hours of tense paddling, I made it to a rocky shore left of the dam where I beached the kayak, got out, and kissed the ground.

For weeks before the trip began, a big worry—second only to concern about the rapids at the border—was how I would get around Grand Coulee Dam with my overloaded pack. The carrying pack, jammed with Klepper parts, and the other gear—life jacket, cook stove, food, utensils—weighs 80 pounds. It is 5 feet tall and strapped into it, I look like an ant trying to carry a sugar cube. To get it on, I sit on the ground and work my arms into the straps. Then I pitch forward onto all fours, and my trembling legs raise me to a standing position.

The week before the trip, I took a trial walk around my block to prove I could carry this pack, but it strained me to the limit. Walking two blocks, also, is not portaging around Grand Coulee Dam, which involved a hike of 7 miles. Relieved as I was to have survived the winds of Lake Roosevelt, I knew I was not home free. My spinal column now faced an almost impossible challenge.

Guardian angels stepped in to solve the problem even before I had to face it. In the parking area above where I landed, two men were sitting by a Ford pickup, drinking beer and enjoying the scenery. Alan and Kurt, old pals on a weeklong vacation, were practically waiting to encounter someone to help. As soon as they learned about my situation, they offered to drive me to a motel. After a nice show of hesitation, I accepted.

As I got into the truck seat beside him, Alan lowered his voice and addressed me very seriously, "You don't have to worry about me. I'm not a mass murderer or anything." He was trying to put me at ease, but his remark put a seed of doubt in my mind. As it happened, he spoke the truth. He and Kurt delivered me safe and un-massmurdered to the Coulee House Motel, just downstream of the dam.

A two-night stay in Grand Coulee gave me a chance to become civilized again with a shower, shave, and laundered clothes. I used the free day to hike around the dam and up onto the three-lane road that runs along the top. I took the tour down into the powerhouse to see the generators, including the largest one in the world, which has a stainless steel drive shaft between the turbine and the generator that is 4 feet in diameter. Deep inside the dam I felt an enormous rumbling and shaking: thoroughly convincing evidence of a million horses at work, generating enough electricity to supply both Portland and Seattle.

When they built the dam in the late 1930s, it was poured in huge 50-foot by 50-foot concrete blocks. Concrete masses of that size take a century to cool and shrink, so to speed up the process, they laid some 17,000 miles of metal pipe in the concrete through which they ran cooling water. When the dam was done they couldn't take these pipes out, of course, so they plugged them by running cement slurry into them.

At the motel in the evenings, I had plenty of time to review my route and study the upcoming segments. My measurements showed I had traveled 137.5 miles from the Canadian border to Grand Coulee Dam. This means that Lake Roosevelt itself is close to 130 miles long, a fact confirmed by using an opisometer on the official map of the lake. I point this out because some sources, including the official Lake Roosevelt Web site, give the length of the lake as 150 miles.

The second lake in the Columbia chain is Rufus Woods Lake, named after the Wenatchee newspaper editor who crusaded for building the Grand Coulee Dam. The river flows into it from Grand Coulee Dam through a channel with steep, rocky sides, so I took a taxi 5 miles downriver to get to the first place where it was possible to put in.

The harrowing approach to Grand Coulee had seriously shaken my confidence, and even after two days' rest, I wasn't over my fears. In the first miles after the put-in, a current of about 3 mph stirred the water, and this was enough to make me apprehensive. Shortly before lunch, I heard a strange, periodic swishing noise down the river. I assumed it was a hidden rapids or waterfall, gripped my paddle tightly and scanned the glassy surface for turbulence. As I approached the source of the noise, I saw buildings off to one side of the river, and paddled over. They were part of a fish farm raising hybrid trout confined in pens in the river. The fish are fed by blowing food pellets into the pens through a long flexible tube. The waterfall I feared so much was the rattling sound of the pellets being blown through the duct every ten seconds and sprayed out over the water.

Rainfall in the Columbia Valley diminishes as one moves southwest toward the rain shadow of the Cascade Mountains. At the beginning of the trip at the border with Canada, the slopes were covered with vegetation and tall trees—mostly ponderosa pines. As I moved down Lake Roosevelt, the land became drier and browner. Below Grand Coulee, on Rufus Woods Lake, the country had the desert feel of the old Wild West. I even found a wrecked buckboard, its bone-dry timbers collapsed on the ground. As I paddled along, I saw few houses or any other man-made structure, and seldom heard a sound of human activity. Only bird songs broke the silence across the water.

One bird that populates the skies on the Columbia is not known for singing, but for acrobatics. It's the cliff swallow. Along Lake Roosevelt, they make their nests in holes in the glacially deposited clay cliffs. On Rufus Woods Lake and downriver, the swallows make their nests out of mud plastered on rock cliffs. These birds are relentless fliers, crisscrossing the skies, dipping, darting, and skimming along the surface of the water, gobbling up stray mosquitoes. My constant companions, they led me to coin my private name for the Columbia: River of Swallows.

Rufus Woods Lake is narrow, only about one-quarter of a mile across, so I could easily switch from side to side. The lake offered a dramatic contrast in temperature. In the blazing sun, the air above the glassy surface was extremely hot, so hot I had to get off the lake at midday for three hours to rest in the shade. But the water of the lake is frigid, because the turbines suck it from the icy bottom of Lake Roosevelt. It felt like refrigerated water. The youth in me delighted in splashing its coolness in the sweltering heat. The oldster worried about the danger of hypothermia if I should turn over.

After two days of paddling, I was camped 8 miles from Chief Joseph Dam where another challenging portage loomed. I awoke to watch the sky light up and to listen to the birds. A dove cooed nearby, while another, way across the river, answered with exactly the same call, a repartee that went on and on. No swallows were about. They are late risers because the insects on which they feed aren't yet flying in the cool early morning air. The morning star was Mars, strikingly large and bright orange in the clear, dry air. It couldn't be mistaken for a star.

I arrived at the boat-launch ramp on the south side of Chief Joseph Dam at noon, the time of the highest, hottest sun of that early July day. I took my time disassembling the kayak and fitting it into the pack. Then I rested in the shade of a tree, had my lunch, and waited. And waited.

I was half hoping someone might drive up and offer me a lift, but the place remained deserted. My rational brain told me that I should wait until the heat abated at sunset, but I couldn't bear the idea of sitting still and wasting the entire afternoon.

I shouldered the pack and set out on the highway. The blacktop radiated heat like a furnace and not a breath of wind stirred to cool me. I plodded steadily for an eighth of a mile up the road, doing well, but sweat began to pour off me in an unusual and alarming flow. I thought it would be prudent to stop and take a rest.

The pack was too big for me to unsling from a standing position. I had to drop on all fours and then fall sideways. I performed this maneuver and wound up seated at the edge of the highway, slumped forward so that the top of the pack sheltered my head from the sun, an odd and pathetic posture.

The first car that came was going the other way, but the driver slammed on his brakes, turned around, and asked if I needed help. I explained that I was just resting. He threw me a bottle of ice-cold Evian water and drove away.

A minute later, a man came up on my side of the road driving a red Datsun pickup.

"I was eating lunch up at my house," he said, indicating a house standing above the road, "watching you from the table. I said to my wife, 'Honey, that fella's going down!'"

What was, on my part, merely a rest stop appeared to be a collapse to onlookers. But then again, maybe it was closer to a collapse than I realized. I didn't refuse Mark Steele's offer to drive me the 3 miles to the boat ramp below the dam. He was a big, chunky fellow, a farmer and contractor—who lived up to his name. He lifted my pack into his pickup with one arm.

So once again, I wasn't able to prove that I could portage around a dam on my own. But then, perhaps that wasn't necessarily required. My job was to make the best effort I could and let fortune, fate, or my fellow man decide what to do about it.

After setting up and launching in Lake Pateros, downstream from the Chief Joseph Dam, I overdid the paddling. Late in the afternoon, when I should have stopped, I saw the town of Brewster 5 miles away, and with it, the promise of a much-needed restaurant supper. I slogged against a brilliant setting sun, my speed dropping as fatigue set in. I didn't reach Brewster until 9:30 p.m. and all the restaurants were closed, except a McDonalds, an especially dirty McDonalds where the food proved to be overcooked and stale.

    I had entered cherry country. The first sign was a puzzling sound that I began hearing as I approached Chief Joseph Dam. From far away, it sounded like a steam shovel dropping a bucket of gravel into an empty dump truck.

    As I drew closer, it became more of an explosive boom and I discovered it was the propane cannons used to scare birds away from the ripe cherries. In some spots, I heard half a dozen of them blasting away, like artillery in a war zone.

    Mark Steele had told me that as the cherries ripen, rain is a disaster because the water sits in the stem well, gets absorbed into the cherry, and splits the skin. So farmers hire helicopters to hover over the orchards after a rain, blowing water away and drying the cherries. Some orchards have towers with big fan blades on them to accomplish the same purpose.

    The fruit-producing area of Washington has a high Mexican population, the result of the need for temporary labor to pick fruit. Many of these temporary laborers have settled, and as a result a visit to a town like Brewster is practically a trip to Mexico. The signs in the stores are in Spanish, the music coming from the bars is Mexican, and the only people I saw on the streets were speaking Spanish. It's a scruffy town, with shacks, run-down mobile homes, and blue tarps over makeshift structures. At the entrance to town, city fathers had put up a huge billboard, "Building Permits Required; Building Code Enforced." This was a great joke because the entire town was obviously noncompliant with any conceivable building code. I suspected a tension between the Anglo city officials, who put up the sign, and the

Hispanic migrants who were taking over the town.

The next day while resting in the shade in the town of Pateros, I saw a tall, lanky fellow riding a bike and pulling a two-wheeled trailer overloaded with camping gear. A lantern dangled from it, and a cookstove, and pots and pans including a heavy cast-iron frying pan, even an umbrella. It must have been a 300-pound load. He was hatless and shirtless, and his skin was toasted to brown leather. He was missing most of his teeth, so he reminded me of Don Quixote, one of whose nicknames was "the Knight of the Sad Countenance" because he lost most of his teeth in an early escapade.

This dour soul was from Marysville, California. He was not talkative, and was eager to get on with his journey, and I had to pry rather insistently to get his story from him. His trip was a loop that would take him over the Cascade Mountains to the Washington coast, and then back down to California. He did this exact route year after year: to me a scary example of perseveration. To drag that monstrous load in the blazing sun, on the same busy highways, year after year, seemed a punishment devised in the third circle of hell, but the challenge obviously suited him.

When I reached Wells Dam, at the base of Lake Pateros, my heart sank. There was no boat ramp, or any other plausible takeout spot. The bank consisted of large, fractured rocks, all the way up to the railway line 40 feet above the lake. A person could barely crawl up this embankment; getting a kayak up seemed impossible.

I managed it by breaking the project into many steps. I unloaded everything from the kayak and carried the items up one at a time. Then I hoisted the lightened kayak a few inches onto the lowest rock and took it apart, stick by stick, and carried up the individual parts. All this took several hours of unremitting labor and at least 20 trips up and down those jagged rocks. To an observer, I must have looked as insanely masochistic as the Marysville biker, except that I never planned to do it again.

Up on the tracks, I packed everything into the carrying pack and lugged it a quarter mile to a patch of green grass and spruce trees that decorated the entrance to Wells Dam. I hid behind the trees until darkness fell, and then set up my tent on the grass. Any green grass in that desert country meant a sprinkling system that might well come on in the middle of the night. I fixed that problem by putting Ziploc plastic bags over the sprinkler heads that might come on. The GPS showed that I had come a total of 201.5 miles from the start of the trip.

The next morning, I had a hurried breakfast of an energy bar, took the Ziploc bags off the sprinklers (they didn't go on during the night), hoisted the pack, and started walking. After three-quarters of a mile I reached a flat area below the dam, the site of a fish hatchery, totally deserted at the early morning hour. Disregarding the weathered "No Trespassing" signs, I made my way to the water's edge and assembled the kayak.

The spot was narrow and dark, hemmed in by cliffs on both sides of the river. The turbines made a grinding, pounding sound, and their discharge erupted in an unnatural boiling of the water in front of me. Water cascaded down the backside of the dam above my head. It probably came from a leaking sluice gate, but in that sinister space it felt like the dam was beginning to break. Escaping into the friendly sunshine, I felt a great sense of deliverance, and exhilaration too, having proven, at last, that I could get around a dam under my own steam.

Several miles below the dam I cruised into a landing spot on shore so quietly that I surprised two coyotes, a mother and a pup, right at the water's edge. They didn't know what to make of me, and dipped their heads up and down in perplexity, before they finally retreated up the hillside, revealing how graceful they are. They don't just walk: they bounce on each step. It reminded me of movies I'd seen of the fox-trot, a bouncy dance popular in the 1890s.

At noontime, at Chelan Falls, I came upon a paragliding rally. The contestants were taking off from the peak of a mountain several thousand feet above the river, looking like a swarm of mosquitoes. Circling round and round, they gradually descended to the river. I beached the kayak and went to the field where they were landing. The best fliers settled as gently as if they were stepping off a bus. The aim of the contest was not to land there, however, but to catch a thermal and ride to a designated landing point 20 miles away. The thermals weren't working too well that day, and most of the fliers came down in the field at the base of the mountain.

My, how the wheel of fortune does turn! A day that saw the morning's victory portaging around Wells Dam and the delight of the paragliders in the early afternoon turned into a paddling fiasco in the evening.

My first problem was food. I needed to resupply, but when I went into Chelan Falls to look for the store I was told was there, I found it had burned down the year before. I was out of bread, fruit, nuts, and energy bars; all I had left was rice and oatmeal for a dreary supper and breakfast.

As I continued down the river, I couldn't find a suitable place to camp. Every landing spot had a house behind it, and the rest of the river was hemmed in by railroad embankment and cliffs. Then the wind against me picked up. I fought that for a mile, until I was unable to make forward progress. Across the lake, I spotted a beach below an orchard, and headed for it, angling into the harassing wind and waves. When I reached it, it was not a beach but tarmac, a remnant of the old highway that ran along the river before the dam raised the water level. The surface was nearly awash, and covered with sharp stones and slimy algae. There was grass in the apple orchard above me, but the irrigation sprayers were going, with tree-high nozzles soaking everything. Oh, and poison ivy grew on the bank between the edge of the lake and the orchard. There wasn't a place to sit down.

I paced up and down the stony, slimy sliver of land, hoping the wind would die down and let me proceed. But it only grew stronger, making it clear I was condemned to this spot. I started to wonder if my trip was over right there, that I would have to walk to a farmhouse and call Judy to get me. It was the lowest moment of the trip.

I watched a muskrat swim out from the reeds and bring hydrilla weeds back to shore, and decided it was suppertime for me too. I piled stones to shield the stove from the wind and, squatting in the stony muck, tried to prepare some rice. Getting clean water was a problem. The waves had been beating against the swampy shore, so the only cooking water I could collect was muddy and slimy. When I heated it, a slick formed on top.

As I finished my miserable supper, yet another hardship befell: the lake began to rise. The water flooded in, covering my sliver of ground and threatening to float away my kayak. It showed how rapidly the level of these narrow, low-capacity lakes could change. Yuppies in Portland decide to turn on their hot tubs, and whoosh, the Bonneville Power Administration draws down the lake to make the electricity for them. When they turn off their tubs, the BPA shuts off the generators and the lake fills up again—rising as much as 2 feet in a manner of minutes.

I grabbed the kayak, carried it to the reeds, heaved it as far up the bank as I could, and tied it to two different bushes, so even if the water rose further the boat wouldn't go anywhere. I hastily repacked the cooking gear before the rising waters overcame it.

I was caught between the rising waters and the sprayers, and a soaking seemed unavoidable. Then I got my first break: the sprayers in the orchard shut off, enabling me to relocate onto the grass, where I could sleep—or at least try. Since the orchard was next to the highway, trucks and cars screamed by 30 feet from my head. A bilingual sign at the edge of the orchard on the highway said, "Danger! Peligro! Do not enter. Poison Spray." Not exactly a luxury campground, but I was a beggar, not a chooser.

Then the sky gave me an esthetic lift. Across the river, the disappearing sun set fire to the clouds in an intricate design of gold and pink, recalling God's promise to Noah to lay off further disasters.

I slept surprisingly well in the orchard. The sprayers didn't come on again, and the traffic on the road slacked way off during the night. In the morning, the wind still blew, but not as fiercely, and with occasional lulls. The healthy sleep gave me confidence to tackle the gauntlet of wind and waves.

I clawed my way along the cliffs for a mile, sometimes losing a few feet when the gusts picked up, but making overall progress. Suddenly, the wind disappeared almost entirely and I paddled freely ahead. I formed the theory that I must have been trapped in a "wind chute," a segment of the river where mountain formations concentrate wind. I applied that theory 8 miles further on, when I came to another spot where ferocious gusts again tried to stop me. Instead of pulling over to wait the wind out, I kept paddling and, sure enough, after I passed that stretch, there was hardly any wind—and occasionally a breeze in my favor.

By afternoon, I reached the town of Entiat, which had a grocery store, and I had the joy of replenishing my supplies. I bought a pound of Bing cherries, and thus enjoyed the product of the exploding orchards I had been paddling past. I stayed at the local campground for $5, and had the blessings of a lawn, a rest room, and a picnic table. I didn't have to crouch on muddy rocks like a savage to make supper, nor flee rising waters. The mantle of civilization fell upon my soul; swear words disappeared from my vocabulary.

I was 17 miles and one more dam from Wenatchee.

Tension mounted as I faced the complexities of getting around Rocky Reach Dam. I pulled into Lincoln Rock State Park, a mile upriver from the dam, to reconnoiter.

At the dock, I met Ted, a burly, sunburned young man who rented, and no doubt rode, Jet Ski boats. He was impressed with my journey and offered me the use of his home and shower—a generous offer I declined.

On parting, he said, "It's great what you're doing—but I still think you're crazy." I was puzzled that such a capable person should view my modest travels with such alarm.

Lincoln Rock State Park's claim to fame is a craggy profile of Abraham Lincoln's face supposedly outlined in the cliffs across the lake. One can stare at it only so long before wondering who's putting whom on.

As the evening shadows fell, I paddled across the lake, found a reasonable takeout spot, and packed up the kayak. The hike around the dam to the put-in on the other side was 1.75 miles, carefully measured on the GPS, and I made it with only three rest stops. On the trek through the grounds of the Rocky Reach Dam—the grandest lawns and gardens I've seen this side of Kew Gardens in London—I learned that I could get up and down quite easily with the pack on my back by hanging onto a pole or signpost. I found myself enjoying the hike in the cool night air and felt almost disappointed that this was to be my last portage.

I reached the downstream boat ramp area at 10 p.m. and walked into a knot of people, with cars, boats, and RVs parked higgledy-piggledy, and a big campfire with flames leaping at the stars. I made friends with the black guard dog, introduced myself to the crowd sitting around the fire, and was immediately given a beer. My hosts were Wenatchee locals who were camping there on this July 4th week. Several of them were roofers (what a job to have in the July sun!).

Tricia quickly became my hostess, and early in the conversation asked me if I thought Wenatcheans were inhospitable. Apparently, a migrant from the Seattle area had created a brouhaha when he criticized locals for being standoffish in a recent letter to the editor. Tricia was a staunch critic of government, and could hardly stop denouncing its wrongheaded policies and transgressions. There were limits to her libertarian creed, however. The local apple industry was being crushed by cheap foreign imports from Australia and New Zealand, and everyone in Wenatchee—the apple capital of the state—was upset and financially affected. Tricia said her dad was about to go bankrupt, so it wasn't the time or place for me to extol the virtues of free trade. After conversation died down, she showed me to an unoccupied tent I was to use that night. Inhospitable not!

The next morning I made breakfast and did a little panning down by the boat ramp, finding some tiny colors. The camping group served no breakfast as such. As they groggily arose one by one, adults and children alike snacked on Cheetos, Sugar Puffs, and soda pop. I said goodbye to those who were awake and struck out for Wenatchee.

As I approached town, I was delighted to see a number of kayakers out on the water on that Saturday morning, members of the local kayaking club. Wenatchee also has an 11-mile hiking-biking trail along the lakefront, where many people walked, jogged, and biked.

One kayaker, a barrel-chested young man, came rocketing out of the boat basin, flailing the water with his paddles and going three times my speed. He made me realize what a leisurely pace I set. Spurred by his example, I increased my efforts, but he still paddled twice as fast as I and soon became a speck in the distance.

I beached the kayak on the grass at the edge of Wenatchee's riverfront park, marking the completion of a trip of 245.9 miles, including portages, rapids, winds and waves. Several people walking along the nearby bike trail stopped to chat with me while I disassembled the kayak. When they learned I had come from the Canadian border, they professed to be amazed.

I told them there was nothing to it.

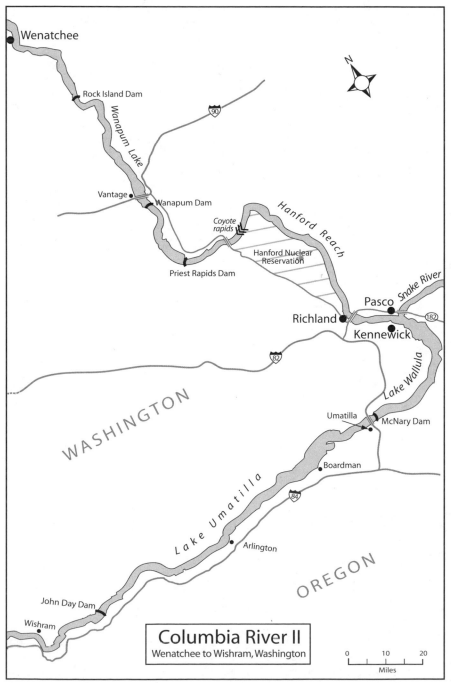

Wenatchee

Rock Island Dam

Wanapum Lake

I 90

Vantage •

Wanapum Dam

Coyote rapids

Hanford Reach

Hanford Nuclear
Reservation

Priest Rapids Dam

Snake River

Pasco

I 182

Richland •

Kennewick

I 82

Lake Wallula

WASHINGTON

Umatilla

McNary Dam

Boardman

I 84

Lake Umatilla

Arlington

OREGON

John Day Dam

Wishram

Columbia River II
Wenatchee to Wishram, Washington

| 0 | 10 | 20 |

Miles

River width not to scale

3

Accidental Terrorist

THE COLUMBIA RIVER II
Wenatchee, Washington to Wishram, Washington (June 2002)

A STRANGE THING HAPPENED to my motivation on reaching Wenatchee: it disappeared.

In the last days of the trip, slogging hour after hour on the glassy water in the blazing sun, I came to the conclusion that kayaking is mostly hard and boring labor and there was no point in inflicting any more of it on myself. I had experienced all the kayaking I needed. I had covered hundreds of miles under my own power. Scared to death, I braved the rapids at the border. I proved my puny frame could pack the kayak around dams. I met colorful personalities, drank in stunning scenery, improvised campsites, and saw a naked woman (waving to me from a fast-moving powerboat). I was ready to turn kayaking on the Columbia into a memory, a safe album of adventure tales to tell grandchildren.

It felt very much like growing up.

Then, less than 72 hours after returning to Sandpoint, I wanted to do more, *had* to do more. It was a little embarrassing to be that inconsistent, changing my mind faster than a politician promising not to raise taxes. What happened?

Simply, the yearning for adventure reasserted itself and pushed all the difficulties and suffering out of mind. Forgotten were all the long, sweat-filled days, the insecurity of being unable to find campsites, the hard ground at night, the unremittingly tasteless food. I had reverted to a youthful outlook, where adventure has only an upside.

As I looked back on this change of heart, I realized that the medical definition of death serves us poorly as a guide to living. To equate a beating heart with life, and to focus on keeping that heart beating for as long as possible is self-defeating. Living means using all your faculties fully and creatively. Someone whose heart is beating but who is in a coma is 99 percent dead. Someone who sits on a couch and stares at television all day long may be 90 percent dead, and so on. Every time a person loses—or doesn't use—a physical or mental faculty, he is a step closer to death. Conversely, every challenging experience makes him more alive (well, okay, facing a firing squad is an exception).

We can be drugged by routines and rationalizations into believing that the rut into which we've settled makes for an adequate life, but we don't know how deeply we can drink from the cup of life until we're fully challenged. I thought I'd had enough adventure until I got home to my usual routines. Then I began to sense that something was missing. On the river, I lived life in Technicolor: everything, whether it was a tree, a sunset, or a principle of political philosophy, was more vivid and more interesting, and I wanted more of that sensation.

The story of Ulysses, the hero of the Trojan Wars, raises this theme of post-adventure blues. Homer's *Odyssey* tells of Ulysses's great exploits as he sailed back from the Trojan Wars to his home in Ithaca, how he escaped from the giant one-eyed Cyclops, how he outwitted the temptress Circe, and so forth. The *Odyssey* ends with Ulysses safely home, reinstalled as king, resting on his laurels, and supposedly living happily ever after.

But was that the end? In his poem *Ulysses*, the English poet Alfred Lord Tennyson took up the story of Ulysses where Homer left off. Tennyson wisely suspects that Ulysses would be not be content to quietly live out his days, but would feel impelled to go back to the sea for more challenges. Tennyson's Ulysses says:

How dull it is to pause, to make an end,
To rust unburnished, not to shine in use!
As though to breathe were life.

A few days of sitting at my computer—merely breathing, as Tennyson would put it—made me hungry for a deeper draught of life. Soon I was making plans to continue the trip down the Columbia.

Early in June the following summer, I began the second leg of the trip in Wenatchee, putting the Klepper back in the water at exactly the same spot in Riverfront Park where I took it out the previous summer. My aim was to complete another third of the journey, approximately 250 miles.

The river in this segment runs through the rain shadow of the Cascade Mountains. Except where irrigation produces lawns or orchards, the land holds nothing but sagebrush, dried-up grass, dead weeds, thorns, and stickers. Next to the river grow scrub trees, especially cottonwoods and a wild mulberry that was fruiting as I paddled by. I found the fruit tasteless and noticed that the birds weren't eating it. The parched terrain was uninviting, but I assumed that it would guarantee dry camping conditions. For this reason, I brought no tent, and no rain gear beyond my nylon jacket.

Well, we live and learn. Or, at least, live.

A strong current powered by the spring runoff from heavy snowfall in the Canadian Rockies rushed me along toward the first dam. In one stretch I sped along at 9 mph, flashing past basalt columns plastered with sparrows' mud nests and apple orchards with tiny green apples just beginning to form.

I had more confidence than the previous year because I had learned how to deal with capsizing. After returning to Sandpoint the previous summer, I took the kayak out to the lake on a warm afternoon and deliberately tipped over in it. The Klepper has two air bladders built into it, so even full of water it still floats. I was able to flip it upright and slither back into the swamped boat without any problem. However, laden with 95 gallons of water, the swamped boat paddles like a cement truck, so if there's a waterfall coming up or a barge bearing down, I would face a Technicolor finale.

I was more confident in facing dams, too, because I had a new strategy for getting around them. I learned from reading Robin Cody's book that an obscure legal provision requires dam operators to portage craft around the dams (since the dam blocks a navigable river). Cody, an employee of the Bonneville Power Administration, knew about this wrinkle and relied on it to get around the dams, phoning ahead to each powerhouse to send a truck to portage his canoe.

It seemed a bit like cheating, but I decided to rely on this "valet portaging" too, especially since I had extra weight in food at the beginning of the trip. Also, this was the summer after 9/11, and I expected more barriers and security hysteria. I would feel exposed creeping around barbed wire carrying a huge black pack that looks exactly like 200 pounds of dynamite. Dam security people might feel less trigger-happy if they knew about me in advance. So several days before starting out, I called the dam control office at the Rock Island Dam and arranged for a portage in the early afternoon.

I reached the dam and stopped at the guard's shack. He phoned the power plant, and two men came in a pickup. They seemed eager to talk and prolong our interaction, as though they were happy to have something to do. They said it's rare that a boater arrives who wants a lift around the dam. The last time they could remember helping a portage was four years earlier, for a group that was sailing down the Columbia in a catamaran, making a film. After they left me at the boat ramp below the dam, I panned among the rocks and found good gold— rather large flakes, indicating the original lode was not far away.

At Wenatchee, I had set out under sunny skies and calm conditions, and paddling up to Rock Island Dam was downright hot in the noonday sun. But during the afternoon, conditions began to change rapidly and dramatically. A mass of chilly air moved in from the north Pacific, bringing strong winds and heavy gray clouds that obscured the sun.

A strong wind sprung up, blowing me from the side, toward the cliffs and jagged rocks that lay on my right. I fought my way offshore, angling against the wind and chop. Occasionally a large wave slammed into the coaming and slopped water into the boat. *If this keeps up,* I thought, *I will eventually be swamped.*

Then began the rain—rain in the desert, just for me! I put on my rain jacket, but it didn't cover my legs. I began to shiver, but there was no place to stop, only cliffs and half-submerged boulders. I just missed being brought down on one boulder by a big wave. If I had hit it, I think it would have capsized me.

After several hours of being lashed by wind and rain, I made it to a cove with a spot of beach and pulled out of the water. I was seriously chilled and needed protection against the rain. Using my paddle as the ridgepole, I made a rough tent using my ground cloth, tying it down to heavy rocks on the sides. I threw my sleeping bag on the sand underneath, crawled inside it, pulled it over my head, and breathed warm air against my shivering knees.

That bag deserves a product endorsement: it's a Slumberjack, a cheap, lightweight nylon sleeping bag, but with a mysterious power to stay dry and warm in damp conditions. It saved my life by allowing me to recover my body temperature.

Eventually my teeth stopped chattering, but I didn't feel well. I hadn't the strength to unpack anything or heat supper. Huddled in the Slumberjack, I snacked on nuts and raisins I carried in my fanny pack. The GPS said I had covered 31.2 miles. I ruefully admitted that I had stuffed the day with more challenges than was wise.

Down the cove a few hundred yards away, two young men arrived in a motorboat and set up a full tent. As dusk fell, they began exploring the area and firing a .22 semiautomatic rifle, apparently shooting at flying birds and spraying volleys in every direction. They made a painful racket for the hypothermia victim huddling in his sleeping bag.

I wondered where all the hundreds of stray bullets were going. I also wondered if the shooters would be satisfied just aiming at birds. For bored and antsy hunters, my blue tarp might make an interesting target. I lay as close to the ground as I could.

The next day was like an Easter Sunday morning, the world made new. I woke toasty warm to a bright and deeply warming sun. The Slumberjack had magically dried my soaked nylon pants. The soldiers of fortune were quietly asleep in their tent, allowing birds to chirp in safety. I pumped up the gas stove and made a cup of hot tea with plenty of honey. Reverently gazing across the shimmering waters of the Columbia, I clutched the warm mug in my hands and gave thanks.

Below the Rock Island Dam, the banks of the Columbia are made of basalt that poured out across Washington in layers so flat and regular that they look like sedimentary rock. In some cliffs I counted over 20 distinct flows. Typically, when molten rock pours out of a fissure in the earth, it moves a few feet an hour, so the rock cools, congeals, and moves slower and slower. The result is a mountain with steeply tipped layers of basalt. In the flows of the Columbia Plateau, the molten rock surged out so fast it didn't have time to cool. It spread out like molasses across a kitchen table. Scientists estimate the tongues of lava moved at 4 miles an hour, a brisk walking pace—and if this stuff were chasing you, you would be walking briskly indeed.

My paddling took me to Vantage, Washington, where Interstate 90 crosses over the Columbia on a long bridge. On the previous day I suffered from bad timing, caught alongside cliffs and rocks when bad weather hit. On this day, I benefited from good timing. Just as I pulled into the boat launch area, the wind picked up and was soon blowing fiercely. I hiked up to a convenience store by the highway to call Judy and was just lifting the handset when the wind exploded from the sky. It blew my eyeglasses off and across the sidewalk and lashed sand into my face and ears. I had to retreat into the store until the fury abated.

I don't know what would have become of me if I had still been on the river when that blast hit because the approach to Vantage has no landing place, only basalt cliffs for 2 miles. The clerk said storms like this have 100 mph winds. I decided not to mention the squall in my call to Judy.

When the winds died down enough to let me on the water again, I headed downstream, crossing the river under the screaming high-speed traffic on the I-90 bridge. My sanity and love of life returned in direct proportion to the distance between my eardrums and that incessant howling.

A few hours later I reached the boat launch above the Wanapum Dam, where I planned to spend the night. As I pulled in, it began to rain. I was tempted to spend the night in the portable outhouse at the boat ramp since it was dry and protected from the wind. The entrepreneurs running portable toilet businesses generally have a sense of humor, and invent droll names for their product. This company was Tee Pee, and its motto was "We're No. 1 in No. 2." I didn't mind the smell so much as the idea of trying to sleep sitting up. So I put together another tent setup at the edge of the parking lot. I found two 4x4s to use as supports and again used the paddle as the ridgepole. It was about an hour's job: digging holes, collecting rocks for tie-downs, and tying the ground cloth. Again, supper consisted of snacking in the sleeping bag. As one index of my hectic bedtimes, I had not been able to brush my teeth for two nights in a row. That hadn't happened since I was 7 years old.

This was supposed to be the desert—but those were real raindrops pattering on the tent. It wasn't torrential, but enough to soak anyone out in it.

The next morning, I picked up the security telephone at the dam entrance and explained my need for a portage around the dam. Two men in a pickup took me to the boat ramp below the dam. They also called ahead to the next dam, Priest Rapids, to alert the security people there and to set up a portage for me.

After a morning of current-aided paddling, I reached Priest Rapids Dam in the early afternoon, and had my first exposure to post-9/11 security efforts.

Since September 2001, we have learned to give "security" a wry, indulgent smile. We are skeptical because time and again we see security officials taking measures that involve great cost and inconvenience, but who obviously haven't asked themselves whether these measures are needed or effective.

On the dams along the Columbia, security officials responded to 9/11 by reflexively closing the dams to the public and putting cyclone fences topped by three strands of barbed wire around them. This was a shame, since it meant that harmless visitors were no longer permitted to see these interesting tourist attractions, with their fish ladders, giant cranes, and crashing spillways. One wonders if officials ever considered why terrorists would be interested in a million-ton chunk of concrete off in the boondocks, and what harm they could do to it if they were.

The other gap in their thinking was the failure to realize that determined terrorists could penetrate their defenses at will. As I was to demonstrate at more than one dam, saboteurs arriving in a boat loaded with explosives, neutron bombs, or trans fat–laden French fries had free access to all facilities.

At Priest Rapids Dam I paddled inside the warning barrier that said "Keep Out" and drew up at the boat launch, as I had been instructed to do back at Wanupum Dam. A security camera on a pole eyed me in the bright afternoon sun.

I walked around waiting for my porters to arrive. Many minutes passed. No one came.

To attract the attention of the security camera, I waved my arms, yelled, clapped my hands, and did everything but take my clothes off. Still nothing happened.

After an hour, I walked up onto the dam, and wandered among the critical dam machinery that would make a terrorist drool, searching for a living soul. Finally, some workmen passed by. I asked them how I could contact dam security. They pointed to a telephone box next to one of the floodgate control motors. I picked it up and dialed the number they gave me.

"Oh, are you there?" a voice said. "We've been watching for you all afternoon."

My eye.

This episode convinced me that in real time, security cameras are probably worthless. Security camera recordings may help solve crimes after they have been committed, but live cameras cannot prevent a crime from taking place.

No human being will watch a live security monitor hour after hour: it's simply too boring to stare at a changeless scene. After weeks and months, these monitors become like wastebaskets, pieces of office furniture barely noticed. Even when security knows the "saboteur" is coming, they forget to watch.

Below Priest Rapids Dam lies the Hanford Reach, a stretch of the Columbia that hasn't been dammed. I had long anticipated voyaging on this part of the river, where the Columbia flows as free as it did in ancient times. Of course, with the free flow came a current. The previous winter, friends told me about a kayaker who took a bad spill on the Hanford Reach and had to be rescued by her companions. I also worried about a "Coyote Rapids" noted on the map.

The people who work at the dams didn't seem to have a clear conception of current. I asked the mechanic who portaged me how fast the river was moving. He looked at it and said 20 miles an hour. It was about 6, which I could plainly see by comparing the water's movement to a walking pace. Even though he spent his whole life dealing with the river's flowing water, he didn't know this elementary fact about it. On the other hand, he knew exactly how many thousand cubic feet of water per second pass through his dam, a number that meant nothing to me.

I didn't go far on the river that afternoon, feeling I should leave Coyote Rapids for morning, when I would be fresh and strong. I camped on a little knoll overlooking the parched desert landscape. I made my first hot supper of the trip, washed a few items of clothing, and brushed my teeth for the first time on the trip. The Hanford Nuclear Reservation lay across the river, its land spanning dozens of miles, all of it closed to the public. The feds are edgy about people even touching the shore on that side. Robin Cody reported that a black helicopter swooped down over him when he briefly landed on this forbidden soil. Looming on the ridge in the distance were towers and buildings where atomic materials were made—and spilled.

Around my campsite I found many broken stones, especially flint chips and half-formed arrowheads: evidence that this was an Indian gathering place in olden days, probably a campsite where members of the Wenatchee tribe fished for the Columbia's salmon, the mainstay of their diet.

The only vegetation in this lonely place was sagebrush and dead stalks of cheat grass with prickly spines that broke off into my socks and pants wherever I walked. One needs cowboy boots for this terrain. The dead grass indicated that the area wasn't full desert and that rain was possible. The sunset echoed the same idea, a red glow shining underneath heavy gray clouds. Since there were no trees to hold up a tent, I broke off branches of sagebrush to put between the ground cloth and the sleeping bag to create an air layer. It protected me adequately against the light rain that came later in the night.

The next morning the water level of the river had risen 4 feet, drifting my drying underwear into the mud, and floating my soap away forever. I spread my wet clothing and equipment onto sagebrush to dry out, only to have the wind blow it onto the dirt. It's not easy keeping up domestic respectability in primitive conditions.

As I paddled that morning I could see that the geology had changed. The first sign of a shift was back near Priest Rapids Dam, where the basalt layers were no longer flat, but sloped steeply, indicating the slowdown of the lava flow. Now, in the Hanford Reach, I saw only sedimentary layers. I had also left the high mountains behind. Alongside the river, the bluffs were only a few hundred feet high. Because of the sedimentary base, the river has a smooth bottom, and flows quietly, even though it moves at the respectable clip of 5–6 mph. The elevation at the beginning of the Hanford Reach was 350 feet above sea level; only four more dams stood between me and the sea.

On the right bank of the river lay the grounds of the Hanford Reservation. Every few hundred yards a post displayed a "No Entry" sign with small print below. At first, I found it an amusing example of bureaucratic mindlessness: a "No Trespassing" sign with print so small you had to trespass in order to read it. As I paddled past dozens of these signs, the insistent repetition of "No," "No," "No" had the predictable effect on the adolescent mind. I began to wonder what the fine print said. I also wondered if it was really true that black helicopters would swoop down on me if I set foot on the property of this tightly guarded nuclear facility.

I pulled the kayak onto the gravel near one of the "No Entry" signs, and walked over to study the fine print. It described in highly technical language the federal statutes under which some unnamed authority was empowered to levy $1,000 and $5,000 fines for unauthorized entrance.

I ate an energy bar. Nothing happened. Then I panned for gold in the gravel along the bank, not finding any. I squinted into the brilliant blue sky. No helicopters seemed willing to appear. The best I could do to defy authority was pee against the signpost.

In Hanford Reach's swiftly moving waters, I let the river do most of the work, occasionally moving the paddles to maintain my self-respect as a kayaker. I couldn't quite sleep or read a book because I had to avoid branches and half-submerged trees, and it could have been dangerous to be caught up in one of those "strainers." Coyote Rapids proved no obstacle, just choppy, agitated water. I expect it would be a true rapid only when the river level is low. By nightfall, I was 9 miles from Richland, having made an easy, current-aided 30.2 miles.

Just before I fell asleep I was treated to two coyote serenades, one far away in the Hanford area, and another, shortly after, on my side of the river. I had heard one the previous night, too. At first their collective howling sounds like cheering coming from a far away football game, then it breaks into yip, yip, yipping and moaning of individual voices. The crooning lasts only about 20 seconds, and then it's over and never occurs again that night. If you miss the overture of this opera, you've missed the whole thing.

I was awakened at first light the next morning by what sounded like a stunt pilot practicing, the snarling motor of a small plane diving and twisting through the air. I lifted my head from my sleeping bag and saw that it was indeed a stunt pilot, but he wasn't wasting his time doing Immelmann turns. He was spraying an orchard, a tricky, dangerous job. To get the spray well down, he put his wheels just at the tops of the trees. At the end of the row he had to leap into the sky to miss propeller towers, power lines, and barns. I watched him closely until he finished the job, made a steep banking climb, and headed for home.

My campsite that night was a queen-sized bed at the Hampton Inn in Richland, Washington. The motel was located on the water, so I moored the kayak at its dock. After my nights in the rain and tramping among stickers, I deserved a little civilized luxury, though perhaps the Hampton Inn was more luxury than I could appreciate. My peanut butter had no need of the room's refrigerator, and I couldn't figure out where, or why, to apply the Special Moisturizing Crème I found on the vanity.

From the point where the Snake River joins the Columbia at the Tri-Cities (Richland, Pasco, and Kennewick), the river is navigable to the sea through massive locks that enable barges to get past the dams. I was keenly concerned to learn whether my kayak would be allowed to go through these locks and what frights of churning water they held for me.

At Pasco, I saw a river tugboat, a strange craft indeed. Alone on the water, the boat looked like a floating lighthouse, with a wheelhouse perched on an ungainly 30-foot tower. Such towers allow the pilots to see over the barges they push. These crafts have no bows to cleave the water, which makes sense, since they normally push a barge. And they have no noticeable hulls, since they do not face big ocean waves. These unseaworthy crafts hardly deserve to be called boats, for they are little more than floating platforms to hold massive engines with propellers. The sight of this tug angrily bashing its square head through the water was the first evidence that my river now had a serious maritime connection with the Pacific Ocean.

A few miles below the confluence of the Snake and the Columbia, I pulled into Two Rivers County Park. It was early for lunch, but the park was such an appealing oasis of nicely mown green grass, towering shade trees, and immaculate picnic grounds, that I couldn't pass it up. How, I wondered, did government create such a blessing here? Soon, I found an answer. I was reading at a shaded picnic table when a man who had been scooting around the park on a three-wheeler checking trash cans drove up and killed the motor.

"This is a lovely park," I said.

"Well, thank you," he replied, as if he were the owner. "I've been working at it for 20 years." He was the one-man manager and do-everything employee of the park. He proudly pointed out the osprey pole he had just erected, and told about the nature walks he organized. Significantly, he broke off the chat, saying he was real busy and had to get to other jobs: most unbureaucratic behavior!

It occurred to me this might be the solution for making government efficient and effective: turn the project over to one person and let him treat it as his own property, without interference from politicians or voters. Then it occurred to me this system would assume that all government officials would automatically be honest, energetic, effective, and responsible. Hmmm. Back to the drawing board.

Below the Tri-Cities, the Columbia opens into a broad stretch 4 miles wide and 10 miles long called Lake Wallula. In the heat of the day, I pulled to the shore and climbed onto the abandoned railroad bed above the river. After eating lunch, I laid down in the shade of a Russian olive tree to take advantage of the peace and quiet for a nap. Before I could close my eyes a comedy of disruption unfolded. It began with two young fishermen who came drifting by in the weak current in a pram. They happened to catch a fish right in front of me, so they had to start their trolling motor to maintain their position, hoping to catch all the other fish they assumed were there.

That wasn't too bad because they were quiet, serious fishermen, and I could respect them in the exercise of a legitimate hobby. A few moments later, however, a large powerboat arrived, driven by a man with a tremendous beer belly. It contained the wives, children and friends of my fishermen. This band of pleasure seekers had bored themselves stiff buzzing in circles around the lake, and decided that the most interesting way to kill time was to bother daddy while he tried to fish. They turned up a stereo to full volume, attempting to reach all four shores of the lake with crashing drums and the heavy twang of electric bass. The fishermen glumly cowered in their boat. Fortunately, the powerboaters were of the television generation, with a limited attention span for any activity, including making a nuisance of themselves. They soon sped away, drinking deeply of renewable and nonrenewable resources, to find some other way to bore themselves.

Just as I started to relax, a red Jeep came roaring along the disused railroad roadbed where I lay. It stopped a dozen yards before running over me and disgorged five teenage boys and girls, several of whom had .22 rifles. They started shooting at fish, birds, and butterflies in the lagoon alongside the embankment, turning my safe haven into a war zone. I lay perfectly still. The kids had seen me, of course, but thus far they had treated me as an inanimate lump. I feared it was only a matter of time before they realized I had a beating heart and was therefore fair game. Thankfully, they also had a limited attention span. After 20 minutes, they clambered back into the Jeep and roared away in a cloud of dust—proving once again that the gasoline engine provides no escape from a boring, pointless life.

I was amused by the cosmic improbability of the scene. How, out of all these empty square miles of lake and shore, did this ruckus descend precisely on me? If a prankster had intended it, he would need a GPS to get the players that close.

At Lake Wallula I again saw the curious effect of disappearing and reappearing motorboats that I first noticed on Lake Roosevelt. I would be aware of a far-off boat buzzing along the water, hear its motor quit, look over, and see nothing. Some minutes later, I would hear the motor start, look over, and see the boat again. Obviously, the boat was disappearing behind something when it stopped and slumped low in the water. I wondered if it might be hiding behind the curvature of the earth, but I was skeptical. Could the earth curve that sharply, 4 or 5 feet in the space of a few miles?

Another theory was that it was an optical effect having to do with humidity near the surface of the water. Back home, I decided to settle the question. I went to the library and got some trigonometry books, and set myself up with a stack of paper, a pencil, and a cup of tea. I quickly determined that I didn't need trig. The good old Pythagorean theorem does the job (along with a computer's calculator that could handle 14-digit numbers). The calculations showed that I was indeed seeing the curvature of the earth.

In the kayak, my bottom is one inch above the water and my eye is 30 inches above that. My calculations showed that my horizon is 1.94 miles away. A piece of paper placed on the water 1.95 miles away could not be seen, no matter how strong the telescope. At a distance of 3.88 miles, I would be unable to see an object less than 30 inches high (like a motorboat at rest); and at 5.81 miles, I could not see an object 10 feet high. This explains why, at this distance, the beaches of a far shore disappear, giving the impression that the trees run right down to the water.

I found these revelations strangely comforting. Whereas I had considered the world to be an abstract vastness beyond my comprehension, I could now see with my own eyes that it was a finite sphere—indeed, a surprisingly small one.

The next day, I was excited to see the GPS indicate a heading of 270 degrees. For landlubbers, that's due west. After all the twists and turns of the past 300 miles, sometimes heading north and even east, I'd finally made the last big turn where the Columbia heads pretty much straight for the Pacific Ocean.

At this westward turn, the river gathers the sinews of national commerce. Running along the south bank in Oregon, Interstate 84 carries a stream of trailer trucks 24 hours a day. And both the north and south banks have railroads. The previous night, I camped next to the Burlington Northern main line on the north bank. I was skinny dipping in the river at sunset, enjoying my supposed privacy, when the eastbound Amtrak passenger train came whisking around a curve with remarkable speed and quietness and caught me by surprise. I could do nothing but wave.

The freight trains were not so polite. With my head only 50 feet from the tracks, they were frighteningly loud. The first one that came by after I fell asleep triggered a nightmare and a rush of adrenalin that kept me awake for a long time.

The next day, I arrived at the lock on the McNary Dam in the early afternoon, consumed with curiosity about whether I would be passed through the gigantic structure. It seemed absurd that they would spill millions of gallons of water to accommodate a 12-foot kayak. The place was constructed for barges, with 15-foot-high concrete walls and no place to land. Not a soul was in sight, but I noticed a cord to pull, and gave it a yank. After a time, a woman in uniform came from one of the buildings and shouted to me that no nonmotorized craft were allowed in the locks. So that was that. Though miffed at the time, I concluded this rule is sound. There's a lot of turbulence, both in the locks when they fill, and also in the dam tailrace just below the locks.

My problem was that since the dam had a lock, the deal about portaging people was off. I was on my own. I beached the kayak at a boat ramp at the side of the dam and, working under the blazing sun, took the boat apart and packed it up. As a result of my semi-collapse at the Chief Joseph Dam, I had formed the rule of never carrying the pack in the heat of the day, since I sweat so alarmingly under those conditions. For five minutes I sat quietly, staring at the pack lying in the sun.

The trouble with people who go around making rules about not doing things is that they fail to reckon with the urgency of action. The idea of wasting the entire afternoon doing precisely nothing became increasingly intolerable, and soon overpowered any worry about sunstroke. I hoisted the pack and began the portage, taking a deliberately slow pace.

I'll never know if I could have survived the hike because a kindly fisherman picked me up and drove me to the put-in. I reassembled the boat, made my way through the angry waves of the dam tailrace, and ended the day at a public park across from Umatilla, Oregon.

In the Umatilla Wildlife Refuge the next day, I pulled toward shore for lunch and paddled into a school of huge bass, some nearly 3 feet long. These monsters hang about in the shallow waters where motorboats and fishermen never go. My boat snuck right next to them before they took fright and darted away, looking like sharks streaking across the surface of the water.

That afternoon, I played cat and mouse with a barge. Most tows were loud and I could hear the tug engines pounding for hours before they reached me. But some coming downriver were able to sneak up on me unnoticed, as this one did. I was in the middle of a wide stretch of river, trying to take advantage of the current, when I looked back and saw a monster bearing down on me less than a mile away.

I shifted course and paddled for the near shore, about half a mile away. After a minute of hard paddling, I inspected the barge closely. I couldn't see either side, which meant it was still heading straight for me. The barge had turned in my direction! I paddled hard some more, and the tug operator continued to turn toward me, as if his one object in life was to run me down. I later realized that the channel ran close to the shore I was paddling toward. If I'd stayed where I was, the barge would have missed me by a half mile. As it was, I was paddling into its course as if—from the operator's point of view—my one object in life was to be ground to pieces under his moving steel walls.

Impending doom motivates vigorous paddling. I ran my boat right into the sand of the shore, where I knew I had to be safe, and the barge passed by less than a hundred yards away.

Barges move at about 8 miles an hour—twice as fast as I can paddle—and produce steep, smooth waves about 4 feet high. When I first saw these waves, they seemed threatening and I took care to meet them head-on. As time went by, I found I could ride over them at any angle with ease. A barge creates a multitude of waves that keep coming for many minutes after it passes, a real nuisance when I beached the kayak at the edge of the water. To prevent the Klepper from being battered and swamped, I had to walk it out into deeper water and hold it there until the harassing waves subsided.

With help from the current, I was making excellent time. I reached Boardman, Oregon, 182.1 miles from my starting point in Wenatchee, on the evening of my seventh day afloat, for an average of 26 miles a day. This excellent progress gave me the idea that I could finish the whole river on this outing, and surprise friends and family back home with an unexpected home run.

I had scarcely begun to enjoy the vision of arriving at Astoria when this rosy scenario collapsed under the weight of a powerful wind that came up from the west, dead against my course. This 25-mph wind blew all night long and was still roaring the next morning, turning the river into a maelstrom of steep waves and whitecaps. I couldn't even consider trying to go against it.

At least I was close to town, where I could get food. I was also near a luxurious shelter. Five hundred yards upriver stood the Riverfront Lodge, a dramatic rustic log structure that identified itself as "a grand boutique hotel." Its PR firm apparently specializes in oxymorons.

On the pretext of needing to get my water bottle filled, I went in to check it out. Dressed in my shabby attire, I was too embarrassed to ask the haughty clerk at the desk the price of a room—a sure sign that I didn't belong. Besides, as my experience at the Hampton Inn pointed up, luxury on a camping trip can be unfitting and down-right uncomfortable.

I wandered about the formless array of buildings that is the town of Boardman, doing my best to kill time. The lady at the café said wind like this could go on for days. The shelters at the town picnic area all had high windbreak walls on the west side of the tables.

I went into the half-sized supermarket for food and a magazine. The magazine selection brought home what ordinary Americans are really interested in—and also what they don't give a hoot about, namely all the policy questions involved in the trillion-dollar government that's ruling their lives. There must have been 150 magazines, but not one dealt with government, policy, economics, history, ethics, morality, philosophy, or social life. Just fashion, house and garden, hot rod cars, motorcycles, sports, stars of screen, and popular music. There were even magazines on soap operas so folks could keep up with the fictitious lives glimmering inside their cathode ray tubes.

I read further in the two paperbacks I had brought along: Barbara Tuchman's *The Proud Tower,* about turn-of-the-century U. S. history, and Tennyson's *Idylls of the King,* a poetic treatment of the King Arthur legend. Schoolchildren used to read this classic, but I doubt many would today, for it's tough going, with a difficult vocabulary and complex sentence structure. I could grapple with only a page at a time.

Thus passed the kayaker's day, a day entirely lost to the huge wind.

The next morning, the wind continued, but I resolved to tackle the waves and go at least as far as a boat basin a quarter mile downriver. It was a quixotic gesture, but I couldn't bear the thought of sleeping at the same miserable campsite three nights running. The waves were 4 feet high, the steepest I'd encountered on the trip. I didn't feel endangered by them, but it took a half hour to slog my way to the boat basin.

The struggle brought home the downside of my kayak's wonderful stability. It doesn't tip over easily because it's high and wide, but these dimensions present a large surface to the wind. The true sea kayak is narrow and low in the water, and so can make decent progress against a headwind.

I moored the kayak in the protection of the boat basin and went for breakfast at the café, where the staff was getting to know me—not an encouraging sign. I returned to the boat resolved to set out down the river and make what distance I could, even if only a few miles. It was my birthday—June 17—and moping around Boardman seemed the worst way to celebrate it. The map showed no towns for 25 miles, just Interstate 84 and sagebrush, but I was stocked up, able to take care of myself for many days if need be. I could always make drinking water by filling my water bottle in the river and dropping two iodine tablets in it.

As I prepared to push off, two boys at summer loose ends came buzzing by on their bikes. My craft fired their curiosity.

"Did you really come all the way from Canada in that?"

"What do you eat?"

"Where do you sleep?"

The questions were the same ones adults asked of me, but the boys had an entirely different point of view. With adults, the tone was usually disbelief, ranging from I-would-never-do-such-a-thing to you-must-be-crazy. These boys showed no such hesitation; they were my soul mates. They saw hard ground, mosquitoes, cold food, and raindrops as no obstacles at all. My voyage instantly appealed to them as a meaningful adventure, a doable project they were eager to attempt as soon as their mothers would let them.

As I paddled toward the outlet of the boat basin, one of the boys ran out along the rocks of the jetty to keep me company as far as possible.

At the mouth of the basin I yelled, "Which way to Astoria?" It was a jest, but also a test. Many children are disappointingly unaware of their environment, and can live on a dammed-up body of water without knowing it is a river, much less which way it flows. Not my hero. He gave a broad smile, wound his arm like a big-league pitcher preparing a fastball, and swooped it in an energetic circle to point commandingly down the river. I wished I could have taken him with me.

I clawed my way against the wind and the waves all that day. In the afternoon the wind slacked off to 15–20 mph, but it was still difficult, exhausting paddling. I couldn't stop for even a few seconds without losing hard-won distance. To rest, I pulled toward shore to find a bit of sheltered water or a tree branch to hold on to.

The shoreline was an impenetrable tangle of scrub trees, offering no decent camping place. It was chilly and overcast, with occasional light rain. Some desert! I put on my sweater and rain jacket. To keep my legs warm and dry this time, I covered them with my plastic ground cloth (I am slow, but not entirely untrainable). I wrested a miserable 12.2 miles from the river that day; given the conditions, it was a creditable achievement.

At dusk, I came upon a rare break in the tangle of brush along the shore, a tiny bay where the water lapped against the base of a cliff. At first glance, it seemed an impossible campsite because there was no place above the water to sleep. Closer inspection revealed that the cliff consisted of loose sand. In fact, a clump of sand collapsed from it into the water as I watched. Using my gold pan as a shovel, I dragged down masses of sand from the cliff, making a mound 2 feet above the water on which I could spread my sleeping bag. Of course, the water would eventually erode this platform, but I figured I had at least one night's use of it.

As night fell, the rain began. My supper was just a snack of dried fruit and nuts, eaten while I huddled under my tarp. Again there was no brushing of teeth. I had to put the mosquito net over my head: I couldn't understand where the pesky creatures were breeding, since I could see nothing but desert and river, and mosquitoes can't breed in agitated water.

As in the Exodus of the old Israelites, my liberation from the fleshpots of Boardman had led me into a wilderness of hardships. I regretted—as I often did in these situations—that I did not have a companion with whom to commiserate. I expect he might have urged me to cheer up because things could be worse. Well, they got worse.

During the night the storm that brought the rain moved east, bringing clear skies—and inviting a big west wind to chase that low-pressure area. By dawn, the wind was howling stronger than ever, whipping the river into a sheet of foaming whitecaps. With a sinking heart, I concluded I was pinned down for yet another day.

This being the case, I told myself, I was fully entitled to stockbroker hours and a lazy, luxurious rest atop my bed on the sand mound, but even that hope was dashed. Big, wind-generated waves pulsed into the cove and attacked the base of my mound, eroding away my bed with alarming speed. I had only a few minutes to cram my wet, sand-covered clothing and equipment into bags, lug them along the shore beyond the cliff, and throw them up between the clumps of brush. Then I thrust the kayak as high as I could into the branches.

I had gone from the frying pan into the fire. At least when I was wind-bound back at Boardman I had a café and a mini-market with hot rod magazines for sale. Here there was nothing but sagebrush and the sun. I was uneasy being trapped so far from any human aid.

The worst part was not knowing when the wind would stop. It could go on for weeks. It seemed a cruel injustice to be pinned down again, after I patiently waited a whole day in Boardman, and fought so nobly against the wind yesterday. But then, Nature knows nothing of justice.

My job became wasting the day. I read a little, tried to nap. In the afternoon, I took a walk in the desert above my campsite. There were no houses, no buildings, no trees: nothing but low rolling hills dotted with sagebrush. From a high spot, I was relieved to see the interstate lying about 2 miles away. I marked it as my escape route, a place where I could walk for help in an emergency. I completely overlooked the obvious way to get help: ride the wind back to Boardman in the kayak. I was so fixated on fighting the wind that backtracking, even in a life-threatening emergency, was literally unthinkable. It never entered my mind.

So passed another day of zero progress. The wind roared and the whitecaps pulsed as if they planned to continue forever. Reaching Astoria seemed an absurd pipe dream. Now my concern was whether I would progress even one more foot down the Columbia. As I lay down for the night, I was troubled by a slight pain in my abdomen. I told myself it was probably a muscle injured when I heaved the kayak into the branches. I pushed other possibilities out of my mind.

Nature may know nothing of justice, but she does have pity. As the hours dragged by during the night, the splashing of the waves against the shore gradually grew less energetic. Keeping a poker face, so as not to attract the attention of the wind gods, I cautiously allowed myself to conclude that this windstorm that could have lasted for weeks was ending after only one day. Before dawn, I began packing my gear. I stuffed the sleeping bag into its sack, and dragged the kayak down from the branches. I didn't bother with breakfast, or even pause to wolf down an energy bar. The only thing that mattered was to accomplish downstream miles and erase the memory of yesterday's miserable purgatory. I shoved off into a light breeze with the kayak cutting over big swells, the river's memory of yesterday's big wind.

After several miles, the exhilaration of being underway faded and I sank into a grim morning-after mood, groggy from a sleepless night, and weak from hunger but not hungry. I stared vacantly at the gray ridges lying far ahead.

Then, hanging in the sky beyond the farthest ridge, I saw a shimmering rosy-pink pyramid. My mind struggled to recognize it. Was it a spaceship or interplanetary object approaching the earth, or the cloud from a volcanic eruption or nuclear explosion whose shock waves hadn't yet reached me? These worrisome interpretations dissolved when I realized it was one of God's mountains, but one so impossibly far away and so improbably high that it seemingly didn't belong to earth's landscape. It was Mt. Hood, 93 miles away, with its snowy eastern slope touched by the sun's first rays. The body of the mountain was invisible in the predawn grayness, leaving just the glowing pink cap suspended in space. The vision was a priceless gift and the reverence of the moment stayed with me for many hours.

The light breeze against me died away in the early afternoon, leaving the water mirror-smooth for the first time in nearly a week. With no waves to disturb balance and coordination, I delighted in paddling. My paddle blades cut the water with precision and the kayak surged across the surface with each stroke. I was flying.

The next morning, prodded by the thought of those dreaded west winds coming up again, I packed up and lugged everything down to the kayak as soon as I could see the blue color of my sleeping bag. Breakfast was an energy bar consumed underway. I deplore eating and paddling at the same time, but I deplore being wind-bound even more.

The approach to John Day Dam that afternoon felt endless. I followed a long bend in the river, expecting to see the dam at any moment. Finally a structure came into view 3 miles away, which I was sure marked the edge of the dam. More sweltering, exhausting miles later, I saw that this structure had nothing to do with the dam. The bend of the river revealed more structures several miles away. My hopes were raised, then later dashed when I saw they had nothing to do with the dam either. I began to wonder if the John Day Dam was a giant hoax.

Just as I expended my last erg in paddling, with no dam yet in sight, a light wind sprang up behind me. I rigged the sail and let it pull me the last 4 miles to the dam at a safe and sedate 2.5 mph. I even nodded off to sleep in brief naps. It was the one time on the trip that the sail really earned its keep.

At the dam I beached the boat at a disused boat ramp and walked around to see what was what. I found myself inside the dam's security perimeter. An 8-foot cyclone fence topped with three strands of barbed wire stood between me and downriver progress. This was another example of earnest, shortsighted security. If the stranger in the scruffy red kayak was bent on mayhem, the fence amounted to locking the fox inside the chicken coop. The innocent kayaker faced the problem of getting past the fence to the river below the dam.

It was suppertime and not a soul was in sight. I walked up onto the dam, and came upon the open door of the control room for the lock. No one was inside. I wondered if a person—an evil-minded person—could open both gates of the lock at the same time, in this way draining the lake and flooding God-fearing communities downriver. I wandered past the spillways and their electronic controls, unable to find anyone. Nor could I attract the interest of any security camera. It was a ghost dam.

Then I remembered the field telephone back on the Priest Rapids Dam, and looked for its counterpart. Sure enough, I found a yellow box with a phone in it, and someone had scratched a number for "Security" on top. I dialed it.

The man who answered was startled. "Where are you?" he asked. "I don't even recognize this station." I explained my location and my problem. To my amazement and delight, the security officer arranged a truck portage for me.

On the way to the boat ramp below the dam, I asked the driver, whose job at the dam was to operate the lock, how he knew when a barge wants to use the lock, since the workers hang out in the control room in the bowels of the dam where they can't see anything. It's all done by radio, he explained.

So if a terrorist has the good sense not to radio ahead, he can expect to have free run of the John Day Dam.

That night I stayed at a private campground 5 miles below the dam, where I beached my kayak on grass that came right down to the water. After a leisurely, humane supper sitting upright at a picnic table, I had the blessings of a shave and a hot shower. I went to bed on top of the world, clean and dry, nestled in my sleeping bag on the lush lawn, gazing up at the sparkling stars. *Here,* I thought, just before I fell into a solid sleep, *is camping the way it ought to be.*

The next thing I know, an avalanche of water is cascading over me. This is not a mere sprinkle, but a copious gushing, as if a torpedo had torn open the hull of my Liberty ship while I sleep in my bunk deep below deck. The surge is so unbelievable that at first I think I am in a nightmare. I calmly wait to awaken. The gushing continues. As a child, I taught myself to wake from nightmares too scary to bear by biting my lip. I bite my lip. I feel the pain but I am still being drenched. The cascading water is apparently real, the perfect storm delivered right into my sleeping bag. The only explanation is I am being drenched by a freak downpour. I look up at the sky: it is covered with stars!

I must be losing my mind! I think. *How can it rain without clouds?*

Finally I see the problem: a sprayer head eight feet from me has come on and is pointed right at me. This was no residential sprinkler, either, but an agricultural irrigation head delivering a thick jet of water. I yank the ground cloth over the sleeping bag to protect it, but my clothes are getting soaked. I look for something to muzzle the sprayer. All I come up with is my paddle, which I hold over the sprinkler head, crouched in wet underpants, shivering in the night, until it stops 20 minutes later.

I assessed the damage. It was only water, of course. Technology had played a practical joke on me—a very good one, as a matter of fact, one that totally frightened and confused me, but did no real harm. I shook the water off the sleeping bag and hung it over a table. After a few minutes, this magical device was dry, and I crawled in and prepared for sleep. On reflection, I realized that this could be considered yet a fifth night that I was rained on in the desert!

Early the next morning, the campground owner came to open the payment deposit box, and I told him about the sprayer going off. After checking the notice board, which said the tent camping area would not have sprinklers going off at night, he gave me my $12 back, which seemed fair.

Explaining my experience to the owner, I was surprised that I wasn't angry or even irritated. In fact, we laughed about it together. I don't believe I would have been so calm in an earlier time of my life. I would have been upset, eager to complain, eager to blame. Where did my composure come from? The answer is I was now a graduate of the Columbia River school of hard knocks. I had been given lesson after lesson that things don't turn out the way you expect, that life isn't fair, that lots of times you just have to endure. As a result of this harsh instruction I was mentally ready to cope when a quiet night's rest became a torpedoing at sea.

Several months later I heard a friend complain about a canceled flight that caused him to spend a night in a hotel away from home. The airline put him up and flew him home the next day. Nevertheless, this 8-hour disruption in his plans so upset him that he was ranting about it 6 months later and writing angry letters to the airline trying to get satisfaction. The Columbia River graduate didn't sympathize.

In the local market the day before, I overheard a customer say there was an Amtrak stop in Wishram, Washington, just 8 miles downriver from the campground. To anyone else it was an offhand comment, but to my ears it was kismet. My stores of energy and enthusiasm were considerably used up at this point in the journey, and I needed a change in focus. Since Amtrak stops in Sandpoint, the voice in the store was telling me I could snuggle in my own bed the following night, and it now seemed a most fitting ambition.

Reaching Wishram was no problem, but getting ashore was. The town is protected against Columbia River floods by a 30-foot high bank of fractured rocks. This levee runs for miles along the river, with not one inch of level ground to land the kayak on.

All I could do was the technique I managed the previous summer at the Wells Dam: pull the boat alongside the rocks, unload each item, heave the kayak onto the rocks, take it apart, and carry the pieces one at a time up the rocky bank. All of this took place at noon on June 21, the summer solstice, the day on which the sun is as high and as hot as it can be, so once again I found myself daring the gods of sunstroke.

After accomplishing that grueling task, I packed the kayak parts into the backpack—a slow, frustrating job because they never fit the first time.

Then, I lugged everything to the railroad station in several trips. Job done, I collapsed on the curb in the shade, drenched in sweat. A thirsty black dog sidled up to me, panting in the heat, too wilted to bark or even growl. I had completed the second leg of my trip, a distance of 246.6 miles from Wenatchee.

Wishram must be the most inconsequential Amtrak station in America. The town has only a dozen dwellings—tarpaper shacks and trailers—and no stores. But whatever it lacks in traveler amenities, Wishram has one thing Amtrak is never expected to provide: free hot showers for customers! The Amtrak waiting room is down the hall from the locker room used by Burlington Northern line crews. After the crews clocked out at 5 p.m., I had the building to myself. I tiptoed into the locker room and shaved and showered. When the train arrived at 6:55 p.m., I was entirely spruced up, a cultured and civilized traveler.

The train followed the river back up the Columbia, giving me a chance to enjoy the river again. The surface of the water was perfectly still, a glassy mirror in the golden glow of the setting sun, beckoning a wind-buffeted kayaker to try his luck again. I noted the landmarks from my journey: the cove where I waited out the wind, the inlet where I washed my clothes, Mount Hood.

We flashed past a feature that charmed me when I came upon it one afternoon, and has remained riveted in my mind ever since. A junked 1960s Mercury convertible had somehow been dragged to a prominence in the desert above the river. It would be an eyesore in a town, but out on the lonely dunes, with no other sign of man near, it was a haunting work of art. On its broken windshield someone had propped a hand-lettered sign that said "Think Always!"

What did the writer intend to convey? It could be an allusion to the moment of inattention in traffic that wrecked this Mercury. The remorseful driver went to all the trouble to position the car on the bank of the Columbia to give the world a graphic "Drive Safely" warning.

I'm inclined to think the advice is aimed more broadly, however. I take it as a reminder to use our God-given brains in everything we do, not to blindly succumb to emotion, tradition, or rules and regulations. It applies to everyone, to youngsters about to rush into marriage, to doctors about to amputate the wrong leg—and to security officials about to set up chain link fences that enclose terrorists inside their dams.

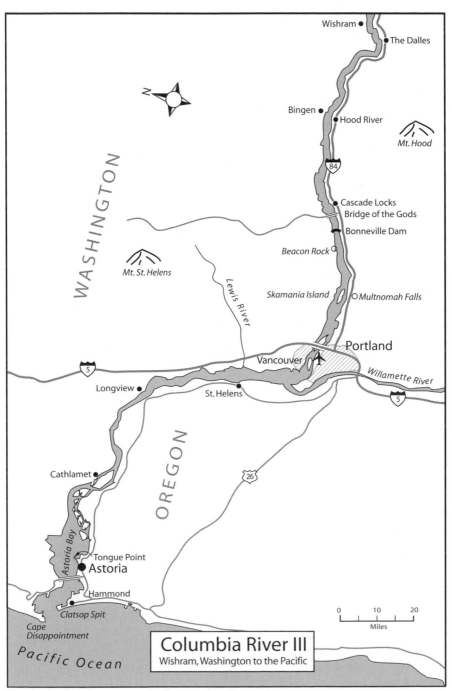

Columbia River III
Wishram, Washington to the Pacific

River width not to scale

4

77 Feet to the Sea

THE COLUMBIA RIVER III
Bingen, Washington to Astoria, Oregon (August 2002)

TWO MONTHS AFTER PULLING OUT of the water at Wishram, I was aboard Amtrak's train again, speeding back to the Columbia. My original idea was to accomplish one leg of the journey to the Pacific per year, but Judy's bout with cancer the previous winter shifted our perspectives. Her illness took us by surprise. One day we were eating granola and drinking herbal tea, doing everything right for health, and the next I was rushing her to the emergency ward at Deaconess Hospital in Spokane with bleeding that would not stop.

Despite a successful operation and recovery, this experience brought home again the reality of human frailty. It wasn't sound to assume I had all the time in the world to accomplish my dream. When I suggested that I tackle the last leg of the trip that same summer, Judy said, "Go for it!"

The seawall at Wishram made assembling and launching the kayak there impossible, so I chose Bingen, Washington, as my put-in spot, 25 miles further down the river. The rail trip was gently frustrating in the way that only Amtrak can be. The train reached Sandpoint 45 minutes late, at 12:30 a.m., and lost more and more time as the journey progressed—a lapse that didn't seem to concern the staff. The conductors dawdled on the platform at each stop, enjoying smoke breaks with Latin insouciance, and eventually we were several hours behind schedule. Somewhere far below my seat, the frame of the railroad car groaned in deep agony on every curve, preventing any possibility of sleep.

When daylight came, I went to the lounge car for a good look at the river. I paid special attention to the topography, since I was to start my trip in the famed Columbia Gorge, where the river cuts through the Cascade Mountain range. One sign that the land was closing in were the railroad tunnels, each of which meant that the builders came upon a cliff so high that it just couldn't be cut away. We passed through the first tunnel just before Wishram; after that they came one after another.

In terms of altitude, my trip down the Columbia was nearly complete, for I had descended from an elevation of 1,318 feet above sea level at the Canadian border to a mere 77, the surface of the water at Bingen. But these last 77 feet contained some formidable obstacles.

The first was wind. For those who care about wind, the Columbia Gorge is a special place. The gap in the mountain range acts as a funnel for westward moving air, accelerating even mild westerly breezes into stiff winds. That makes this area, especially Hood River, Oregon—across the river from my stop at Bingen—a mecca for windsurfers. My interests were diametrically opposed to theirs, of course. I watched the river carefully, apprehensively looking for any sign of wind. So far, the water was glassy.

At the mouth of the gorge stands Bonneville Dam, the last dam before the sea. I didn't know anything about the portage around it, except that it was bound to be difficult. Once past the dam, I would enter the estuary where the Columbia becomes a natural river again, with its current influenced by the tides. The climate changes as the river leaves the rain shadow of the Cascades and enters Oregon's notoriously rainy coastal zone. To be ready for that, I brought along a one-man bivouac tent.

Knowing that I would be living rough in the coming days, I savored my last minutes of luxury in the lounge observation car, relaxing deep into the cushions of the armchair, enjoying a ham sandwich and a cup of coffee. I read Barbara Tuchman's *The Guns of August*, a history of the beginning of World War I, which was to be my entertainment for the journey, looking up every few moments to drink in the panorama of the Columbia Valley in the early morning sun. As we approached Bingen, the vegetation changed dramatically, transitioning from desert to heavily forested hillsides in just a few miles.

When I stepped off the train in Bingen at 10 a.m., I learned that the river was two miles away from the station, which meant I had an hour-long struggle to haul my kayak, food, and equipment to the put-in. The air was calm when I began the trek, with hardly any sign of wind. But with each step of this interminable hike, the wind showed more life, puffing then dying, then gusting a bit harder. By the time I reached the water and completed the laborious assembly of the kayak, the river was being torn into whitecaps by a stiff west wind. I stood hands on hips, staring at the leaping waves and muttered in a low voice compound curses drawn from realms of theology, human reproduction, and canine breeding.

On the previous leg of the trip I had stayed on shore in such windy conditions, but now, after a 10-hour train trip, the idea of sitting still was unbearable. I launched into the wind, paddling vigorously, angling across the river to the Oregon side. The waves were breaking over the deck and washing back into the cockpit, soaking me in my bathing suit. It took me an hour to claw across the river, making no net downriver progress at all. I landed on a stony beach tucked next to Interstate 84. Between the roar of the wind and the howl of the traffic, I could hardly hear myself think.

In this way, I found myself in the same kind of dreadful purgatory I had experienced on the previous leg: pinned down by the wind, squatting among rocks at a deplorable campsite, trying to find a way to kill time, wondering all the while if the wind intended to persist forever. It was painful to recall that just a few hours earlier I was relaxing in a cushioned armchair, sipping coffee in a railroad observation car. I thought, *This adventure is getting underway all too quickly!*

Though being wind-bound was familiar, I was on this day in a different frame of mind, determined not to give in to Nature. I was eager to make some sort of progress, and also less afraid of waves than before. So, after eating a quick lunch, I launched into the waves again, a bolder, angrier kayaker. It took me several hours to creep one mile to the main beach at Hood River. There the wind gathered strength, so I beached the kayak and passed time watching windsurfers jump the waves.

I asked one of them how fast the wind was blowing.

"It's a five," he replied. Windsurfers rate winds according to the size of sail they need; he had no idea how that translated into miles per hour. My estimate was 25.

Several hours later, I overheard one of the sailors saying something about needing a "seven" and I saw that the wind had let up a bit, so I headed out again. To proceed down the river, I had to paddle through a heavy traffic of windsurfers scooting back and forth across the river, a turtle trying to cross a six-lane highway. It was their job to dodge me, which they did with fine ability.

Another group that had to dodge me was the kiteboarders, guys—I saw no women doing this—surfboarding while hanging from a gigantic kite. The boys—I saw no older people doing this, either—were hooked by harnesses to the kites that pulled them along at water-skiing speeds. They darted back and forth over the water like dragonflies. Watching the kites—dipping, dashing, almost crashing into the water—was a show in itself. Every so often, the performers took a heart-stopping leap off a wave top, soared 10 or 15 feet into the air, and did a somersault before slicing back into the water in a joyful exhibition of athletic skill!

With all their ability, the kiteboarders had no problem missing my kayak. I was in about as much danger of being hit by one of them as by a swallow.

After a long slog that practically pulled my arms out of their sockets, I made it to a secluded island that afforded dry sand to sleep on and a bank of ripe blackberries to snack on. My total gain in down-river distance for the day was 3.6 miles. I had proved that I could at least go against a 20-mph wind and the 3-foot waves that go with it, but I knew this was something of a Pyrrhic victory. At that rate, I wouldn't make my 77 feet to Astoria until Christmas.

I battled against wind all the next day, making it to Cascade Locks by evening, my aching shoulders testifying to a creditable day's labor. I moored the kayak next to a 35-foot cabin cruiser that was tied up at the marina for the night, and told the owner and his wife—who were planning to sleep on board—that they wouldn't have to worry about any rowdy parties on my boat disturbing their slumber.

Cascade Locks is the choke point in the river. A major earthquake and landslide 700 years ago—which the native tribes remember in their tales—dammed the river here, creating a temporary land bridge that the Indians called the Bridge of the Gods. The river soon overflowed and cut through the blockage, forming rapids. All river traffic had to portage around this spot until the Corps of Engineers built locks to bypass the rapids in 1896. The locks are still standing; the water in them is now nearly still since the Bonneville Dam, 5 miles downriver, has backed up the water and drowned any rapids.

The next morning, I got a look at myself in the restroom mirror after returning from the restaurant where I had breakfast, and saw unbelievably spiky, tangled hair—the result of swimming in the evening and then sleeping on wet hair without combing it. I then understood the apprehensive glances of waitress and patrons at the restaurant, for I looked highly dangerous. I scolded myself for not taking care of my appearance, but I doubt the lecture had any lasting impact.

A stiff headwind harassed me as I headed down to Bonneville Dam, starting my route by paddling through the gateless old locks. Indian salmon fishing platforms lined the shore of the river, but no one was fishing from them now. The gorge is extremely narrow at this point, with cliffs on both sides, and no stopping places for a kayak. I went under the famous suspension bridge over the gorge, also called the Bridge of the Gods—a privately built, privately owned toll bridge.

I was apprehensive about the portage situation at the dam. The previous week, I had called the dam from home to check the possibilities. I first talked to a lock operator, Bernie, who was strangely guarded, as if his job depended on having nothing to do with me. He mentioned that earlier in the summer he had shown a kayaker from Idaho (!) how to get around the dam, then hastily added, "but don't tell anyone I said that." Then I talked to someone in the manager's office who said it was against their policy to give lifts around the dam.

I already knew I couldn't go through the lock, being a nonmotorized craft. My hope was that I would encounter a pleasure boat willing to take me through the lock in tow. I was prepared to wait several hours for one to arrive, because the map indicated a horrendous portage.

It took me all morning to reach the dam, bucking gusts of 20–25 mph and agitated waves. By the time I reached the lock, I had concluded that the chances of a pleasure boat turning up were slim, for I had not seen one all morning—perhaps not surprisingly, it being a Monday. I could wait all day and have nothing to show for it.

The other option, portaging around the dam, was extremely forbidding. To start with, the only place I would be able to take out was a rocky embankment, steeper than any I'd ever contended with. It would be a job of many hours to disassemble the kayak and pack it up that bank, piece by piece. I moored the kayak at the edge of the rocks, clambered up to a dirt road above, and confirmed that I would have to portage many miles before I could access the water again. At the snail's pace at which I lug the kayak pack, that could take days. I could practically hear the spinal fluid spurting from my crushed vertebrae.

Since it was lunchtime, I dawdled by eating raisins and an energy bar, hoping for a miracle to solve my problem. Finally, I bit the bullet and started carrying food and equipment up the embankment in preparation for whatever hellish portage was in store. I was just coming up with my second load when a blue van came bouncing along the road.

It turned out to be my hoped-for miracle. The driver worked for the Union Pacific railroad, tending train signals. He claimed a portage was impossible because the nearest place to put back in the water was 10 miles downriver, and locked gates blocked the route anyway.

However, he had an idea, and a cell phone. *Oh noble cell phone!* I thought. *Never again shall I thee disparage.* He called the Corps of Engineers ranger's office and explained my plight: "This guy has come all the way down from Canada on the Columbia in a kayak and can't get around the dam." After a bit of conversation he hung up. "They said they'll send someone."

There's nothing like having someone else make your case for you.

I wait at the road, expecting a pickup truck. Five minutes later, a boat approaches the kayak on the water below. The rangers are going to take me *through* the dam in the lock! I'm thrilled, not just because I will be spared a dreadful portage, but also because I'm going to go through a lock for the first time.

We load the kayak onto their boat and motor into the lock. Skip, the mate, loops a line around the bollard on the side. The bollard is on a vertical track so it can go down as the water level in the lock falls. However, because of the slight danger that the sliding bollard might stick, and leave a tied-up boat dangling, he has to hand tend the line as we descend.

The giant gates thump shut behind us. The lock is huge, a football field long, nearly as wide, and 60 feet deep—the drop of water level at Bonneville Dam. Our descent takes 15 minutes. Then the giant front gate quietly parts like the curtain on a stage, opening to a vista of the dancing waters of the estuary!

The water is turbulent below the dam, where the current of the tailrace fights the wind and waves coming up the river. Greg, the driver, suggests taking me down a few miles to a cove at Beacon Rock. I heartily assent to this. As we slam across the big waves and buck the gusting wind streaming through my hair, I say, "Come to think of it, how about taking me to Astoria?"

As we motored down the river, Greg asked me if I was the guy who had called earlier in the week about a portage, which I confirmed. Apparently my case had been discussed at higher levels, and they deviated from the policy of not giving lifts around the dam. He didn't say what their reasoning was, and I didn't ask, sensing that this miracle was a delicate conjunction of psychology and bureaucracy that the least bit of curiosity might throw out of alignment. Perhaps they were worried about their legal obligation to provide portage; perhaps they wanted to avoid embarrassment and negative publicity; perhaps they simply said stuff bureaucracy, let's do the right and natural thing.

At Beacon Rock, Greg and Skip unloaded my kayak alongside the dock. I thanked them profusely, barely able to restrain myself from violating the taboo against kissing grown men.

Beacon Rock is where Lewis and Clark first noticed a tidal surge in the river, which must have caused them great joy because it meant they were done with all the Columbia's horrendous rapids—they portaged around Cascade Rapids—and now had clear passage to the sea. Following in their paddle strokes, I felt a similar joy. I had all 11 dams behind me, and no more portages to worry about. My sense of relief was especially keen since just a few minutes earlier I believed I faced a bone-crushing portage.

My trip was far from over, though. I was still 140 miles from the Pacific Ocean and, according to Greg, 17 feet above sea level. Among my worries was the prospect of traversing Astoria Bay, with its winds and tidal currents. My second concern was dealing with the notorious Columbia Bar, where the Columbia's massive current collides with ocean breakers.

After saying goodbye to Greg and Skip, I set out downriver to see what the estuary had in store for me. The wind was moderate but the waves were 8 feet high, the highest I'd ever been in. They had built up over a fetch of 20 miles, and gave me the feeling of having already arrived at the ocean. Fortunately, they weren't breaking and therefore didn't slosh into the cockpit. In fact, they were fun to ride: like being on a roller coaster—except that with a roller coaster you know the operators want to keep you from harm, whereas here I was in the hands of Nature, who had no concern for my safety.

Late in the afternoon, I came upon Skamania Island, a campsite well worth my struggle to reach it. The island is a mile and a half long, with broad sandy beaches, and uninhabited, with no buildings, because it is completely covered at flood time. Way out in the middle of the river, the island was secluded and secure, cut off from hikers and automobiles.

Looking north toward Washington State, I enjoyed a vista of forests and jagged precipices. The Burlington Northern line was over half a mile distant and almost entirely hidden behind trees. On the other side of the river, looking toward the Oregon side, was the same kind of spectacular mountain panorama with an additional treat: I was directly opposite world-famous Multnomah Falls, a dramatic 600-foot cascade that spills down a cliff face. The sky was deep blue, with a delicate tracery of cirrus clouds. I went for a swim, and then sunbathed on the sand as normal people do in the summer, letting the mellow afternoon sun relax my face. For the first time in the entire journey on the Columbia, I seriously considered stopping for a day just to enjoy my campsite, and take an actual, ordinary vacation. In the end, though, the hunger for action won out.

I placed a rock at the edge of the water to gauge the tide cycle, though I suspected that erratic flows from Bonneville Dam would probably obliterate any pattern. In the middle of the night a light rain began falling. This time I was prepared, ensconced in the bivouac tent I had added to my equipment for this leg of the journey. Dry and warm in my sleeping bag, I tried to keep awake to enjoy the delicious sound of raindrops spritzing on the roof.

Peering out of the tent the next morning, I felt a gentle drizzle on my nose and saw fog-shrouded mountains. The air was perfectly calm, the stillness absolute, without the slightest sound of any highways or trains. Just me in the primeval mist. After all the miles of paddling through parched desert and blazing sun, this coastal climate was a dream.

Eager to experience the magical moment on the water, I skipped breakfast, packed, and pushed off. I paddled past the last railroad tunnel of the gorge, as the land opened out into a plain, with only low hills to the west. The rain soon stopped, so I could put on my glasses and see the lush vegetation. The trees were mostly deciduous, particularly oak and ash, a sharp contrast with the conifers that covered the slopes at Hood River. It was another sign I had paddled into an entirely different climate zone.

I burned up the river that day, covering 25 miles. I had never gone that far in a day of pure paddling. Though I benefited from a slight current, I was also countering a moderate breeze, so the two factors about canceled out. It was clear that I had more strength than I did in June.

I attributed this better performance to work I began with a nutritionist several weeks before starting this leg. She put me on digestive enzymes, and I found they made a significant difference in my strength, as measured with weight exercises at the gym. The theory is that as we get older, our bodies don't produce enough enzymes to break down the food we eat, so we can't fully absorb it. A plate of scrambled eggs becomes, nutritionally speaking, a plate of scrambled wood chips. Out on the river, the enzymes were helping me get more energy from my food, and as a result I was paddling faster and needing fewer rests.

My speed on the river brought me all the way from Skamania Island to the Portland area by late afternoon, giving rise to the challenges of urban camping. These include the possibilities of being rousted by police for sleeping where camping isn't allowed, being molested by a gang of youths looking for entertainment, and being attacked by an out-and-out robber. Another chance for trouble, or at least embarrassment, is attracting the attention of a dog that finds it necessary to bark his head off when he finds a human being in a sleeping bag.

I drew up on a beach on the Washington side, directly across from the Portland airport, at a county park posted with "No overnight camping" signs. I lurked among the trees, carefully observing passersby, trying to read their character and motives from the interest they took in my kayak lying next to the water. Everyone seemed quite innocent: a couple of dog walkers, young lovers, and a group of moms and their kids.

When darkness gathered and the visitors left me alone on the beach, I set up my tent. Lights came on around the airport, shimmering across the water like an impressionist painting. The row of approaching planes hung in the sky with their landing lights blazing, forming a staircase of lights against a red sky. The wind dropped and tiny waves lapped at the shore. Across the water rose a nearly full moon, fat and orange.

The following morning I again started without breakfast, unable to resist another romantic moment on the river. At 5 a.m., it was still dark, and not a breath of wind stirred the waters. No one else was up; nothing was moving on the roads or on the river. The airport was perfectly silent with no planes taking off or landing. I had the whole city and its shimmering lights to myself.

The tide had come up over 8 feet during the night and floated the kayak, even though I had dragged it high onto the bank, to be on the safe side. Fortunately I had also tied it to a stone. It was apparent that I had no feel for either the timing or height of the tide.

Before leaving on this leg of the trip, I had considered bringing a tide table, but concluded it would be unnecessary. Living on the river 24 hours a day, I reasoned, I would be able to directly observe what the tide was doing. Well, it's not so easy to figure out.

For one thing, the tide times vary with the distance from the sea. The tides around Portland are 8 hours later than near Astoria on the coast. For every 15 miles I traveled downriver the tide times changed by about an hour. Also, tides in an estuary are asymmetrical. It's not 6 hours to high and 6 hours back to low as it is on the seacoast. On the Columbia, high tide comes 5 hours after low tide, and the next low is 7 hours later. Finally, all tides shift half an hour later each day, owing to the rotation of the earth compared to the moon. The upshot of this complexity was that I never had any idea when to expect the tide.

As day broke, I reached the Lewis and Clark Bridge connecting Portland, Oregon, to Vancouver, Washington. Beneath the bridge, a dock with a stairway leads up to a Red Lion Inn: the perfect setup for a kayaker hungry for breakfast. During the meal I mentioned to the waitress where I came from and how I traveled. Minutes later, she came from the kitchen and walked right to my table, obviously with something on her mind.

"I have one question," she said. "Does it ever happen that you get up and just don't feel like doing it? That you'd rather just stay in bed?"

I told her it hadn't happened, that every day I was excited by the prospect of what lay around the next bend in the river. Later, it occurred to me that she was probably projecting her own situation as a waitress not too crazy about getting up at 4 a.m. each morning to carry plates of pancakes around the Red Lion. I hoped she concluded from our exchange that the obvious solution to her early-morning blues was to take a kayak trip beyond the horizon.

At Vancouver I encountered my first oceangoing freighter, a dream I had carried in my mind's eye since the beginning of the trip. It was docked at a grain elevator, loading up with wheat. I paddled up to the bulbous protuberance of the bow, and snapped a picture of my kayak about to hit the freighter's giant nose. Friends who see that picture assume it documents a mid-ocean collision and are amazed I survived.

Downriver from Portland and the confluence with the Willamette River, the Columbia takes a right bend and becomes wonderfully peaceful and rural. The highways and railroads have all gone somewhere else, and, with them, the thumping, humming sounds of industry. Suddenly, the air is still, filled only with the chirping calls of ospreys.

Still, oceangoing ships pass by, about six a day, each an awesome monster. The ships utterly dwarf the motorboats. In fact, they dwarf the river: the Columbia seems too small for them. One evening, I was washing my cooking pot at the shoreline when the water suddenly retreated, exposing 40 feet of bare sand. I was trying to understand this strange event when I heard a low rumble and looked up to see a giant container ship approaching. Containers on its decks were piled five high—I estimated it carried 1,000 containers above decks, and at least that number in the hold. I had to crane my neck to see the top of the ship looming above me as it passed. I sensed that the disappearance of water from the beach was somehow connected to the ship, but I didn't see how it applied to me until it was too late. As the ship drew past, a steep wave 3 feet high came sweeping up the beach like a tsunami, bashing and overturning my kayak, which I had pulled well up on the beach.

That ship was the only one that produced this curious "advance suction" wave, drawing water off the beach a minute before the ship itself arrived. The other ships generated waves akin to powerboat wakes, though in most cases larger.

I stopped at St. Helens, Oregon, for supplies. The town was plastered with "Private Property, Keep Out" signs, and many unnecessary fences and gates around lawns, docks, and decks. I had noticed the same thing several years earlier on a visit to the Oregon coast. The signs give the impression of a self-centered, possessive attitude toward property, an "I've got mine" mentality. In a world of considerate people, one would think private property would be turned to a degree of public use. For goodness sakes, let the occasional passerby walk on your lawn and smell your flowers. And let the forlorn kayaker sleep on your beach.

Camping across the river from St. Helens, I picked up a white rock to use as a weight on my ground cloth. It was as light as Styrofoam; in fact, at first I thought it was Styrofoam, or some other man-made plastic. The beach was covered with these curious lumps, which ranged in size from a walnut to an orange. I nibbled at the edge of it to test its texture, and it was not any kind of soft plastic. The little bits that came off were scratchy like sand, hard as quartz. It occurred to me this might be pumice, an unusual volcanic rock full of gas bubbles, supposedly so light it would float in water. I carried it to the edge of the river and dropped it in. It bobbed up and down like a cork, a true floating rock, one that made a mockery of the expression, "to sink like a stone."

Solving one puzzle gave rise to another: How could there be so many of these rocks on the beach? It seemed obvious that pumice doesn't hang around very long, because it washes out to sea with the river's floods. Geologically speaking, these stones had to be very recent. So where were they coming from? I could think of no answer at the time

but many months later I made the obvious connection: St. Helens—
Mount St. Helens. Duh! This mountain, just 30 miles away, exploded
in a volcanic eruption in 1980. I looked at the area using the satellite
photos on Google Earth and saw how it all must have happened. The
volcano spewed pumice into the nearby Lewis River, and that stream
carried the rocks to the Columbia, and thence to my campsite, which
was just one mile downriver from the mouth of the Lewis.

The following day the lesson changed from geology to anatomy.
I stopped for lunch at what proved to be a nude male homosexual
beach. My first clue was a muscle magazine in the woods behind the
beach. The second indication came from a fully clothed Asian boy
who came by and warned me. Sure enough, a few minutes later, a
young man wearing a T-shirt and no bottoms came sidling by. He
didn't say hello, and I didn't either.

This display reminded me of the other exhibitionist I saw on the
Columbia, near Brewster. I was slogging along, bored and fatigued,
when a cabin cruiser came whizzing up the lake, quite close to me.
On it stood a young woman totally nude, standing spread-eagle facing me. As soon as she reached me she shrieked and tried to cover
herself with her hands. I guess she wasn't mentally ready for prime
time as a streaker—though her physical endowment was more than
adequate. So another realization of this Columbia adventure was to
view the nude male and female forms—though perhaps not with
equal interest.

Now that I was nearing the end, I was making a habit of starting each day very early without breakfast, eager to make distance and
to take advantage of the early-morning calm. On my seventh day, I
started at 4:30 a.m., well before daylight, and navigated by the light
of the bright moon reflecting on the mirror-like river surface. How
delightful it was to be on flat water for a change. Grappling day after
day with coastal winds, I had almost forgotten the sensation of power
and grace that comes from kayaking in perfectly calm water.

I was right to get an early start. In the morning, I made excellent time in light winds, covering 18 miles before noon and fully expecting to turn in a record day. But then the wind came crashing down, forcing me to inch along in fits and starts, spending much of the time sitting ashore watching whitecaps. The total for the day was 21.1 miles.

In the evening I pulled onto a beach that presented an awkward camping situation. It was private property, with a fishing shack and a "No Trespassing" sign. The beach was too exposed to be a dependable commando camping location. But with a stiff wind blocking further progress, I had little choice.

I lay down on the sand to rest and to assess the social environment. Sure enough, sounds of shouting and laughter soon came from up the beach. I peeked over the sand dunes and saw two boys playing in the waves. A large black German shepherd—no doubt a protective, uptight guard dog—was playing with them. I lay back on the sand and debated whether to introduce myself, or remain a secret camper. I concluded that sooner or later the dog would get around to ranging far enough to find me, and explode in a frenzy of indignation when he did.

I went up the beach to meet the boys. The dog panicked of course, barking hysterically, hackles up, threatening to tear open my throat. I studiously looked out across the river, avoiding his eyes as if I didn't even notice him, while the boys tried to call him away. These efforts calmed him down and Buddy was soon licking my hand.

I explained my plight to Rico and Tom, whose family owned the property. They were interested in my trip and eager to help, welcoming me to use the beach and urging me to sleep in the fishing shack.

They reported that this was a very windy stretch of river. "Everyone has wind generators they use all the time," Rico pointed out. They were shivering in the wind in wet bathing suits but took no notice of my urging them to get into some clothes. Of course, when it comes to avoiding hypothermia, I'm probably not entitled to give kids advice.

I slept well on the beach, preferring my bivouac tent to the strange-smelling fisherman's hut the boys urged me to use. Retiring into my tent each night always gave my morale a boost. It was a little piece of home away from home, a piece of private, personal space in a lonely universe—with the added virtue of protecting me from harassing wind and warding off heavy dew of the damp coastal climate.

I had no idea when I awoke the next morning that my travels that day would catapult me so far. Astoria Bay lay ahead, and I intended to approach it in a cautious and responsible way. For safety, I intended to hug the south side of the bay, but I had to make one exception to this plan: Tongue Point. As the name implies, this peninsula is a formidable mile-long tongue that sticks out from the south into the middle of Astoria Bay. To round it, a kayaker has to give up all protection, enter the shipping channel, and expose himself to the full force of the westerly winds and waves. If anything goes wrong, the tidal current is waiting to suck him down the bay into the maelstrom of the Columbia Bar.

The challenge of rounding this point had concerned me for days; every time I glanced at the map, this huge tongue made its ugly, taunting gesture at me. My plan was to cover a modest 15 miles this day, and camp before reaching Tongue Point, leaving rounding the point for the following morning, when the wind was low and I was fresh.

Ready to begin my attack on Astoria Bay, I peeked out of the tent and saw it was nearly calm. With Rico's remark about everyone having wind generators still ringing in my ears, I immediately packed, put to sea, and headed through the mist to the town of Cathlamet, Washington. There I obtained a sit-down hot breakfast—very necessary as I'd been only snacking for several days, too tired, too windblown, and too eager to move on to bother with setting up the stove and cooking a meal for myself.

Setting out after breakfast, I dialed in the coordinates for Astoria: the GPS showed that Astoria was 18.8 miles away as the crow flies. At Cathlamet, the Columbia broadens into an area of wide channels and islands. I crossed the river to the Oregon side and followed the Clifton Channel, a meandering route screened from winds and waves by a series of islands. In addition to protecting me, the Clifton

Channel took me away from the fishermen. This was a big salmon fishing time in the lower estuary, and the river was crowded with motorboats. Where the riverbank was accessible, rows of fishermen sat in deck chairs waiting for a bite, their casting poles held upright in white PVC pipes.

I stopped on one of the islands for lunch. I had looked forward to camping on the islands in Astoria Bay, encouraged by my fine experience on Skamania Island, but I soon realized that camping on these islands was impossible. Higher up the river, where Skamania is, spring floods tear out vegetation and leave sandy beaches after the water retreats. In the slack water of Astoria Bay, the islands are choked with grasses and shrubs, difficult to penetrate. And they flood at high tide, a point I learned at lunchtime when I landed on a sliver of beach at the edge of one island. Even as I ate lunch, that bit of beach disappeared rapidly under the incoming tide. I barely had time to finish my peanut butter sandwich and clamber back into the kayak before the whole island became a semisubmerged mass of grass and brush. Watching this island flooded by the tide brought home to me the difficulty I would have finding a viable campsite that night.

Navigating the ambiguous fingers of the Clifton Channel was not easy. I ran into a sandbar that stretched for acres in every direction covered by an inch of water. As far as my eye could tell, the entire channel was blocked, and I began to wonder if I would have to retrace my route for many miles. Fortunately, a motorboat came buzzing up a channel half a mile away, revealing deeper water.

Early in the afternoon I met four kayakers, out for an afternoon of paddling. While exchanging greetings, we had an interesting demonstration of the principle of relativity.

"Where are you headed?" one woman asked.

"Astoria."

"Oh, you've got a long way to go! Where did you start from?"

"Wenatchee."

"Oh," she said, "Then you're practically there." We all laughed.

Later in the afternoon, my route took me away from the shelter of the islands and followed the edge of the bay. In the open water, I was assailed by waves that seemed to come from all directions, jumping and jolting at random. In all of the Columbia's lakes, the waves had an underlying regularity. Even if they were high, they were predictable. In Astoria Bay, the water seems to have a long memory, retaining the different pulses of wind waves, ocean waves, tidal currents, and ship wakes, all intersecting and interacting in unpredictable jolts. As the waters slapped against me, I felt like a tired boxer being jabbed by half a dozen opponents from all sides. The jabs were not violent. My opponents were only sparring and pulling their punches. But I had the unnerving feeling that at any moment one of them might tire of being patient and land a haymaker.

As the sun sunk lower in the sky, I approached Tongue Point, looking ever more desperately for a camping place. Since the islands were out of the question, the only alternative was the shoreline, but this was a steep continuous railroad embankment, composed of jagged rocks. At one point, I stopped to see if I could find a way to use it as a campsite. I struggled up a steep bank of slippery, jagged rocks, wondering how I would carry any gear to a campsite, since I needed both hands to climb. Once on the tracks, I found the disused railroad line choked with blackberries. It was impossible to turn around, sit, or lie down without being sliced and bled by this devilish stuff. Even if the brambles could be conquered, there was nothing but stones and railroad ties to sleep on. And what would I do with the kayak? It could not remain tied up, because the severe tidal drop would leave it hanging by the mooring rope in the middle of the night. I returned to the kayak and set out toward Tongue Point. If the alternatives were trying to camp on that railroad bed or pushing on into the risky unknown, which would you choose?

The sun was setting as I pulled through the waters of the bay. A tourist excursion boat from Astoria came around the point, racing right toward me. It missed me, but not by much. I wondered if the pilot had failed to see me in the dim light. I felt exposed, vulnerable.

As I got closer to the point, it occurred to me I could round it "just to have a look." If the wind and waves were severe, I'd scurry back into the lee of the peninsula. I was not thinking too clearly, for I had forgotten about the tidal current. This had been a negligible factor in the entire trip, but in the last mile before the point, the tide was running out strongly, with a current of 5 miles an hour. I couldn't return to the lee of the peninsula if I encountered bad conditions. The tide would suck me down the bay regardless.

Another danger loomed into view: a mammoth container ship was passing in front of me in the channel right off the tip of Tongue Point. If another came while I was rounding the point, I would be directly exposed.

Just a few hundred yards from the point, the tidal current grabbed me and I understood too late my miscalculation. As I shot out into the bay, I heard the sound of rapids several hundred yards off the point. Peering intently through the dim light, I could make out whitecaps and breakers. It was a tidal maelstrom where the current of the side bay I was following collided with the main tidal current in the channel.

What on earth am I doing here? I thought.

My general policy is to have a leeward shore to which I could drift if I should happen to turn over, but here I had no margin of safety. If I overturned, I would be in the shipping channel in pitch darkness where no one could see me to help. Even if I managed to slither back into the swamped kayak, I would be unable to paddle the boatload of water to safety before the tidal current swept me down the bay right out to the Pacific and the dreaded Columbia Bar. I felt I must have made a wrong choice somewhere along the way to end up in this dangerous situation, but even today I can't identify the error.

The tide swirled me out past the point into open water. I shuddered to think what would have become of me if the usual 25-mph wind had been blowing up the bay, but it wasn't. There were plenty of waves and chop from the tidal currents, but the air was calm. The excursion boat raced by me again on its return trip, again rudely close. *"On your left, ladies and gentlemen, a drowning kayaker overturned by our wake."*

Elated to be past this obstacle that I had been dreading for days, I paddled past the lighthouse on the point and headed for the lights of Astoria a few miles ahead.

I spotted a small cove and resolved to make that my camping spot, come what may. I had pushed my luck far enough kayaking in tidal currents in the dark. The little bay had no park or public land, and had buildings all around it, but unusual circumstances demanded a degree of boldness. I beached the kayak behind a house and went to the door and knocked, ready to ask whoever answered it if I could camp in the backyard. Expecting resistance and suspicion, I was floored when the young man who opened the door invited me in for a cup of coffee!

Jon was divorced, had no children, and made his living as an independent contractor installing telephone lines. His home was an old gillnetter's shop, and it stood alongside a warehouse of some 15,000 square feet where nets were once stored and repaired. Jon had bought the property for a song 10 years before when it was almost derelict, and had been repairing it, putting on a new roof, and replacing the dozens of rotting wooden piles that the buildings stood on. When restoration was complete, he planned to resell it.

He had a new computer, which he invited me to use to send an email to Judy. There were also chess sets in every room, even one in the bathroom, and a three-dimensional board in the living room, evidence of his mastery of the game as a member of the Longview, Washington chess club. He had even worked out a three-dimensional chess game he wants to market on the Internet.

Jon lit his woodstove—it's damp and chilly in these parts, even in August—and we chatted about the local society and economy. Astoria is an old town, founded in 1811 by the Pacific Fur Company, whose president was John Jacob Astor. It thrived as a seaport, then declined as shipping moved upriver to Portland. Jon said the town is reviving a bit on the basis of a strange "disaster" tourism. When a Pacific storm hits, people fill up the hotels and motels to experience the coast's lashing winds and rain.

Suddenly, Jon asked, "Would you like to go to a party?"

Of course I said yes.

"I hadn't planned on going," he said, "but I thought it might be fun to show you off."

The party was a series of bands playing in a grange hall, a potluck affair organized by a portly woman named Linda. "Mostly by email," she said. A heroic volunteer effort: I gave her ten dollars to help defray expenses.

Jon introduced me around as the kayaker going down the Columbia. "Oh, I read about you in the paper!" said one woman. This was impossible since no reporter knew of my existence, but I was enjoying the pseudo-celebrity so I didn't contradict her.

I chatted with a couple that participated in competitive sailboat races in Astoria Bay, listening with dread and fascination to their tales of high waves and horrendous tidal forces in the body of water I planned to cross the following day.

It was well after midnight when we returned home and I said goodbye to Jon, then retired to my tent on his lawn. In a 19-hour day, I had covered 29.2 crow-flies miles and probably 40 on-the-water miles, living three or four lifetimes in the process.

The next morning, I opened my eyes to a dark, overcast day, relieved to see there was no wind. Given the challenge I faced, this was a vital piece of good luck. I scrambled out of my sleeping bag, packed as fast as I could, and got myself on the water.

I had given a lot of thought to finishing my trip down the river. My original idea was to paddle into the Pacific Ocean, turn left, and land on the coast. Even without knowing the details, I sensed this plan had dangers: I could be hammered in the surf, or be pushed out to sea by the wind or tide and end up a boatful of sun-bleached bones in Hawaii four months later. As I studied the problem, I learned of an even greater danger in trying to go out the mouth of the Columbia.

"Stay away from buoy 10."

I first heard this mantra from an elderly woman at a campground near Longview when I told her I was headed for the Pacific Ocean. Her husband was a fisherman, and the fishing community knows that the mouth of the Columbia, where buoy 10 is located, is a dangerous spot.

In earlier times, the Columbia Bar was an unbelievably challenging hazard. The river washed millions of tons of sand into a system of meandering, changing channels. From offshore, the mouth of the

Columbia looked like a beach, with a continuous line of surf—which explains why early explorers kept missing the entrance. Once the entrance was found and the port of Astoria was established, ships came through, but with extreme difficulty and much danger. The bar has been the site of over 2,000 shipwrecks.

At the turn of the century, the Corps of Engineers built gigantic jetties on either side of the river's mouth to funnel the current and flush out the sand, thus maintaining a stable channel. The South Jetty is five stories deep, seven miles long, and took over 20 years to build. The jetties clear away the sand bars, but they can't prevent the clash between the river's powerful current and the massive swells of the Pacific Ocean, which heaves up crazy waves as high as 30 feet. Salmon fishing is best in the mouth of the river, and many fishermen run this gauntlet—and many are overturned, even in large boats. The Coast Guard station at Cape Disappointment averages one rescue a day.

I agreed it would be a good idea to stay away from buoy 10!

My plan was to cross the bay from Astoria to Clatsop Spit, the neck of land between the bay and the ocean where Lewis and Clark spent the winter of 1805 after coming down the Columbia. Jon's tide table had shown an 8-foot tide running out that morning until 10:30 a.m., so I had to make it across the bay before the tide changed. The sky was overcast, with a heavy layer of fog just a few hundred feet above the water.

Approaching downtown Astoria, I was amazed to spot sea lions draped along the rocks. The previous night I had heard their distinctive moaning, but because my brain was still wedded to the inland, desert environment, I never considered these sea animals as the source. I thought the sound came from wooden pilings rubbing against each other in the swell.

The city was still asleep in the early morning, but the bay was buzzing with motorboats of sport fishermen angling for king salmon. As I paddled past the Astoria waterfront, the outrushing tide created an 8-mph current with whirlpools and waves that cascaded through the pilings of the piers. The churning reminded me of the turbulence at the Canadian border where I began on the Columbia over a year earlier. My trip had come full circle, rapids to rapids.

The current rocketed me under the suspension bridge that spans the bay and sucked me into lower Astoria Bay where I passed several oceangoing ships—I hoped I was staying well out of their channel, but I could see no buoys to confirm this. After an hour, I had crossed the swirling, bumpy waters of the bay, not a nervous wreck, but feeling that the past 36 hours of dealing with Astoria Bay and Tongue Point had depleted my reserves of courage.

I hung close to the shore, still being sucked toward the mouth of the Columbia by the vigorous tide. I was looking for Hammond, which the map showed as the last town on the peninsula. I almost missed the narrow opening to the boat basin, and had to turn around and paddle furiously to escape the tidal current and reach safety.

It was a Sunday morning during salmon season at the boat ramp closest to the mouth of the Columbia, and the boat ramp was jammed with fishing boats unloading in six parallel lanes. Fortunately, a kayak can go where motorboats fear to tread, and I worked my way to the land in the shallow water behind the boat slips. I had gone as far as I could go in my kayak.

On the last leg, I covered 155.4 miles, making the grand total since the start at the Canadian border 641 miles. The total time spent wandering this watery wilderness was a biblical 40 days and 40 nights.

I left the kayak at the dock and walked to the only motel in town, the South Jetty Lodge. Its "No Vacancy" sign was brightly lit, but I had no intention of going back across Astoria Bay to look for lodgings. It was either sleep in this motel or sleep in a ditch.

I decided to be philosophical, have a good breakfast in the café next door, and see what developed. When I came out an hour later, relaxed and well fed, the "No" part of the sign was turned off, bowing, it seemed, to the powerful will of the successful kayaker. I rented a room and prepared to finish the last two miles to the Pacific on shoe leather.

Walking to the Pacific was more of a chore than I imagined. The roads on Clatsop Spit run north-south, and impenetrable vegetation caused by the huge rainfall and temperate climate meant I couldn't cut straight across the remaining 2 miles to the sea. The foliage was so thick it blacked out my GPS, so much of the time I didn't know where

I was. I wondered how the men of the Lewis and Clark expedition made their way around. They must have spent a lot of time chopping paths. At one point, I was on a path parallel to the ocean and could hear the breakers just several hundred yards away, but access to the ocean was blocked by a tangle of brush and high grass. I had to continue on the path for over a mile to reach the entrance to the beach.

It was a beach worth getting to. At most places along the Pacific you find narrow beaches or cliffs, but this beach was many hundreds of yards wide, thanks to millions of tons of sand washed down by the Columbia. With an almost imperceptible slope to the sea, it looked like Daytona Beach on the Atlantic Coast.

I walked to the water's edge where spent surf was spilling across the sand, dipped my fingers into it, and tasted its salty message. I had achieved my objective. My mind filled with images from two years of paddling this river: the water in all its moods, from mirror surface to spitting waves, the dams, the locks, the marinas, the swallows darting after mosquitoes. I took a deep breath and thought, *Columbia, I know thee.*

Sunday visitors dotted the beach, some playing gaily in the sand, others staring quietly out at the thin line of the sea's horizon. The metal bones of the *Peter Iredale,* a grand yacht shipwrecked in 1906, loomed out of the sand. Children climbed as high as they could on its rusty girders while their parents snapped pictures of them waving proudly in their achievement. The sun came out for the brief afternoon visit it makes between morning and evening fog, and showered the beach with its glistening light.

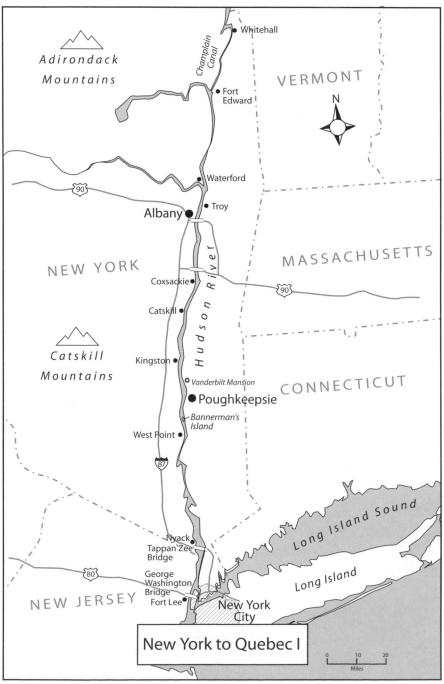

Adirondack
Mountains

Champlain Canal

● Whitehall

VERMONT

N

● Fort
Edward

● Waterford

90

NEW YORK

Albany ●

● Troy

Hudson River

MASSACHUSETTS

90

Coxsackie ●

Catskill ●

Catskill
Mountains

Kingston ●

○ Vanderbilt Mansion

● Poughkeepsie

CONNECTICUT

Bannerman's
Island

West Point ●

87

Long Island Sound

Nyack ●
Tappan Zee
Bridge

80

George
Washington
Bridge
Fort Lee ●

New York
City

Long Island

NEW JERSEY

New York to Quebec I

0   10   20
Miles

River width not to scale

5

Surprised by Samaritans

New York City to Quebec (May–June 2004)

THE HUDSON RIVER

"WHY ARE YOU GOING *up* the Hudson River?" friends asked when I described the projected journey. "Wouldn't it be easier to go down it?" Time and again I patiently explained the logic of my trip in terms of the hydrology of the river, and of my psychology in dealing with an urban area. The hydrology answer began with the observation that the Hudson is an estuary, a drowned river. Ages ago, a stream did flow down the Hudson Valley, with crystal clear water bubbling over rocks and dashing down rapids. Then the land fell, and the Atlantic Ocean invaded the Hudson Valley, all the way to Troy, New York, creating a body of water that is many times wider and deeper than needed to drain the Adirondack Mountains watershed. There is no "down" on the Hudson, no perceptible river current in it. It's practically a level lake.

The Hudson does, however, have a tidal current that pushes in and out, and I was given a rude introduction to it right at the beginning of my trip. After paddling furiously for an hour, I was a mile further from my destination than when I started!

Months before, I had downloaded the Hudson River tide table from the Internet, and I carefully chose my launch time to coincide with low tide, figuring I wouldn't have to fight any tidal current coming down the river. This was more forethought than I usually exhibit on my trips and I was rather proud of myself. The table showed that low tide at my put-in at the Dyckman Street Marina, at the north end of Manhattan, would be at 1:52 p.m.

Arriving there at 1:30 p.m., I saw something was wrong. Instead of calm water, a massive downriver current was gushing and sucking through the pilings. Unfortunately, I wasn't free to sit around for several hours to let this unexplained current dissipate because I had an audience. My daughter Ellen and her family, who lived in an apartment in upper Manhattan, had come to see me off. Ellen was snapping pictures, her husband David was eager to help me assemble the kayak on the grass alongside the river, and the two girls were waiting to see Granddad sail away on his adventure. I had to pretend I knew what I was doing and go ahead with it.

The marina made a miserable launch site: sharp stones, garbage, a dead fish, broken glass, and an old tire that nearly blocked my exit between two pilings. But it was a portal for my escape from New York. The current seemed especially strong against the bank on the New York side, and instinct suggested I would find a weaker current across the river, by Fort Lee, New Jersey. I struck out on an angled course upriver, paddling like mad in the brilliant Sunday afternoon sunshine, 2 miles upriver from the George Washington Bridge, watching nervously up and down the river for powerboats seeking to slice me in two. In the middle, I stopped paddling for a moment to check the drift. The GPS said the current against me was 2.4 miles per hour.

When I completed the crossing, I was a mile downriver from my launch site, but the current was much less, around 0.5 mph, and I soon regained the lost ground.

I needed a rest after all this struggle, so I pulled onto the edge of a mudflat and stepped out, thinking I could walk to dry land. Now we come to the psychology part of what's wrong with going "down" the Hudson River. An estuary is a static body of water. It doesn't flush out, so any pollution that gets into it sloshes back and forth for months.

This pollution includes sewage, algae thriving in water much too rich in nutrients, and silt churned up by powerboat wakes that continually beat upon the shores. The water of the lower Hudson is smelly and stagnant, and so opaque I could not see my paddle tips 3 inches below its surface. It is water one wants to escape from, to leave behind. Paddlers who go down the Hudson from the hinterland to the city face the unappealing prospect of moving day by day into an increasingly contaminated environment.

And it's not just the water. New York tends to be a dirty city, with trash continually collecting in gutters, and graffiti appearing faster than authorities can paint over it. Ears are offended, too: sirens that make it seem the city has a murder every few minutes, busses with roaring exhaust, subways with screaming brakes. Years earlier, I had lived in New York City and adjusted to the urban environment; but after many years in the village of Sandpoint, Idaho, my biorhythms had calmed down and the city seemed stressful. It made a good starting point for my journey, a place to get away from. I couldn't see making it the destination of a long, arduous journey.

And now, as I stepped out on that mudflat, I experienced another dimension of New York grime. It wasn't honest mud my foot stepped upon but slippery, slimy muck. I tried to step toward the shore but discovered my foot was stuck. I finally wriggled it free, only to discover that the other foot had sunk all the way to my calf in the process. I was mired in quicksand—well, nothing so hygienic as quicksand: this was a special New York quickmuck. It suddenly occurred to me that this ridiculous predicament was life threatening. If each attempted step left me mired deeper, then the muck would eventually close over my head.

Fortunately, I was still close enough to the boat to fall back on it, and use its support to extricate my feet. I clambered aboard, my shoes and socks full of this stinking, black muck. It must contain ground-up coal dust in addition to a bouquet of blended Hudson slimes. I was never able to rinse my white socks clean.

Several hours later, I was 5 miles up the river, resting alongside the parkland of the New Jersey Palisades. I couldn't see any buildings or people on my side of the river, just trees and cliffs. It was hard to believe I was only a few paddle strokes away from the crush of humanity in New York City. Birds were twittering energetically in the forest. The Paulownia trees were in bloom, displaying masses of purple blossoms along the base of the cliffs. Normally, these trees don't grow this far north because they can't stand subzero temperatures. I suspected that the water of the lower Hudson (which doesn't freeze because it's brackish) warms the cold air coming down from the north, and the cliffs keep this warmer air confined around the trees.

The slog against the waning current gave me time to figure out where my calculations about the tide went wrong. There's a big difference between (a) low tide and (b) the end of the tidal current flowing out the estuary. Just because the water level at Dyckman Street stops falling and begins to rise—the point of low tide—that water level is still lower than the water level higher up the river, which will therefore continue to drain. So the end of the outrushing tidal current comes several hours after low tide.

In the late afternoon, I had covered 12 miles and reached Piermont, just below the Tappan Zee Bridge, and I needed help. I had used up my first bottle of water (I carried only two bottles total) and needed to resupply before dark, but I could see no landing place—just a 20-foot concrete wall with houses perched on top. I spotted a man out on his lawn, and paddled over.

He was amazed that I had come all the way from New York City in just an afternoon. He had me throw my empty bottle up to him.

"Would you like some extra?" he asked.

I was touched by his eagerness to be of help, but politely declined, as I already had a spare bottle. That was my first human contact since leaving New York and it augured well for the journey.

Darkness had fallen by the time I crossed under the Tappan Zee Bridge, which carries the New York State Thruway across the Hudson River at Nyack. That bridge is a good way of marking the outer limit of the New York metropolitan area, so I felt I had accomplished my escape from the city. I continued paddling in the darkness, trying to find a place to rest my weary head. All I saw were houses, concrete walls, and embankments of broken stone. I toyed with the idea of sleeping on one of the many sailboats moored in the Tappan Zee, the wide stretch of the Hudson by Nyack. I wasn't thinking of breaking into one, just sleeping on the deck. However, they rock pretty badly in waves, and the halyards clang noisily against their masts, making sleep difficult.

I finally reached a patch of sand with no houses nearby where I pitched my tent. It was a marginal campsite: junk and garbage were strewn about, and there was an odor of rotting flesh—animal, I hoped, not human. The no-see-ums were eating me alive before I was able to crawl into the tent.

Far off to the east, I saw faint reflections of lightning in the sky, the remnants of a slow-moving front that passed through New York City the previous night. In between the noise of the trains, I heard the faint rumble of thunder 50 miles away.

Choosing the Hudson River as the setting for my trip was a reaction against the loneliness of the Columbia River. While I reveled in the solitude and privacy of that trip, I also missed contact with people. In the sparsely populated desert of Washington and Oregon, I passed days without using my voice at all and seldom saw human beings, except for fishermen in their distant boats. As I contemplated taking another trip, I found I yearned for a social dimension. This need turned my thinking to the densely populated eastern United States where I would surely be thrust against my fellow man.

I also missed history and culture on the Columbia. When you do see a work of man on that river, it is a 20th-century creation. The towns, streets, and structures have a 1970s feel, with not one penny spent on ornamentation or flair. Enough of western rivers, I said. Like Dinah Shore, who years ago sang a song of a disillusioned western homesteader, I craved "eastern things with buttons and bows."

What, I thought, could be more eastern, cultural, and historic than the Hudson River, arguably the center stage of American history in the founding years of the country? The waterway was first explored by Henry Hudson in his ship *Half Moon* in 1609. Hudson was looking for a water passage across the North American continent—the same goal that animated the Lewis and Clark expedition that explored the Columbia two centuries later. When Hudson came upon the broad waters of the Tappan Zee, 15 miles north of New York, he at first thought he had found the connection. But sailing further, to the Troy area, he found his way blocked by rapids.

Hudson gained fame in having a river and a bay—and an automobile—named after him. Few seem to know that he was a deplorable captain, unable to lead and manage men. Mutinies marked all his voyages, and he was finally done in by one. On his fourth voyage in 1611, the crew he had badgered and mismanaged put him and his son adrift on the icy waters of the eponymous Hudson Bay and they were never heard from again.

In colonial times, the upper Hudson River-Lake Champlain region was the arena of conflict during the French and Indian Wars, a conflict waged intermittently for nearly a century, ending in 1763. Fort Edward on the upper Hudson was the base of English operations, and Fort Ticonderoga on Lake Champlain was the French stronghold—though the British later took it.

During the Revolutionary War, the river was a bitterly contested prize. To keep British forces from sailing up the river and dominating the valley, Revolutionary forces stretched chains across it at three places. The first was at Fort Lee, just across the river from where I launched at Dyckman Street; the second chain was at Fort Montgomery, near Bear Mountain Bridge. The British managed to capture these forts and destroy both chains, but they never took the third one at West Point. This was a massive structure, with links weighing over 100 pounds each, and the whole—kept afloat by big logs—weighing 186 tons.

On the second night of my trip, I saw a remnant of that West Point chain at my campsite. I had eaten supper at Highland Falls, the village a few hundred yards down the road from the Military Academy where cadets go AWOL from institutional food. After finishing my spaghetti and meatballs, I crossed the river to set up camp in undeveloped parkland on the other side. A park ranger came by in a four-wheeler and showed me that my tent was pitched just 30 feet from the bedrock where the chain was attached. All that was left of the iron support that anchored the chain was a stub of metal cut flush from the rock with an acetylene torch: some rapacious moron had recently appropriated the historic chunk of iron for his mantelpiece. The ranger was furious about this act, his anger probably fed by the fact that the vandalism reflected poorly on his ability to protect the park he was supposed to manage.

When I enquired about what to expect upriver, the ranger told me this was the famed Hudson Highlands section, the most scenic part of the river. On the next day, I had my camera right at hand when I set out, paddling along the S-turn around West Point. I saw masses of trees on the hills, but nothing that prompted me to remove the camera from its Ziploc bag. Later I reached Storm King Mountain, supposedly the scenic climax of this stretch. Storm King Mountain was the site of a big environmental battle in the 1960s, when Con Edison, the electric utility company, wanted to build a storage reservoir nearby. The environmentalists—who won—opposed it on the grounds that it would detract from the natural beauty of the place. The dispute seemed weirdly irrelevant based on what I saw from the river. Storm King Mountain was already incredibly defaced. A railroad had been gashed into the mountain's base at river level, and not one but two "scenic" highways had been hacked into the middle and upper levels—producing naked, blasted cliffs and talus slopes of waste rock. The place looked like a well-used atomic test site. I did take a picture of that.

After passing Storm King Mountain, I crossed the river to see the famous castle on Bannerman's Island, on the east side of the river. I paddled up close to the island in the shallow water to get a close-up of this fascinating structure. Built in the early 1900s by Scottish businessman Francis Bannerman, the imitation Scottish castle looks like a Hollywood set, with just the façade remaining after a fire. For a western kayaker craving buttons and bows, this was it: a deliciously over-the-top structure laden with medieval turrets and crenellations.

Photography and kayak safety don't mix. To get pictures of the castle I had to pass the island on the landward side. A strong wind at my back, waves going in the same direction, and a powerful tidal current all combined to rush me along the water lickety-split, a great free ride if I had wanted one at the moment, which I decidedly did not. Between the island and the mainland were rows of closely spaced pilings that supported the causeway that once connected the castle to the mainland. The tops of the pilings were barely submerged, and waves were breaking on them. The current was too strong for me to turn around and go back: the pilings were my destiny. With bad luck, I could have been pinned against them and tipped over by the current, or the skin of the kayak might have been ripped open while I tried to scrape in between them. I snapped the shutter, quickly slipped the camera into its plastic bag, and gave my full attention to navigation. I picked out what seemed to be the widest gap and hurtled through, or over, the pilings—I don't know which: I blinked in the moment of crisis.

I wasn't the only voyager to face a crisis at Bannerman's Island. The travel writer William Least Heat-Moon (best known for *Blue Highways,* an account of an automobile journey) visited the place when making a trip up the Hudson in a motorized dory (described in *River-Horse*). Eager to visit Bannerman's Castle, he and his friends tried to get close enough to land their boat, but wrecked a propeller, probably on the same pilings that threatened me.

Later that afternoon, I developed a pain in my right shoulder—a cause for considerable alarm because arms are the engines on a kayak trip, and if they don't work right, the trip is over. The truth is my paddling stroke is deficient. One day back home on Lake Pend Oreille, I was paddling alongside a highway bridge when I heard a shout from a speeding car: "YOU-ARE-PADDLING-WRONG!" I understood that my critic intended no insult; he was trying to help. However, at 65 miles an hour, that was all the advice he could give. It was like being sentenced to jail without ever being told what crime you committed.

Over the ensuing years, I've done my best to deduce what my drive-by mentor would have told me if he had had more time. One principle of paddling, it seems, is that you should vary your stroke, to use muscles differently. So occasionally I break my normal rhythm to take a few very high strokes, or some low, sweeping strokes. Every so often, I pretend I am a rower, and reach way forward on the stroke and pull back with my entire body. I have even spun the boat around and paddled backward for a few hundred yards, albeit awkwardly.

Despite these diversions, I find myself using a normal stroke about 95 percent of the time. Clearly, this basic stroke has to be right to avoid injury on a long trip, and must take the strain off the shoulder and elbow joints by using torso muscles. If the body doesn't twist enough, the arms and shoulders are left to do all the work. When this pain surfaced in my right shoulder, I knew I'd fallen into a lazy habit of paddling with my arms. To correct the problem, I locked my elbows, tightened my gut, and started twisting back and forth from the waist. The pain lessened noticeably, and well that it did, given the scope of the trip I had set for myself.

The Hudson River made a good start for my eastern trip, but I wanted a longer, more challenging journey than the 120 miles from New York to Albany. At first I thought of continuing on the Erie Canal, but was put off by the idea of paddling for weeks confined in a canal. Then I noticed a short canal that branched off at the beginning of the Erie, going north: the Champlain Canal. This would take me to Lake Champlain, a body of water that ran 113 miles to the Canadian border. I determined to follow that route, excited by the prospect of traversing Lake Champlain, though apprehensive about facing its wide waters.

All that was lacking was a suitable destination, a target worthy of my paddling effort. The point that stood out on the map was Quebec, the capital of the French-speaking Canadian province of the same name. To get there, I would follow the Richelieu River from Lake Champlain, and then join the Saint Lawrence River, which ran to Quebec. All together, from New York City to Quebec, the route was 490 miles, plenty long but a manageable challenge if I could remember to paddle with my stomach muscles.

Finding a suitable camping spot is a challenge on most kayak trips, but on those first days on the Hudson River, it was a grueling struggle. I had to contend with rain, uneven ground, tides, boat wakes, mud, biting insects, and screeching New York Central trains blasting past like 500-pound bombs only a few feet from my head. From this pageant of camping woes, one night stands out as especially miserably memorable. It happened on my third day out.

Really bad camping experiences usually begin long before nightfall. They start in the late afternoon when you aren't seeing any possible camping situation and are consumed with mounting anxiety about finding a suitable place. I was approaching Poughkeepsie, along a stretch where railroads ran along both sides of the river with steep, rocky embankments blocking access to the land for miles and miles.

I made a first effort to find a stopping place on the west side, where CSX trains run, by investigating a tiny bridge under the tracks. I dragged the kayak under the bridge and paddled for a few yards in the stagnant pool on the other side. All I could see was swamp, and a steep bank that came right down to the edge of the swamp. No camping there. I retraced my steps, having wasted an hour in this fruitless search for a campsite.

A mile further along, I saw a spit of land between the railroad and the river that looked like a plausible camping spot. As I approached, I realized it was a deserted, yet lived-in hobo jungle, with blue tarps and bundles spread around. Not being a hobo myself, I figured that I wouldn't have a good read on the people and dangers involved in trying to join this situation.

As I looked ahead along the east side of the river, I saw nothing but steep, rocky railroad embankment for miles and miles. Despite blustery wind and worrisome waves, I crossed the river to Poughkeepsie on the east side. After a long slog, I came up to the municipal pier at the center of the city. I disembarked to use the restroom and drinking fountain, then visited with a young man from Peru who was full of questions about my trip. He was surprised to learn that I had kayaked all the way from New York City, and even more surprised to learn that I had lived in Peru. He urged me to camp in the nearby park, but after weighing the matter, I concluded that an urban park isn't a safe place to camp, since even if the police leave you alone, there are teens, drunks, and thugs to worry about.

In the gathering darkness, I launched again. All afternoon I had been watching the clouds building in the northwest, a mass of thunderheads that advertised a classic cold-front formation approaching. It really was time to find a place to camp!

I continued along the Poughkeepsie waterfront. The shore was a mass of jagged rocks and rotted pilings, adorned with twisted metal and old tires. After a half mile, I found a slight break in this forbidding shoreline, a sloping steel ramp that extended to the water. At least I could land the boat without ripping the bottom. The shore was crowded with a mass of brush and weeds, sumac, and poison ivy, but this was no time to be choosy. I made my way through the brush and found an abandoned industrial site, with wide areas of tarmac with seedlings pushing through, and empty buildings, including one like an airplane hanger with its massive doors open. I was leery about going in there, not knowing what weird kind of life—human, animal, or vegetable—might be encountered.

Strong floodlights pierced the blackness in different places around the site. I saw no one, but suspected this was the kind of place that might be infested by homeless squatters and drug dealers. I wondered whether my lipstick-size vial of pepper spray would provide meaningful protection.

I concluded that, for better or worse, this abandoned industrial site in the heart of the city—with police sirens howling on the streets just a few blocks away—was to be my home for the night. I unloaded the boat and lifted it into the trees well above the tide line. I couldn't drive stakes for the tent into the asphalt but I found chunks of 4x4 lumber onto which I tied the support lines. I took care to stay in the shadows in case a night watchman was about.

With the tent set up, I stuffed my gear, and myself, into the tent. My last chore—a delight, really—was to check the GPS to see how many miles I'd made. I hadn't looked all afternoon, being too busy with the stress of finding a place to camp. The screen said 23.4 miles, a respectable achievement, especially considering this was linear mileage, not taking into account four river crossings and bends in the river. I was proud of myself for having at last found a workable shelter against the coming storm and looked forward to falling asleep to the sound of raindrops on my tent.

Soon the rain arrived, but it was no restful pitter-patter. Above my head, frigid air from the Arctic tundra collided with steamy humidity swept from Louisiana bayous, producing an end-of-the-world tempest. Lightening cracked and pounded, wind lashed the trees almost to the breaking point—I could only hope the kayak wasn't being blown to kingdom come—and the rain hammered down in gushing torrents. I feared the tent wouldn't stand the pounding for long. I ran my fingers over the inside surface. It was damp but no drops were falling on me. There was no question of trying to fall asleep. All I could do was grit my teeth and hope the storm's fury would soon abate.

After several minutes I suddenly became aware of a new and alarming sensation. My arms and legs were floating, just like in a waterbed. I unzipped the tent flap and touched the ground. The tent was standing in water three inches deep!

I closed the tent and lay back. My first thought was that I must not move, to avoid stressing the seams of the tent and letting water in. I lay frozen in position for some minutes, but it wasn't clear what improvement I could hope for. My tent was in the low spot of the property, which would collect runoff all night, even after the rain stopped.

When the rain eased somewhat, I peeked out of the tent again. I was lying in a lake that extended 30–40 feet, and it was now four inches deep. That open airplane hanger was looking better and better. I collected my sleeping bag, put on my shoes and made a dash through the rain in my underpants to the whatever-infested hanger.

Inside, I found a dry spot where the roof hadn't leaked and spread my sleeping bag on the concrete floor. I moved quietly, hoping not to disturb other inhabitants of the hanger. My hip hurt as I lay down against the concrete floor. Through the gloom I could see the silhouettes of two storage tanks and the place smelled strongly of diesel. It occurred to me that I probably had stumbled into a Superfund site where the land was too contaminated with PCBs, or something, to sell or use. That would explain the absence of people. Out on the street there would be a 12-foot cyclone fence topped with barbed wire, and signs that said "Danger, Toxic Chemicals" along with a skull and crossbones. I was savoring urban camping cordon bleu.

I was appalled by my bad luck, to find myself soaking in the middle of a lake after all the efforts I had made to secure a protected night's sleep! It was Job's story: you do all that's right, and you still get dumped on.

The night wore on. My apprehensions about the airplane hanger proved groundless. In fact, the place was a blessing, a dry shelter from the continuing rain. As for companions, I heard a cat squealing at some point in the night, but that was all.

The next morning the world was new. The cold front did what it's supposed to do, clearing out the muggy air and leaving crisp weather with a crystalline blue sky. I had a north wind to buck, but I enjoyed battling the spray on this bright day. It never ceases to amaze me what a difference sunshine makes in kayaking. The same steep, pitching waves that are menacing thugs in gloomy light become friendly playmates when the sun is out.

By midmorning I ran out of drinking water, but rather than wasting time trying to find a source, I made some iodine-flavored water from the river, using my purifying pills. The river had cleared up somewhat: I could see the paddle tips about 2 feet below the surface. The water didn't have the burden of silt that it has in the New York City area. The banks are mainly rock, so the tide and the waves don't stir up so much dirt from the banks.

I passed a racing shell of four local college girls coming down the river. They were warming up, taking a few strokes, coasting, then stroking some more. They spent only 10 minutes in this relaxed mode before they went all out. I typically needed the better part of an hour to fully warm up. The pain in my shoulder was still there, but not worse. I was being careful to lock my arms and twist from the gut.

The Hudson Valley is the setting of hundreds of grand estates, and my aim that afternoon was to visit one of grandest, the Vanderbilt Mansion, which lay close enough to the water for me to reach. When I reached it, I left the kayak at a boat basin off the river, and hiked up.

Cornelius Vanderbilt bought the property in 1895, and tore down the existing mansion in order to build a bigger one. The property is thought to be the first landscaped estate in the Hudson Valley. On the curving drive leading to the mansion I saw white oaks 6 feet thick, a size rare in the East where forests have been cut and recut. The family donated the estate to the federal government in 1940 and it is now run by the National Park Service. Its gardens, which the government allowed to go to ruin, were rescued in the 1980s by a local volunteer group, which now lovingly tends them.

The Beaux-Arts mansion is adorned with glorious artwork, sculpture, and carvings created by old-world craftsmen brought from Europe to make everything look thoroughly French. Mrs. Vanderbilt's bedroom is an exact copy of Marie Antoinette's bedroom (one wonders how thoroughly Mrs. V. intended to follow in Marie's footsteps). The furniture, decoration, and artwork have been left the way they were when the mansion was used around the turn of the century, making the place great for time traveling in the imagination.

We tour members rolled our eyes with moral superiority as the guide described the extravagance of the owners. This 40-room mansion with its staff of 60 was the smallest of four mansions the Vanderbilts owned, and was used only a few weeks out of the year, in spring and fall. Surely, we supposed, if we had that much money we would use it more constructively.

Walking around the Italian Gardens afterward, I realized that this matter of ethical spending is complicated. If a member of the middle class buys a powerboat and uses it one week of the year, is that a wiser use of money? If a child buys a toy and breaks it the next day, isn't that as wasteful? Maybe we're all guilty of wasteful consumption; it's just that we do it on a less noticeable scale than the Vanderbilts.

Besides, how do you define a "good" use of money? Surely, it doesn't mean fully consuming everything you buy. Someone who buys 5 pounds of chocolates and eats them all in one afternoon is not using money wisely.

Reaching for an answer that covered most situations, I settled on the idea that wise spending is that which gives the greatest possible creative opportunities and constructive pleasure to the human race (including oneself and one's family). By this definition, Vanderbilt would come off rather well. He gave work to all the painters, carvers, and other workers who built and decorated the mansion. He motivated them to create and achieve. And his descendants, in their philanthropic gift of the estate to the public, have given pleasure to all the tourists who now visit the mansion and grounds.

I owed a special thanks to Vanderbilt for building his mansion because, in addition to the pleasure of seeing the house and grounds, I managed to shave in the visitor center bathroom, my first time since leaving New York City.

At the end of the day I settled in the Margaret Lewis Norrie State Park, another property donated to the government by a philanthropist. At the nearly deserted campground I took a hot shower, and spread my wet sleeping bag and tent over picnic tables to dry in the sunshine, completing a happy recovery of the status quo ante flood.

Another monument of philanthropy on the Hudson was one I spotted in the first minute of my trip after shoving off at Dyckman Street: the tower of The Cloisters, the medieval monastery-museum John D. Rockefeller, Jr. donated to the Metropolitan Museum of Art. The 67-acre park in which The Cloisters stands, Fort Tryon Park, was another Rockefeller gift to the city. He had the park constructed—stonework, roads, stairways, embankments—during the Depression to provide work for the unemployed. These kinds of donations reminded me that there are two systems to get the wealthy to contribute to the common good. One is to try to tax their money away and have the politicians spend it; the other is to let them be creative and generous on their own.

In Kingston, I had arranged to meet with old family friends. I'd never done that before on a kayak trip, setting up a meeting time days in advance, and it added a degree of anxiety, since guaranteeing a schedule on a kayak trip is difficult. But this meeting had a compelling justification.

In 1936, my parents bought an old farm near Grahamsville in the Catskill Mountains of New York. Every year, we spent the entire summer there in fun-filled days of games and outdoor exploration (after we had finished our chores). The Furmans owned the dairy farm a mile below us on Glade Hill, and we depended on them at every turn: for providing milk, bulldozer work, sawed logs for firewood, and for pulling our stuck car out of the mud. The Furman children, Frances and Pete, were our playmates since before I can remember.

In an odd way, kayaking had kept me in touch with Frances. Over the years I sent her accounts of my trips and she read them to her mother Emma, then in her mid-90s. She reported that Emma enjoyed these tales, so I kept sending more. When Frances learned of my trip on the Hudson, she suggested a meeting in Kingston, which is about an hour and a half from their home.

As I paddled toward Kingston the next morning, I recalled a childhood fantasy that had slipped my mind for a half century. When I was nine years old our family visited some friends in Kingston. In the harbor among the other crafts, I spotted a stubby little workboat with a boxy cabin a person could stand up in. Even at that tender age I detected that the boat was amiably underpowered with its putt-putt inboard engine: it was no relation to the slick powerboats meant to pull water-skiers. On the spot, I became determined to buy such a boat and to travel up the Hudson River in it with a friend, exploring creeks and bays, sleeping in the cabin, completely self-sufficient. This dream fell by the wayside, since I was too young to be allowed to accomplish it at age nine, and later became laden with too many responsibilities. It had dropped from my mind until that moment paddling toward Kingston, when I realized with a start of delight that I was living this boyhood ambition now.

Gene, Frances's husband, told me to meet them at the Kingston waterfront by a "tugboat in the air." This puzzling direction was spot-on: there was a real tugboat hoisted in the air in front of the Hudson River Maritime Museum. I reached it a few minutes before 10:00 a.m., tied at the dock, and came up to the street level of the museum grounds. I soon discovered I was locked behind wrought-iron gates that didn't open until 11:00 a.m. (This is a common situation on waterfront properties: places that are locked tighter than a drum on the street side are wide open to the water.) There on the sidewalk were Frances and Gene. I had to hug Frances through the iron bars of the fence, like a jailhouse reunion. To escape the bars I went back to the kayak and paddled up to the municipal dock.

Emma was frail and unable to speak, but gave a sweet smile of recognition when she saw me. Gene and Frances treated me to a breakfast that filled me up for some time to come. At the table, I think Frances noticed me filching a couple packets of jam: these were needed to provide variation from the honey and peanut butter sandwiches that were the mainstay of my diet.

I pulled out what people on the river call a water chestnut, and asked Frances and Gene to guess what it was. When I first came across these black, walnut-sized objects floating in the river, I thought they were broken pieces of a child's plastic toy. They had sharp, pointed arms, or horns, that suggested the head of a Martian warrior. They wash ashore by the scores of thousands, their sharp spines making it necessary to wear shoes on the beaches.

Gene had the same idea, thinking they were some kind of defective plastic part dumped into the river by a careless manufacturer, but Frances, more familiar with plants, guessed they were seedpods—which they were—the fruit of a waterweed that grows in shallow waters.

After breakfast we said good-byes, and I promised Frances and Emma a copy of the Hudson River account—in which they would now figure as characters in the tale.

I paddled down Kingston's Rondout Creek to find the Hudson lashed by a strong south wind and jumping with the highest waves I'd seen so far. I put on my life jacket, zipped all pouches closed, and attached the rain skirt that Robin the Sandpoint seamstress had made for me, and plunged into it. As so often happens in these situations that seem dangerous at first glance, the turbulence was no problem, just vigorous wind and waves that, along with the incoming tidal current, added 2.5 mph to my speed. Soon I was roaring along, having a great time.

Then—I guess the Hudson gave me two white-knuckle moments that morning—I happened to spot both a green and a red buoy lying between the near shore and me. That was a shock, for it meant I was either sitting in the shipping channel, or even beyond the channel toward the middle of the river. *Well,* I thought, *I'm in no immediate danger as long as no ships are coming.* On the Hudson, oceangoing traffic is rather rare, with only three or four ships passing a day. I looked up the river to make sure I was alone. A tanker was coming down the river at me!

I was in a game of elephant and mouse. I didn't have enough faith in the buoys to believe I would be safe paddling toward the middle of the river (which was in fact the case). I was determined to reach the near shore. But to get there, I had to paddle across the tanker's course. I flailed at the water, all the while watching his towering steel bow pointed directly at my heart, slicing closer. My reason told me that, given the shape of the river and the position of the buoys, the tanker had to turn, but the hair standing up on the back of my neck wasn't listening to reason. I paddled until I hit the bank. Still he came on, headed right at me, and the thought flashed into my mind that perhaps the pilot was suicidal, an al-Qaeda recruit who had hijacked the tanker to bring jihad to Kingston, New York. At the very last minute, the monster gently veered to the right and glided by: I could almost touch it. I wondered if pilots of these ships think it's funny scaring wee kayakers and seeing them flee.

In planning my trip the previous winter, the first point of interest I circled on my map as a "must-see" destination was Cedar Grove, the home and museum of artist Thomas Cole in Catskill, New York. Cole was a leading 19th-century painter who inspired the Hudson River school of landscape painting. His greatest work is *The Voyage of Life,* on exhibit at the National Gallery in Washington DC. These four 6-foot-high canvases are richly detailed, stupendous landscapes depicting life as a boat trip down a river. The second panel, *Youth,* shows a young man cruising along a calm river toward what he thinks is a shimmering castle. Alas, it is only a castle of clouds in the sky. In the distance, the river takes a sharp right turn and plunges down steep rapids. We can see the danger, but the youth, his gaze fixed on the castle, has no inkling of what's in store for him. The painting speaks to all water voyagers who have taken an easy trip for granted. Many times over the years I stood in awe before those paintings in the National Gallery where they have their own special room, so when I saw the Thomas Cole home noted on the map, I had to make a pilgrimage.

I paddled into Catskill and learned that the Cole house was miles away from the harbor, too far to walk. However, one of my informants mentioned that it was near the Rip Van Winkle Bridge. After a hearty lunch, I went back out to the river, and paddled up to that bridge. The bank was steep and covered with a thick tangle of vegetation, seemingly impossible to scale. Then I spotted a 75-foot wooden stairway that came right down to the water. No one was about and the rickety, moss-covered steps hadn't been used in a long time. I couldn't resist the conclusion that the stairway had been placed there to accommodate Thomas Cole kayaking pilgrims. Since there was no high ground to beach the kayak, I attached two lines to heavy stones to hold it when the tide came up.

I tiptoed up the stairs and found myself in a backyard with laundry flapping on the line. I sidled past that to a driveway, which led to the street, and hence to the Thomas Cole home.

The house, which Cole bought in 1836, has been rescued from demolition by a voluntary group that runs it as a museum, and which is raising money to restore Cole's nearby studio. Being the only visitor, I was given a private tour by Sybil, a volunteer board member. It was a thrill to be in the rooms where Cole lived and worked. On the tour I learned of another Cole sequence painting, *The Course of Empire*. In five panels it shows an imaginary country (very much like Rome) going from a primitive agricultural society to imperial greatness and then to ruin (I made a note to see the canvasses some day, which are at the New York Historical Society Museum in New York City). After visiting with Sybil I signed up to join the historical society that runs Cedar Grove. Then I made my way back to my boat, which was floating in the rising tide, still attached to its stone anchors and guarded by fishermen who had volunteered to watch over it.

About once on every kayak trip, I hit a paddling rhythm that is positively intoxicating. Human limitations seem to drop away: I feel no aches, discomfort, or sense of fatigue. I become a machine capable of paddling smoothly and effortlessly forever. I had one of these paddling highs that afternoon, boosted by the exhilaration of reaching Cole's house. It helped that the tide was flooding up the river, and the wind and waves were going in my direction, all combining to give a great feeling of speed and power. Soon I was tearing up the river, slaloming past buoys like a water-skier. I didn't even want to pause to slide out the GPS to check what record-breaking speed I was attaining.

Other kayakers have noted these moments of high-energy paddling. Paul Caffyn, a legendary paddler who circumnavigated Australia in 1982, described a memorable high on his grueling 9,420-mile journey in his book *The Dreamtime Voyage*. Caffyn's biggest challenge was getting past Zuytdorp, 106 miles of unbroken cliffs that required an all-night paddling session. Caffyn took No-Doz tablets to stay awake, since falling asleep would have let the wind and waves dash him against the cliffs. As the harrowing passage neared completion, the exhilaration of success gave him unusual energy:

> I had anticipated being at my wit's end during the final few hours to Kalbarri, mind frazzled by lack of sleep, body drained of energy. . . . The contrary was the case. Now 32 hours since launching, I was literally going for broke with all the stops out. Drenched with spray as the bow plunged into the chop, I experienced a strange but marvelous, overwhelming feeling of being unstoppable.

To top off the afternoon of glorious paddling after Cedar Grove, I came upon the first good primitive campsite of the trip that evening, an area called the Hudson Islands Park. The park was a large, heavily wooded peninsula with a sandy beach above the tide line where I could safely leave the kayak and set up the tent. It had only one slight drawback: three boatloads of fishermen just offshore were still fishing at dusk, and unavoidably observed my nighttime preparations. I always feel embarrassed setting up my tent and retiring in plain view of other people. It's like having strangers in your bedroom.

The next day, I stopped to investigate a tower—a big chimney actually—standing at the edge of the water. It proved to be the remains of a powerhouse connected with an old ice operation on Nutten Hook, opposite the town of Coxsackie. Natural ice was a big industry along the Hudson in the 19th century. When the river froze, they would cut the ice into slabs and drag them into an icehouse the size of a football stadium, where the ice was packed in sawdust. In the summer, it was barged to New York City. The industry collapsed around 1890, as mechanical refrigeration took over. The icehouse burned down long ago, and forest has reclaimed the land, with hardwood trees now a foot thick. Except for the chimney and some decaying pilings in the river, you'd never guess this used to be a major industrial site.

In the afternoon, I stopped to ask some fishermen what they were going after. I'd been seeing scores of boats of anglers, which puzzled me because I thought the Hudson was polluted. In fact, there's a health warning against eating fish from the Hudson, especially because of mercury pollution. One marina owner told me the authorities have now raised the threshold and declared that it is safe to eat one Hudson River fish a month.

He scoffed at that: "They're saying if you eat two of these fish you will die, but it's okay to eat one of them. Yea, right."

Understandably, no one fishes for native Hudson River fish. The fishermen were going after "stripers," that is, striped bass. The striped bass live in the ocean and come up the river only to mate and spawn, so they are safe to eat. Sometimes as I paddled along, I saw striped bass jumping all around me. They don't dart into the air as they would if they were chasing prey. Instead they do a squirming roll at the surface, which the fisherman told me is part of their mating ritual. Once, one thumped heavily into the bottom of my boat, apparently mistaking the sleek black neoprene of my kayak bottom for a fishy femme fatale.

You don't need a fishing license on the Hudson, they told me, because being a sea level part of the ocean, it's considered federal coastal waters, and not under New York State regulation. The U.S.

Coast Guard operates the icebreaker that keeps the channel open in the winter.

On the morning of my sixth day, I tried to outsmart the tidal current. After slogging for 4 hours against it and making only 7 miles, I pulled ashore determined to wait it out, conserve my strength, and pour on the coal when the current changed in my favor. I placed a stone at the river edge to gauge the turn of the tide, pledging not to go back on the river until the stone was covered.

To pass the time I did my stretching exercises and read the book I had taken along, *The Last of the Mohicans* by James Fenimore Cooper. The novel is set in the upper Hudson-Lake Champlain area at the time of the French and Indian Wars, and seemed a worthy piece of literature to tackle. Cooper's writing style is flowery, which was considered the proper way of writing in the 19th century. He wouldn't say, "They talked in a friendly way." Instead he writes, "A few sentences were exchanged that served to establish the appearance of an amicable intercourse between the parties." This style makes for tough reading: at times, it is almost like solving a cryptogram.

All of my waiting that morning accomplished very little. After 2 hours my stone was finally covered and I set out again, but only a weak current moved in my favor. And since the north wind I had been fighting had become stronger, I was no better off than before. I suppose the lesson was you can't fool Mother Nature. Eventually I made it to a marina at New Baltimore late in the afternoon. When they found out I needed a cash machine, the owner and his wife drove me 9 miles to Ravena and back.

Their assistance further underscored how friendly everyone was along the Hudson. The dozens of people I approached for advice and directions were all eager to help. I had asked for water at three places, and each time my helpers wanted to give me extra bottles. The openness and friendliness seemed very western, and contradicted my image of easterners as standoffish. Perhaps that used to be the case, but now it seems the country is developing a national culture of helpful, easygoing people.

In the evening, I camped only 6 miles short of Albany, near a highway bridge roaring with traffic. I was careful to drag the kayak well up the bank because the tides were rising higher. Near New York City, the water rose only 1–2 feet, whereas in the Albany-Troy area the surge was 4–5 feet. As the river narrows, it constricts the water and that amplifies the rise of the tide.

I reached Albany on Sunday morning, a week after setting out, proud that I had vaulted 123 miles from one major city to another under my own power, without benefit of oil, electricity, or even horses. I paddled alongside the towering buildings and the concrete spaghetti of freeway bridges, off-ramps, and skyways. I pulled under the stern of the full-sized replica of Henry Hudson's ship, the Half Moon, which was moored on the east side of the river. It was brightly decorated with a red-and-white checkerboard design and had a big half-moon painted on the stern. The tourists standing on its deck waved at me and I waved back.

I continued up the river toward the first lock of the Erie Canal at Troy. I approached the spot with apprehension, unable to see anything but water pouring over a wide dam. I had no idea what to do. Did I register somewhere? Would I be allowed in the lock? Did I have to pay? A half mile before the dam, I pulled over to get some information from a young man who was fishing.

"How do I go through the lock?"

"What?"

He apparently didn't understand what a lock was, so I rephrased my question. "How do I get up the river above the dam?"

"You can't. That's as far as you can go. The boats come up the river to the dam and turn around and come back."

Well, at least I knew there was a lock at Troy, the famous Federal Lock, which was more than this Trojan knew. I continued up the river and approached the lock. I saw nothing but high concrete walls—no place for me to moor, no way to ask questions, just three pleasure boats lined up waiting in front of a red light. When it turned green, they motored into the lock, and I followed along, pretending I knew what I was doing. I entered the lock, and the big gate thudded closed behind me. I grabbed a slimy iron ladder as the water started to boil around me, and had to change my grip every few seconds as the water level rose. Fifteen minutes later, we had gone from the dingy dungeon of the empty lock into the brilliant sunshine of the lake at the top, 14 feet above sea level. This first lock on the Erie Canal system is under the jurisdiction of the feds, being a sea-level facility, and it's free for all boats. Higher up the canal, powerboats are charged, but kayakers go through free.

After leaving the lock, I paddled my way against the river's weak current to Waterford, 10 miles up the river. This is where the Mohawk River joins the Hudson, and where the Erie Canal branches off to the west. The Hudson continues north, but it's not a free-flowing river. In 1915, the authorities decided to improve on the narrow, century-old Champlain Canal with a big-capacity route that would use the Hudson River itself. They drowned its rapids and falls with a chain of dams, and installed locks to let barges pass the dams. This staircase of dams and locks extends to Fort Edward. From Fort Edward, authorities dug a canal and lock system that rises to 139 feet above sea level, then descends to Lake Champlain, 95 feet above sea level.

Although this expanded Champlain Canal was built for big barges, it came too late in the transportation cycle to be of much use: trains and trucks had taken away the commercial business. The last commercial load was an oversized electric generator that went through on a barge in the 1990s. Now all the traffic consists of pleasure boats, and the system is oriented toward tourism. In one of the lock houses, I noticed a list of instructions on the bulletin board that directed lock-keepers to greet each boater, and, at the end of locking through, to bid boaters goodbye. And they do it: the lockkeepers were all friendly and helpful.

Early summer is normally a wet time in the Hudson Valley, but the rain was breaking records the year of my trip. Heavy showers were falling practically every night. As I pulled into Waterford that evening, storms were threatening again.

My first choice for a campsite was a little low island at the mouth of the Mohawk River—a gravel bar lying about 18 inches above the water level. It seemed wonderfully private and secure. I wasn't worried about it being low because I was now out of the tide's reach, and no boat traffic could speed by and make waves. When I attempted to land, however, I found my way blocked by a stony, shallow bottom extending far out from the island. I started to drag my kayak over these stones, but found this was too much work, and too hard on the fabric of the kayak, so I gave it up. I had no inkling that I had dodged a bullet.

My solution for a campsite was the day campground on a peninsula between the Hudson and the Mohawk. Overnight camping was forbidden, the sign said, and the park was supposed to close at sunset. I reconnoitered the place, and figured how to locate myself out of the attendant's line of vision when he came to lock up the restrooms. Quietly creeping through the twilight, I set up my tent, being careful to choose higher ground.

It was well that I did, for this was another night of Poughkeepsie-style thunderstorms and heavy rain. The next morning I took advantage of a lull in the rain to take down the tent and pack up my gear, but before I could stow it in the kayak, another downpour hit. I only had time to pull out the tent and draw the material over my head against the rain.

Huddled against the downpour, I passed the time examining the line of cabin cruisers tied up across the water at the entrance to the Erie Canal, their owners warm and dry, watching TV and petting their poodles. You might suppose that I envied them; let me explain why this was not so.

Many years ago, at the age of 18, I spent a summer traveling around Europe. I was on a tight budget, seeking to spend only a dollar a day, pressed to economize on food, lodging, and transportation. That meant that many times I had to settle for considerable discomfort and uncertainty: sleeping in odd places, waiting long hours to catch a ride as a hitchhiker, being caught in the rain, and so forth. Occasionally, I would treat myself by taking a train, staying at a hotel, or eating a meal at a restaurant. In this variation of conditions, I began to notice a pattern: the more difficult and uncomfortable the situation, the more interesting and rewarding the experience. When I sought out a barn to sleep in, for example, I would meet a farmer and his family and be introduced to their wholly different world, whereas if I stayed in a hotel, I found it boring and sterile. Hitchhiking was uncertain and difficult, but it gave me a chance to meet many interesting people. A train ride, on the other hand, was comfortable and dependable, but was almost always uneventful. Over the years, I've seen the point confirmed on many other journeys and expeditions: the more comforts and conveniences you do without, the more invigorating and fulfilling the journey.

I don't know how far you can press this principle. Would, let us say, slithering from New York to San Francisco on your belly lead to a more fulfilling journey than just walking it? Come to think of it, it might, when you take into account that more people would be interested in, and help out, the belly-traveler (assuming he had some rationale for doing it). But one needn't go overboard in applying the idea: some attention to comfort is warranted.

The denizens of the cabin cruisers are not just seeking some comfort, however. For them, it is the premise of their journey. Their approach is to maintain all the conveniences of suburban life while traveling, to bring along air conditioning, Internet, television, plush pile carpeting, the hair dryer, and the cat. But what kind of recreation—re-creation—can they have when they've brought their entire old world along? How are they to get a new perspective on their lives? How do they get solitude with the TV blaring and the microwave beeping? How do they test their willpower, patience, and ingenuity when no difficult or challenging problems arise?

What of nature can be seen from a cruiser? Several times a day I see goslings hustling after Mama Duck, and their eagerness always brings a smile to my lips. They don't just follow; they practically run up her back. Is the suburbanite sitting atop his hammering twin Volvo diesels aware of these creatures?

And riding those hundreds of horsepower from place to place, how does he get his exercise? The evening before, I noticed some women resolutely taking their constitutionals up and down the dock. It was encouraging to see they valued exercise but ironic that on their vacation they obtain it exactly as they do in their suburban lives.

No doubt, those who travel by luxurious and secure means will occasionally face an unexpected crisis, one that challenges their abilities and gives them an interesting experience to tell the folks back home. Fuel pumps on a Volvo diesel occasionally fail. But for the most part, I'm afraid those who strive to travel in comfort are missing out on most of what recreational travel has to offer. That is why I felt sorry for the residents of the cabin cruisers—even while they would no doubt have felt sorry for me if they happened to spot me huddled against the early-morning downpour.

As I paddled away from Waterford that morning, I glanced back to the mouth of the Mohawk River and saw something that made my jaw drop. The low island where I intended to camp the previous night had disappeared! It was under several feet of swirling floodwaters, with the tops of the bushes dragging in the surging current. The torrential rains had raised the water level in the Mohawk River to flood stage—a possibility that never crossed my mind the previous evening. My guardian angels must have paused a bit the previous night before countering my thoughtless attempt to camp there. I could see them gathering in the auditorium to attend the debate on the deep theological point, namely, "Do the willfully stupid deserve divine assistance?" Thank goodness the bleeding hearts won.

The excess rain was confounding everyone's travel plans and making workers on the canal system jittery. When I reached Lock 1 on the Champlain Canal, 3 miles north of Waterford, the water was pounding over the lip of the dam. Mike, the lock operator, urged me not to continue, saying more rain was expected and the canal might be closed. He pointed out that there was nothing to stop a person going over the dam; even the dinky warning buoy hadn't been put up yet that summer. Perhaps he was afraid of having me on his conscience, or on his service record. He invited me to camp on the grass of the lock grounds. I was strongly attracted by the idea of a campsite where I wouldn't be an intruder for once, but I couldn't see the validity of stopping so early in the day. Just because he was nervous didn't mean I should be. With an it's-your-funeral shrug, Mike said he would telephone up to the next lock operator to expect me.

I made about a mile against a moderate current. The high water had crept up onto people's lawns, and flooded back into the forest—making for a very unpromising camping situation. While resting, clinging to a tree to hold myself against the current, a volley of thunder erupted in the northwest. The swirling black sky said Mike had been right about more rain. I reversed course and paddled hard back down the river, the raindrops starting to fall just minutes before I made it back to Lock 1. I pulled the kayak onto the grass and sprinted over to a blue porta potty unit. Safely inside, I blotted my soaked pants with toilet paper, listening to the rain clatter down on the plastic roof. It was a wheelchair-accessible unit, quite large, and the smell wasn't too bad. Any porta in a storm, I say.

An hour later, the storm had passed and I went to the lock house to say goodbye again. Mike came out to meet me and pass along the bad news. He had just gotten word that the system all the way to Port Edward was closed! The high water hadn't left enough clearance for boats under some bridges. So I was stuck at Lock 1 for the duration. I told Mike I would just have to kill time by writing poetry; perhaps "Ode to Lock One" would be my first opus. He invited me to use the shower in the lock office, an offer I eagerly accepted.

The next days were spent exploring Waterford, a town with certain, if diminutive, historical achievements. One claim, as a plaque on the main street says, is that it is the birthplace of Ethelda Bleibtrey. Perhaps if her name weren't a tongue twister she would be better remembered. She was the first American woman to win an Olympic event, taking three gold medals in swimming in the 1920 Antwerp games. This remarkable woman took up swimming as therapy to recover from a childhood bout of polio. In 1919, she entered a swim meet without wearing the requisite stockings and was cited by the police for "nude swimming." The subsequent controversy led to doing away with stockings as a requirement for ladies swimming attire (they still had to wear skirts, however).

At the historical museum I learned that Waterford was the site of the first bridge across the navigable Hudson River, built in 1804. A covered bridge 797 feet long, it was built by local businessmen who charged a toll to recover their investment. The placard under the picture of the bridge said, "They assessed a one-dollar penalty for crossing this bridge faster than a walk, riding or driving any horse or carriage"—an interesting example of a traffic regulation on a private roadway. Like Cedar Grove, the Waterford Museum is in an old, historic house saved from demolition by a voluntary group. As is my custom, I joined the society.

On the second day in Waterford, I was joined at Lock 1 by two men from Quebec on a sailboat. Guy had bought the sailboat in Nyack, New York, and was motoring it home, with the mast unstepped and lashed horizontally to get the boat under bridges. They were in a rush to get back to Quebec—Guy worked in the steel distributing business—and the closure of the canal had disrupted their plans. Guy spoke good English, but his companion didn't speak any, so he was rather left out of our conversations.

One of my aims in taking a kayak trip in the East was to meet people, and Waterford certainly filled that need. I couldn't help but compare it to the time on my Columbia trip when strong winds stopped me for an entire day near Boardman, Oregon. In that western landscape, I camped in a thicket beside the river, 15 miles from the nearest town, and didn't use my vocal cords all day. By comparison, my enforced stay in Waterford was a social whirlwind. The first morning, I hitched a ride into town with Glenn, the supervisor of the locks. He'd been up all night regulating the dam's spillways to let more water through, because boatyard owners above the dam were complaining about the high water. At the Erie Canal pavilion I met Val, a volunteer who invited me to use the computer there (which I used to churn my Charles Schwab account on the Internet). Jo—Josephine—was another volunteer at the Canal Center who kindly drove me back to Lock 1 in the afternoon.

I was learning that on a kayak trip social contacts have a quality of provocative mystery. My status as an unusual traveler caused people to open up quickly, and give me a deep glimpse into their lives. Yet it was, perforce, only a glimpse, leaving me to speculate how the pieces of their lives fit together. One of the more puzzling encounters was with Caleb, the relief lockkeeper I met on my second night in Waterford. Caleb was black, and was amazed to learn I had started my kayak trip at Dyckman Street, since he had grown up in that area of New York. He remembered going to the famous Apollo Theater at age 10 and seeing Ella Fitzgerald. I wondered why a black should leave New York City to move to lily-white upstate New York, but he gave no clue about his motives for the move. He spoke proudly of his three children, whom he had brought with him from New York, but didn't say anything about a wife. Was he a single dad raising a family, or did marital tension lead him to avoid mentioning his wife? I found myself becoming a social detective, looking for the tiniest clue to infer a larger picture.

After two days in Waterford, I took stock of my situation. The canal was still closed, and likely to remain so for several days. It was time to get a move on! I was not like Guy in his sailboat, compelled to wait for the canal to open. I had a foldable kayak that could be packed up and put in a car. I called a taxicab company and arranged to be picked up at 6:30 a.m. and taken 30 miles to Fort Edward, where the canal was open.

Though Waterford can justly boast of its friendly and helpful people, the food in the eateries was deplorable. At a pizza place I went to the first night, I had intended to buy pizza by the slice, but the slices looked so gray and wilted I concluded they must be left over from several days before. So I ordered an entire fresh pizza. When it arrived at my table, it was as wilted and dingy as the slices I rejected! It had no flavor except that it tasted tinny. As soon as it cooled, I couldn't bear to eat any more. I couldn't finish the breakfasts, either. The eggs were laden with grease and the sausages turned into wood by overcooking. That was another reason to leave Waterford promptly: foodwise, I was wasting away.

On the last night in Waterford, I splurged and visited the highest-price restaurant in the area. Alas, the almighty dollar wasn't strong enough to overcome the regional culinary blight. The salad bar was below the standards of a fast food joint, the broccoli was heavy with oil and overcooked, the steak had no taste, and the baked potato had been cooked last Thursday.

As I was struggling to put some of this fare into my stomach, Guy and his friend came in and sat at the next table. To his enquiring glance about the quality of the food I gave a surreptitious thumbs down. After they started to eat, his friend made grimacing faces: remember, these men were used to the French cooking of Quebec. I teasingly asked Guy how it tasted and he made a joke out of overpraising it while the waitress, unaware of the subtext, looked on. *"Magnifique!"* he said. *"Superbe! Formidable!"* He put his fingers together and kissed them, like a chef making the ultimate gesture of approval. His friend looked down at his plate and grimly shook his head back and forth, feeling, I think, that such food shouldn't be praised even in jest.

The taxi ride to Fort Edward cost $89—perhaps too much, but it was a valuable service from my point of view. The driver was terribly overweight and when he got into the car it listed heavily to the left. He was also tattooed, and had shaved his head, which gave him a dangerous look. However, once I started talking to him he proved to be a sweet guy. When I told him I had kayaked from New York he said, "You must be in awesome condition!" Well, perhaps compared to him I was.

At Fort Edward, my route left the Hudson River. The river continues on to the west, where, since men have no further interest in its transportation potential, it is allowed to be a free spirit with rapids and falls. My route continued north on a dug canal to Whitehall, where Lake Champlain begins. This stretch gave me the experience of pure canal travel, with one added benefit. Normally, a kayaker on a canal has to contend with powerboats and their wakes. On this day, I had the canal entirely to myself, since all other boats were waiting for the locks below to open.

What a fine paddle it was! I zipped along, just skirting the overhanging branches on the shady east side. The canal was fairly wide, about 75 yards across, heavily treed on both sides. Some flowering bushes —I think mock orange—smelled heavenly. I could hear the faint rumble of machinery from a factory some miles away; otherwise, the only sounds were the twittering of birds. All worries and distractions were removed. The course was obvious. My brain had no decisions to make about cutting across a bay, or angling across a river. No waves upset my stroke, no current added to or subtracted from my mileage, and, because of the sheltering of the trees, no significant wind hastened or retarded my passage. It was a setting where you get exactly what you deserve. Quite unlike life, in other words. Paddling in such a cocoon could get boring, but that was not an issue. For one soon to face 113 miles of wide-open Lake Champlain, I was happy to accept an interlude of peace and security.

I came to the first lock on my route, Lock 8, went to the stop line, and—nothing happened. I pulled out the little silver referee's whistle I carry for emergencies and blew three shrill blasts. The lockkeeper appeared and waved me into the lock, which I had all to myself. Going up in a lock produces a delightful sensation of redemption. I start out in a deep, dark pit whose sides are dripping with water and covered with slime. The doors close behind me with a great, thudding clank that sounds like I'm entering a maximum-security prison for life. The water level rises, about an inch a second, the light gradually increases, the breeze stirs my hair, and suddenly I'm blinking in the dazzling sunlight. It's like a religious conversion.

At Lock 9, the summit of the canal, I experienced the reverse sensation. This was the first lock taking me down toward Lake Champlain. I started in sunshine, but lost the faith and descended into the Slough of Despond.

By evening I had made it to Whitehall, passing through four locks, every one of them operated for the exclusive benefit of Little Lord Fauntleroy in his postage-stamp kayak, tooting imperiously on his silver whistle. One lockkeeper said the three blasts on my whistle sounded like a drum major starting a parade.

As I paddled into Whitehall, I noticed Skene Manor, a dramatic, three-story Victorian mansion high on the hill overlooking the town. It's listed in the National Directory of Haunted Places, thanks to the ghost of Mrs. Skene. As the legend goes, Mrs. Skene was wealthy and her husband was to receive an annuity from her estate as long as she was alive, but this was expressed legally as "for as long as she remains above ground." When she died, her husband contrived to keep the annuity by keeping her lead-lined coffin in the house—above the ground. Alas, not receiving a decent burial, Mrs. Skene was forced to wander about the house on chilly nights, moaning about the misspent annuity. The magnificent granite mansion was saved from destruction by a voluntary group that raised the money to purchase it. From one of the volunteers, I learned that the ghost legend, however delightful, is pretty much hokum, since apparently no one named Skene ever lived in the house.

This stop on my trip gave me the answer to a question that would baffle most quiz show contestants, namely, What is the birthplace of the United States Navy? To collect his prize, the winner would have to reject the famous maritime locations along the eastern seaboard like Boston, New Haven, and Annapolis, and name a village 100 miles inland in the mountains of New York State. In 1776, the British were threatening to cut the colonies in half by gaining control of Lake Champlain. To counter this threat, the Revolutionary forces hastily built a fleet of 16 ships at Whitehall, thus marking the town as the cradle of the U.S. Navy. This fleet, commanded by Benedict Arnold, fought an important naval battle against the British fleet off Valcour Island, near Plattsburgh. It was a losing battle, but useful in delaying the British advance for a year.

Whitehall has a mid-America feel and seemed brimming with friendly people. I went into a hardware store to find the equivalent of an air mattress: my sore hip was informing me that I had pushed my doctrine of travel and suffer too far. The clerk turned the store upside down and came up with a swimming pool float that looked like it might do the job. I went into a waterfront bar down by the lock and asked Sue, the owner, if I could tie up at her dock overnight. She did me one better and invited me to sleep on the covered porch that overlooked the water. I moved the tables and chairs aside to make a sleeping nook, where I was cozily protected from the inevitable nightly rainstorm.

Québec City

Neuville

Portneuf

Deschambault

St. Lawrence River

Batiscan

Cap-de-la-Madeleine

Trois Rivières

Lake St. Pierre

Sorel

Saint-Ours

Chambly Canal

Montréal

Richelieu River

Chambly

Saint-Jean

CANADA

UNITED STATES

Rouses Point

Plattsburgh

Valcour Island

Willsboro Pt.

Burlington

Sand Point

Lake Champlain

Whallons Bay

Westport

NEW YORK

VERMONT

NEW HAMPSHIRE

Port Henry

Crown Point

Fort Ticonderoga

Chipmans Point

New York to Quebec II

0   10   20
Miles

Whitehall

River width not to scale

LAKE CHAMPLAIN

I had long looked forward to paddling on Lake Champlain, to relive the early colonial times of soft-footed Indians stalking the deep forest in the days of the French and Indian Wars. Where it begins at Whitehall, the lake is winding and narrow, only a few hundred yards wide, with trees overhanging the water. I could almost believe I was paddling with Hawkeye and the Mohicans to rescue Cora and her sister—though the historical mood was somewhat broken by the sound of a highway a few hundred yards behind the trees.

One part of my romantic vision of Lake Champlain was flatly unfulfilled. I had expected to paddle on crystal blue waters of a pristine mountain lake. Instead, the water was as brown and muddy as the canal had been—not surprising since the lake was taking the muddy discharge from torrential floods. I held out hope that the water would clear further down the lake.

I had come 192 miles from New York and noticed with a thrill that green channel buoys were now on my right. Before, the right-side markers had been red, following the ditty every sailor knows, "Red on the right, returning." That is, when you are returning upstream to home port, the right-side markers are red. So when I saw a green buoy on my right, it meant I'd crossed a divide and was now heading toward the sea. In one sense, I'd passed the halfway mark on my trip.

My map called the area at the head of Lake Champlain "The Drowned Lands," and when I went by, that's exactly what it was: forests drowned under several feet of water. Lake Champlain's water level follows a natural pattern, climbing 4 or 5 feet above normal with the spring runoff, and dropping lower all through the summer. A month after I passed, the drowned trees would be on dry land.

On that first night on the lake, I didn't get a chance to try out the vinyl inflatable as a mattress for the simple reason that I slept on a real one. On a real bed, in a Vermont farmhouse. It happened in this way.

In the late afternoon, I'd come to the usual evening crisis of not finding a suitable place to stop. The lakeshore was solidly lined with homes—mostly empty summer homes, of course, but still not quite trustworthy as campsites from a trespasser's point of view. As I nosed along the shore, I heard voices from up above, indicating people out on the lawn: a promising situation for the weary traveler. When people are sealed up in a house, there's no easy way to prove you are a normal, lovable person. They watch you from their windows, puzzled and worried, their fingers reaching for the telephone to call the local sheriff. I'd found on this trip that whenever I actually met someone and asked for help, they always gave it, so I pulled ashore and went up to the house to see if the residents would let me camp on their shore.

I reached the yard and discovered I had walked into the middle of a Memorial Day weekend drinking party. An older woman, rather tipsy and trembly, was standing by the door. Before I had a chance to say anything, she took my hand, stroked my arm and shoulder, and drew me into the kitchen. It was the lone kayaker magic at work, getting me instantly accepted by a complete stranger, but the warmth of the response surprised even me.

Inside, I began to explain my situation, and Daisy thrust a cell phone at me with an unsteady hand, saying, "You must call your wife and let her know you are all right." Heavens knows what interpretation Judy placed on the message I left saying I was at Daisy's party and was all right so far.

The group included five men, longtime friends of Daisy's, who had come up from Connecticut to stay with her in the farmhouse, to fish and to drink. Daisy also had a husband, but he was not part of the party. The party had gone through a great deal of ethanol by the time I arrived and everyone was in a highly confidential mood and included me in their circle.

Daisy said that she had known one of the guests, Nick, for 51 years. She repeatedly told me, "He's my main man."

"You must have been high school sweethearts," I suggested.

"Well, we dated," said Daisy, "and I was very fond of him, but I never had sex with him."

"No she didn't," Nick confirmed. "I even kicked her out of the car and made her walk home one night."

Later in the evening, Daisy's husband came through the kitchen, large and scowling, and went straight to the bedroom without saying a word. Everyone, including Daisy, ignored him. The episode left me wondering how the pieces of this marriage fitted together.

Daisy had been through a lot. She spoke of having been quite suicidal in connection with a divorce 20 years back. She drinks pretty heavily now, by her own admission, and smokes a lot. Her memory is weak. Throughout the evening she kept saying, "You must call your wife," and each time I gently reminded her that I had. She takes care of two vacation rental cottages on this property, an unused dairy farm. Judging from her flawed memory, and the clutter of her kitchen and house, I don't think these cottages would get too many Michelin stars.

Later in the evening, Daisy showed me up the delightfully steep stairway to a bedroom I would be sharing with Jack. So I slept between flannel sheets, and slept well. Since it was an extremely cold night, I was fortunate to be inside.

Nutritionally, it was probably well that I got away from Granite Hill Farm. In the evening the only solid food was potato chips and dip, and I tried to have enough of that to call it supper. The next morning I ate as many white English muffins as I dared without appearing rudely voracious. Nick came down and had a Coke for breakfast, and Daisy and Walt had cigarettes and coffee. Principles of modern nutrition had apparently not penetrated this neck of the woods.

After breakfast, I thanked Daisy for her kindness, gave her a big hug, and promised to send her a postcard from Quebec.

Ten minutes after launching, I was crossing the lake when who should appear, passing within 50 yards of me, but Guy and his friend, chugging along in their unmasted sailboat! The canal had reopened and they were trying to make up for lost time. We waved madly at each other but since we were on diverging courses, we didn't stop and talk. Quite a coincidence, since normally I'd be paddling along the edge, far away from the middle of the lake.

When I came upon Fort Ticonderoga that afternoon, towering majestically above the water, I was impressed by its sense of power.

Enemies of olden times must have quaked at the sight, because the fort's cannons commanded deadly coverage of the strategically important narrows of southern Lake Champlain.

For months, the fort had been on my list of must-see attractions. I took it for granted that a dock would be available for visitors who arrived by water. As I paddled toward it, I looked carefully for such a facility, or any pathway that led to the fort, but there was nothing but cliffs and a jungle of trees.

"Where a goat can go, a man can go; where a man can go, he can drag a gun." This was the war cry of British General William Phillips when he attacked Ticonderoga in 1777, dragging cannons up neighboring Mount Defiance, to bombard the fort from higher ground. I adopted a similar attitude of defiance toward the fort, and played the goat. I landed on a sloping slab of bedrock—I could see the deep north-south grooves scraped in it by the glacier—and dragged the kayak as high as I could against the brush. Grabbing onto tree trunks, I pulled myself up a 15-foot cliff, and made my way through patches of nettles until I came to the base of the fort. I could see tourists looking from the ramparts above and hoped they didn't notice me. I clambered up the rocky, blackberry-covered hill to the empty moat, followed that around until I came to a chain designed to keep tourists from going where I was coming from, and ducked under. Whistling nonchalantly, I was now in the fort.

I couldn't relax to enjoy it, however. I kept worrying about my kayak back on the rock, vulnerable to speedboat wakes. I took a quick look around, listened to about 10 minutes of the guide's narration, and then retraced my steps to the kayak.

I did learn from the guide's talk that Fort Ti, as the locals call it, is owned and operated by a voluntary group. Philanthropist William Pell bought the ruins of the fort in 1820. Even that long ago, tourists visited the site, including, of all people, artist Thomas Cole! In the early 20th century, Pell's descendents began fort restoration, and purchased a large tract of surrounding land for preservation purposes. In 1931, the property was turned over to a voluntary group, the Fort Ticonderoga Association. When I found out that I had cheated a voluntary group of the $12.00 admission fee by sneaking in, I resolved to send them the money and become a member when I got home.

Earlier in the day, I had found a kayaker's oasis at Chipmans Point, on the Vermont side of the lake. Slogging against a north wind, exhausting myself almost to no avail, I came upon this blessed spot, a little mom-and-pop marina—the mom in this case being a helpful, sunny woman named Pat. Vacationers keep coming back to the marina year after year, using their boats mostly as summer cottages. Joyce, who owned the cabin cruiser next to my mooring spot, works in the admissions office of Castleton State College nearby, and sleeps in the boat in the summer. She confessed that she had yet to learn to drive it. She did note one drawback of marina living. A few days before, she was cooking supper when she was knocked to the floor by a large, unexpected wave created by a fast-moving powerboat out on the lake.

The long-stay vacationers at the marina formed an extended-family community, one that included children, who visited with me while I did my laundry—Joyce lent me detergent and fabric softener. Pat let me use the shower. I shaved, did my exercises on the lush, green lawn, and had a relaxed lunch. I also bought a bound volume of detailed charts of Lake Champlain. Equipped and refreshed, I paddled away ready for anything the lake had in store.

I camped that night on the New York side on a pebbly beach on the property of a big paper mill, which stood about a mile away. Except for the drone of the mill, the secluded campsite was superb, with a panoramic vista of Vermont dairy farms across the lake.

The noise of the mill defeated my hope of finding a place where no man-made sound could be heard, an aspiration I formed during my first days on the Hudson. I noticed that even when it was calm with no sound of wind and when most human activity ceased in the late evening, I could still hear a faint rumble coming from a far-away highway or factory. This contrasted with my Columbia trip, where no noise of man disturbed the solitude on most nights. It became my goal to find a corresponding condition on this eastern journey. I had failed in this quest all the way up the Hudson, and I was hoping that rural Lake Champlain would provide this moment of sonic inviolability, but it was not to be. Not on Lake Champlain or anywhere else on the way to Quebec did I truly escape the sound of man.

I gave the swimming pool float I had purchased in Whitehall a trial that night. It served as a useful mattress, but overall proved utterly impractical. Inflating it required an hour's huffing and puffing, and in the morning, stomping and squeezing the air out of it required a similar labor. Even after all this work it remained a bulky mass that did not stow compactly.

On my way again the next morning, I spotted another kayaker out in the early-morning calm. I angled over to meet Rick, a boy of about 10, keen on kayaking and fascinated by my long-distance journey. He invited me to have breakfast at his family compound, where a reunion of several dozen friends and relations was taking place. I was warmly welcomed and urged to partake in a massive brunch. Among the guests was a young Peruvian woman studying early childhood education—the second Peruvian I met on this trip. She was amazed to learn that I had lived on La Colmena Avenue in Lima (when I was researching a book on the labor movement), near where she grew up. I omitted mentioning that I had lived there before she was born. I discussed Lake Champlain with several of the guests who knew local conditions. They mentioned that I should expect 5-foot waves, especially by Westport where I was headed the next day. I invited Rick to accompany me a few miles down the shore, but his father vetoed the idea, fearing that I was the pied piper of kayaking and he would never see his child again—and perhaps he was right!

I battled waves most of that afternoon, passing Crown Point and hammering my way under the Chimney Point Bridge, where, I was relieved to see, the lake water finally lost its muddy appearance. I dragged into Port Henry, New York, where I settled for staying at the municipal campground on the lake. The site caters to lower middle-class families who stay all summer and return year after year, creating their own friendly community.

Esthetically, it was a deplorable campground. RVs were jammed in cheek by jowl, the streets were dusty dirt, and the open spaces were barren sand and gravel. The half-clad children were having a great time playing together, though the scene reminded me of the slums of Lima. The worst part was the smell. In New York State, authorities have declared campgrounds and picnic areas pack-it-in-pack-it-out parks with no trash receptacles. This saves money on their budgets, but it leads to dysfunctional behavior. People try to get rid of their trash by burning it in their fire barrels, half-charring wet cardboard, plastic, and the broccoli Johnny wouldn't eat. A stinking pall hung over the area like a city dump.

My campsite, Number 26, was a joke, a space 12 feet wide between two RVs. It was available because it was too small to accommodate even a car. They charged me $27.50 for this slot of dirt, a price so outrageous it was funny.

The family in the neighboring trailer invited me for ice cream in the evening. A group of their friends gathered in the living room of their RV to learn about my trip. One man's reaction on hearing that I was kayaking from New York to Quebec was, "You must be nuts!" He was emphatic and sincere, not teasing at all: he really thought I was mentally defective. I was rather dismayed to be thus accused, but upon reflection I concluded that the remark said less about me than about his own narrow and fearful perspectives.

"Do you ever feel lonely?" Nora asked. It was a question I often heard.

I explained that *lonely* wasn't the word, as I was having plenty of social contact on this trip. This day was a good example, sharing breakfast in the morning with one group of people, and ice cream in the evening with another.

What I do feel sometimes on a kayak journey is forlorn, lost from human awareness. Heading out across an open stretch of water, I imagine myself an observer on shore, watching me get smaller and smaller until, at about three-quarters of a mile, I become invisible in the waves. I've ceased to exist: swallowed up, disappeared—like someone sent into outer space. This is only an occasional feeling, but unsettling when it hits me. It suggests that I need some contact with other human beings—or other living things like animals—to confirm my existence.

Nora also asked how well I was sleeping, and thus pried from me the hip situation. She pressed me to take two Tylenols. Whatever the reason, I got a fine night's sleep.

The next morning, goaded by fear of those 5-foot waves at

Westport, I was out on the water at 4:30 a.m., taking advantage of perfectly calm conditions. An orange-colored band above the mountains in the east had chased away all the stars. The birds started to twitter. I snacked on grapes, walnuts, and an energy bar as I paddled. I was not going to waste precious calm-water time on a proper peanut butter sandwich breakfast.

I had to put on my shoes to launch my kayak because of the sharp stones underfoot, and as a result, soaked my $139 New Balance combination walking-jogging shoes again. For the umpteenth time on this trip I kicked myself for not buying kayaking booties. When I saw them in the supply catalog, I thought it silly to spend $59 for these neoprene slippers. (And, if the truth be told, I was put off by the unmasculine name.) On the Columbia trip, I didn't seem to need any. Almost everywhere, I could step out barefoot onto sand, or with shoes onto rocks or dry land. On this trip, I'd needed foot protection to wade for many launches and landings, and that meant sacrificing my cherished NBs, which were now badly mud-stained as well as perpetually damp.

As I paddled along, the light gathered intensity at one point behind the Vermont mountain they call Camelback, like a glowing coal fanned into white heat. Then the edge of the sun flashed into view and the day was born.

I made it across the dreaded Westport Bay in fairly calm water. At the other side I found a dock and children playing with a black lab. It felt like private property. I asked the children if I could land and they invited me ashore. It was a private estate, jointly owned by at least three families, from Boston, Connecticut, and Pennsylvania. The children exhibited an attitude of ownership and command, and also an inbred politeness. I asked the favor of filling my water bottle and several of them ran up to the house with it. When I was making my morning sandwich in full view of the group, one of the boys blurted out, "I love peanut butter sandwiches."

"Would you like some?" I offered.

His training kicked in, "Oh, no thank you."

So began another day of the social whirlwind that is eastern kayaking.

For a kayaker nervous about large expanses of water, traversing Lake Champlain from the south is a study in mounting suspense. Narrow at first, the lake gradually broadens until it's a mile wide. Then, at Chimney Point it makes a quantum increase in width—to about 2 miles. Twenty miles further up, at Whallons Bay, the width doubles again. As I rounded the point there, I felt dismay. Looking north, I could see no sign of land at all! The horizon ahead of me was water, just like on the ocean. Though the air was calm, one-foot waves bounced me about. What would happen, I wondered, when the wind began to blow?

I crossed the wide bay and by late afternoon landed at a spot called Sand Point, 2,100 miles from my hometown of Sandpoint, Idaho. This eastern Sand Point is a peninsula where, just like at home, a glacier left behind a massive deposit of sand. As I approached the place from the water, I saw matching brown cottages, obviously a compound or camp of some kind, but it was completely deserted and therefore a potential campsite. I beached the kayak and explored. I didn't unpack anything, because something—maybe it was the freshly mowed lawn—told me someone had an eye on the place. Sure enough, Dave, the manager of these rental cottages, arrived in his pickup truck 20 minutes later. I explained my predicament, and he said it would be okay for me to sleep on the lawn. He also told me nasty weather was forecasted.

I set up my tent at the edge of the lawn and turned in. About midnight, I awoke to a ferocious wind hammering at my tent and creating ever-mounting waves that lunged at my kayak. I had pulled it 6 feet above the waterline, but the waves were already wetting it. I staggered out, worked the boat higher up the beach, retied it to driftwood logs, and slid back into the sleeping bag. I tried to clear my mind for sleep, to no avail. Like a mother whose teen daughter is out on a first date, my mind couldn't be at ease until I had the precious one safely home. I went down to the shore again, undid the lines, unpacked the kayak, and carried it up to the grass right beside my tent.

The next morning I didn't want to face the lake. I was weak from lack of sleep, rain was spritzing against my tent, and a strong south wind was kicking up waves and occasional whitecaps. It felt like the perfect time to sleep in. As the day turned out, I should have listened to my body, as the yoga teachers say. But, driven by the Western, mechanical goal of achievement, I instead launched into the pulsing waves.

At first, the going was manageable. The wind was variable, strengthening at times to 20 mph, and then dropping back to 5 mph, pushing 2-foot waves at me from behind. I continued in these conditions for several hours, somewhat outside my comfort zone but making good time.

All of a sudden, the wind speed jacked up several notches to 30 mph, and it didn't drop back. The water surface erupted in whitecaps. Waves began breaking over the stern and water sloshed against my back. *These,* I thought, *are the famous 5-foot waves of Lake Champlain, and here I am in the middle of them!*

The storm caught me off Willsboro Point, far from shore. Sensible as the idea of hugging the shore may seem, I just couldn't adhere to it because it made my route twice as long. On Lake Champlain, I was at least a half mile from shore most of the time, as I was now. I paddled hard for land. After a bit, I rechecked my position against the shore and I seemed to have made no progress at all. Was some strange current drawing me back? By carefully lining up houses and treetops I confirmed that I was moving in the right direction. I had apparently discovered the converse of the maxim "Time flies when you're having fun," which is, "Time stands still when you're scared." I thought I had been paddling a half hour since the storm hit, but it was probably only a few minutes.

Finally the shore drew closer, a windward shore with waves crashing against concrete walls that protected the vacation homes. No landing in sight. No bay, no cove, no dock. I continued angling toward shore and finally spotted a little indentation that partially shielded me from the waves while landing. I managed to beach without taking on too much water—again soaking my precious shoes—and dragged the kayak onto a slab of glacier-scraped rock. The wind was howling in the trees above.

I walked up to the house and asked the owner, Gary, if I could leave my kayak on his lawn until the storm abated. I decided I probably needed and deserved a motel at this point, especially since I might have to wait out the storm for several days. Gary offered to drive me to a motel several miles away. He dropped me at the motel and drove away, a perfectly innocent thing to do, except that after he left I found the motel was closed.

Here was a fix! I had no lodging, and my tent and sleeping bag were back at the kayak, miles away.

Nearby, I heard the sound of a tractor, and went to ask the driver about the motel. Harry gave a pained smile when I asked him about the motel. "I don't think he's serious about it," he said, nodding toward the motel office. He pointed to a torn-up sewer line coming from the motel. "It's been that way all spring."

When he heard my story, Harry invited me to his house to warm up with a cup of tea and to meet his wife Marie. The couple lived in Connecticut and were spending a few days at their summer home on Lake Champlain. They left me in the living room to enjoy my tea and cookies while they withdrew to discuss my fate.

Ten minutes later, Harry returned. "You're going to stay here," he said.

I couldn't deny that I was hopelessly homeless, but I was flustered by such generous hospitality. "Oh, I couldn't possibly. . . ."

"No, no. You're welcome here. Later today we'll take the trailer and get your kayak."

So I joined the family. Harry was a tool nut, crazy about machines, a self-taught jack-of-all-trades. At Pfizer, the chemical and drug company from which he recently retired, he worked in the research department, though he had never been to college. He used his native inventiveness to diagnose and fix bugs in the production process. On this day he proved his skills of mechanical improvisation by getting the jackknifed flatbed trailer (on which we retrieved my kayak) out of the mud with a hydraulic jack.

One of Harry and Marie's interests is the Avalonia Land Conservancy, a voluntary group that preserves land in the southeast corner of Connecticut. They were busy that weekend making elegant signs for walking trails on a newly acquired property of the Conservancy. Started in 1968, the Conservancy has over 70 parcels and 1,400 acres.

Of course I joined.

They were Lutherans, which was another common tie. Another was the fact that their grown son is a major kayaker. "He's out on Long Island Sound in the middle of the winter practicing Eskimo rolls," said Harry. "He holds the record for most Eskimo rolls in one minute." To some extent, I think, Harry was treating me the way he would want someone to treat his son if he were a castaway. They put me in the guest bedroom, where I had a wonderful sleep on a real bed with a real mattress.

The next morning, Harry prepared deluxe oatmeal laden with fruits and nuts for breakfast, of which I had two helpings. I paddled away from their home into a calm, misty morning feeling on top of the world, my paddle blades cutting the water with firmness and authority, exhilarated at recovering from a desperate, difficult situation through the generosity of others.

Paddling along Lake Champlain, I found I was taking very few pictures. I would pull out the camera knowing that I wanted some pictures of the landscape to show friends back in Idaho. But each time I looked through the viewfinder, it wasn't worth snapping the shutter.

The locals are unaware of the photographic shortcomings, never having seen—or not remembering—scenery in the West. The ranger I met at a campground opposite West Point raved about the Hudson Highlands and urged me to have my camera ready. But as I've reported, that stretch was a bust photographically. At the Vanderbilt Mansion, the guide showed us what she called a "gorgeous" view off to the northwest. It was the reason why the mansion was sited on this spot. Other members of the party swooned, and whipped out their cameras. I kept my peace because they were in a lynching mood about the vista. All that lay before us was flattish, rolling land, uniformly tree-covered, and, in the distance, a low, flat ridge: a pleasant and peaceful scene, to be sure, but not containing features that make for a great painting or photograph.

The biggest disappointment for me was Cedar Grove, the property that landscape artist Thomas Cole bought, as the brochure said, for its inspiring, scenic view. I wanted to believe that the vista off his front porch had magic and power, but I have to be truthful. There's just a fuzzy mass of trees, and a ridge rising about as high as your fingernail in the distance. I concluded that art historians have it backwards: Thomas Cole's paintings weren't inspired by the local scenery. His fantastic landscapes were an escape from its dullness.

As I paddled along, I mulled over this contrast, trying to identify why eastern scenery is lacking in drama.

For one thing, the East doesn't have the vertical relief of the West. Its long-eroded mountains rise gradually from the valleys. In the West, ridges loom 10 times higher in your field of vision. The West is a land of dramatic cliffs and soaring mountain peaks.

A second problem in the East is the dense deciduous foliage. Eastern trees are bushy and blend together in a featureless mass. Western trees, almost all conifers, grow tall, separate, and spire-like. They make any mountainside look like a cathedral.

Then there's the difference in atmosphere. On a typical summer day in New York, the relative humidity is around 80 percent. In Idaho, it is about 40 percent. The higher humidity—and pollution—in the East makes the air hazy, blurring details of scenery. On the Columbia River, the reader will remember, I saw Mt. Hood's breathtaking snowy pink cone 93 miles away. At the farm in New York's Catskill Mountains where I spent childhood summers, we seldom could see the ridge 15 miles away, and on many days couldn't see hills 5 miles away.

The sky, too, is different. Dry western air often produces skies that are not cloudy all day, as we have all sung. But clouds appear on many days as well, and these formations can be stupendous, with multiple layers consisting of bands in one place, delicate wisps in another, and towering castles in another part of the scene. Even in the middle of the day, the intricate tracery of swirls and scallops can make an exciting picture; add the colors of sunset and the result is a sacred vision.

The East occasionally has interesting skies, especially when wisps of high cirrus clouds portend a warm front, but such times are rare. The skies I saw on my trip were usually whitish, not a sharp blue, and had watery, ill-defined clouds: nothing to excite a photographer. I couldn't help thinking that if he had lived in the East, Ansel Adams would have been an insurance salesman.

Of course there are exceptions and qualifications. In the fall, eastern hardwoods take on colors and thus become individually distinct, like western trees. Then the hillsides become glorious mosaics of color and design. And nature can occasionally contrive stunning vistas anywhere. The night after leaving Harry and Marie's, I saw a spectacular moonrise that started as an orange rectangle just above the horizon, looking like a roof on a monstrous barn, an effect caused by cloud strata that blocked the moon's top and bottom. As it rose higher in the sky, it made a shimmering silver pathway all the way across the lake to Burlington, Vermont, on the other side.

As I paddled along the lake, I saw many "Vs" of Canada geese, with huge numbers in each group, all migrating north for the summer. They looked like bomber squadrons heading for Berlin. The formations became larger further up the lake, as smaller groups joined forces. One formation was flying just a few feet above the water, perhaps to avoid the resistance of a strong wind higher up. For a moment I worried that there could be quite a collision if the geese on this water-level course didn't notice a boat ahead, but then I remembered they are skilled aviators.

I reached Plattsburgh in the late morning—having taken the same narrow strait alongside Valcour Island that Benedict Arnold used to protect his smaller fleet from the larger British forces in the 1776 battle. I went into the local marina, and explained my need for a motel on the water to the clerk. Overhearing the conversation, a customer kindly offered to drive me to just such a motel. I registered, came back to the marina, and got in the kayak to paddle across a mile-wide bay to the motel.

This almost trivial project proved to be life threatening. When I set out, the sun was shining, but once I was committed to the crossing, black clouds gathered and headed my way. About a mile ahead of me, a Hollywood-quality bolt of lightning smacked down from those clouds. The hair on the back of my neck bristled. I couldn't believe the startling turn of events. One minute I'm registering in a motel like any other guest, with nothing on my mind but unpacking and lunch, and suddenly I'm trapped in the middle of a lake in a lightning storm. I tried to comfort myself by remembering that death this way would be painlessly instantaneous. I paddled as hard as I could, until my arms screamed with pain; I kept paddling and unaccountably the pain went away. Blessedly, there were no more lightening bolts and a few minutes later I was parking my kayak, unpacking and thinking about lunch.

I spent an extra day resupplying and relaxing in Plattsburgh, a nicely unpretentious town. One of my projects was to find some kind of water footwear to serve as booties. I had in mind to buy flip-flops, but none of the downtown stores carried them. The only waterproof footwear I could find, and which, with terrible angst, I bought, were a pair of shocking pink ladies' puffy Styrofoam beach clogs for $3.49. Anyone dressing a kayaking clown for the circus would look high and low and not come up with footwear as ridiculous as these clogs. They were my punishment for being too proud and too cheap to buy regular kayak booties when I had the chance.

In the evening I watched the movie *The Barbarian Invasions* at Plattsburgh's old-fashioned Strand Theatre. It was a thought-provoking movie about the value of personal relationships in a cynical, bureaucratic world. Set in Montreal with French subtitles, it was the perfect film for me to see on the day before I entered French Quebec.

On the second morning in Plattsburgh, I went to the nearby McDonald's for breakfast at 6:00 a.m., when it opened. Being Saturday, I was the only customer there for a time, and it made me realize what an amazing service this was. The building, the lights, the gleaming floors and tables that someone had cleaned last night, the aroma of food prepared by cooks who got out of bed early: all this so that a scruffy kayaker didn't have to crouch in the sand forcing down a cold energy bar. It was ludicrous to say my $4.45 paid for all this effort and attention.

I told the server, "Thank you for coming to work today."

She was puzzled. "I mean it," I continued. "I really appreciate you and everybody coming here to serve me breakfast." Her puzzled look continued.

"Look," I asked, "When did you get up this morning?"

"About a quarter to five."

"Well if you hadn't gotten up and come to work, I'd be standing out on the street, hungry. So thank you!"

She got the point. "Thank you for saying that," she said. A sweet kid—her name was Katy—a music student at the state university at Pottsdam. Later, I overheard her passing the compliment on to the cooks.

At Plattsburgh I decided to do the leapfrog act again and take a taxi to Rouses Point, 18 miles away at the Canadian border. The weather was highly unsettled, with thunderstorms cropping up at the drop of a hat—as I learned when trying to paddle to the motel. To continue safely, I would have to wait a lot when confronted by threatening weather, and also religiously hug the shoreline. I knew that in practice I wouldn't be that patient, so I would undoubtedly end up in danger. I wrestled with the decision, not liking to admit that I was, to a degree, chickening out. I concluded that since I'd already survived one windstorm and one lightning storm on Lake Champlain, it was time to cash in my chips. I knew my concerned sisters would approve of my decision, even if *Outside* magazine might cluck its tongue.

THE RICHELIEU RIVER

The U. S.-Canadian border cuts across the northern end of Lake Champlain, where the lake narrows to about a half mile, and a slight current marks the beginning of Canada's Richelieu River. A border checkpoint stood on the west side of the river. I suppose I could have snuck into Canada by paddling unobserved on the east side, but I had nothing to hide, and besides, I was hungry for any crumb of human contact. So I opted for legality and pulled over to the customs dock. An attractive woman in uniform came out. My kayak was such an unusual touring craft that she forgot, for a bit, that she was a cog in a government machine.

"Aren't you afraid to be in that little boat?" she asked with a charming French accent.

"A little," I replied.

"Don't you get lonely? Isn't your family worried about you? Where do you sleep?"

I was just starting to bask in all this feminine concern when she abruptly handed back my passport. In a clipped tone she said, "Enjoy your stay in Canada, monsieur," and turned away.

Quebec was a language shock for me, for I had assumed that everyone spoke English, and had made no preparations to deal with a foreign language. I hadn't even brought along a French pocket dictionary. In Quebec City, English is spoken widely, and the Anglo tourist can get along, but in the small towns along the Richelieu and Saint Lawrence rivers, one has, for all practical purposes, arrived in France. This was charming in its way, to land in Bordeaux when I thought my ticket said Detroit, but I had to scramble to deal with the language.

Some French was lodged in my gray matter. On my European trip as a teenager 46 years before, I had hitchhiked across France. Armed with a dictionary, a grammar book, and coaching from friends, I developed enough French to get by. I desperately tried to recall this skill as I met boaters, waitresses, and shopkeepers of Quebec. Alas, this linguistic faculty was blocked by many decades of disuse, as though wrapped behind a layer of cellophane. Some of the speech came back, but my ear was totally dead. In the first few days, I couldn't recognize a word. Even when people said "*bonjour*," and I knew that's what they must be saying, I didn't hear it as such. It sounded like "xkfclyp."

On my first day on the Richelieu, the driver of an excursion boat yelled something at me. Trying to make sense of the syllables I thought I heard, I guessed he was saying that the restaurant in town had good pizza. Several minutes later, I spotted the channel buoys and realized he was telling me that I was, at danger to myself and everyone else, in the middle of the channel.

I developed a technique to finesse the language difficulty. Instead of trying to speak English—which I thought might give offense—I started with French, asking, "*Parlez-vous anglais?*" (Do you speak English?). This established my helpless state. Almost everyone would reply, "*Un petit peu*" (a little bit), and it really was only a little bit. Then I would speak in my broken French and they replied in their broken English.

I made good progress along the Richelieu, although the boat wakes were a nuisance. I had expected the area to be rural, with few people. In fact, it's Montreal's water playground. Summer cabins line both sides of the river. Every urban refugee had a powerboat, and they were all roaring up and down the river at top speed on this fine weekend afternoon.

With riverside homes blocking the shore, finding a campsite was not easy, but a good one cropped up by happenstance at the end of the day, a mothballed state park just a few miles from Saint-Jean. The park wasn't staffed, the restrooms were locked, and the grass hadn't been cut, but a fisherman told me—I think he told me—that it would be okay to pitch a tent on the grass.

I was just settling in when two teenage boys arrived and began collecting wood for a fire at a spot 100 yards away. Then other youngsters began to arrive, some walking, some in cars. Except for the boys and me, the park was deserted. They looked over at me from time to time, obviously aware of my presence. I had no reason to believe they were hostile, but groups of youths, like grizzly bears, are not predictable. What especially worried me was the language gap. If approached by a similar group of American youngsters, I think I could deal with their curiosity, and defuse a tense moment. But I would be pretty helpless with these kids, for my limited French left me with little ability to joke around or engage their interest. They might ask if I liked the sunset, and I might think they were asking for my wallet.

I withdrew into my tent, carefully peeking out from time to time to gauge the social and moral evolution of the group. As I feared, more youngsters kept arriving until there was what a nervous observer might describe as a "gang" of over 25 kids. Most were boys, but some girls came too, which I took as an encouraging sign for what it implied about the civilizing effect of the female of the species. Some of the boys started playing hacky sack in the light of the bonfire, another sign of a healthy, positive disposition.

As the time passed without any signs of aggression from the group, I gradually relaxed, though their shouts and radio noise made sleep impossible.

Several hours later, the youths dispersed and I had the park to myself. But not for long. A vehicle entered the park and drove right up to me, stopping only a few feet away, shining its headlights directly on my tent. I assumed it was a law enforcement official about to roust me from this officially closed campground.

I decided to wait for some kind of summons before coming out of my tent. No one spoke. The car lights went off, and then I heard a man talking and a woman giggling. They were loud enough for me to hear every word—but of course I didn't understand a thing. This secluded corner of the park was a lover's lane, and this was a tryst. They must not have seen my tent: not surprising really, since I had chosen its dark olive color specifically to be unnoticed in commando camping situations.

The talking and giggling, with pauses, went on for about an hour before the car finally left at 1 a.m. I assumed I had at last earned some peace and quiet. But no, dance music began blaring from a brightly lit house directly across the river. A major party was taking place—and it went on nearly 'til dawn.

So it was another night in the naked city for a kayaker—but, except for the noise, a perfectly harmless one. As I pulled away early the next morning, I noticed a tent beside the remains of the bonfire. Apparently the two boys who began the youth powwow were camping out for the night and their friends came to see them off on this adventure.

At the first lock on the Chambly Canal at Saint-Jean, the Canadian flag was flying at half-mast—to mark Ronald Reagan's death I later learned.

Entering the lock, I met Vicki, one of the lockkeepers.

"You surprise us!" she said, laughing. "We don't expect such a little boat."

She spoke good English, and we had a long conversation, as locking through was delayed waiting for other boats to arrive. She was excited about my trip and asked many questions. An attractive young woman, she had been quite a traveler, lived and worked in Mexico, the Dominican Republic, and Guadeloupe, but was now in a rut.

I asked her if she had seen *Barbarian Invasions*. She hadn't. She said she didn't watch any TV—which I said was good—but she also wasn't going to any movies. She said she was in an apathetic, inactive mode, lived way out of town, and didn't have much contact with anyone. We were clearly on the same wavelength about the virtue of travel in opening up new horizons. Seeing me had apparently stimulated her thinking.

"How old are you, if you pardon my asking?" she asked. I told her 64.

"It's amazing!" she said. "I mean, I'm 31. If you can do what you are doing"—she was too polite to finish the phrase with "at your age"—"then what should I be doing?"

"You," she said pointing to me, "inspire me," she continued, tapping her forefinger on her chest.

Perched on my shred of faded red canvas, overshadowed by the sleek, shiny cabin cruisers in the lock, I was well aware that I was low man in the pecking order of the waterways. Vicki gave me a moment in the sun.

At the second lock of the Chambly Canal I got almost more adulation than I could stand. As I was entering it, a man on the deck of a three-story cabin cruiser towering over me asked, with a French accent, "Did you really come from New York?"

"Oui."

"Bravo!" he replied, and then he and a dozen other people on the yacht, as well as another dozen standing alongside the lock, applauded!

I felt like Lance Armstrong finishing the Tour de France. Apparently Vicki had phoned down the canal and everyone at this lock knew about me.

Speaking of Lance Armstrong, the Quebecois are keen on bicycling; it's the national sport. That Sunday morning, the canal towpath was busy with hundreds of cyclists of all ages: toddlers shepherded by their parents, young adults on bike dates, and courtly seniors who waved graciously as I paddled by.

The Richelieu River was tame water, narrow enough to keep wind and waves from being a significant threat, and with locks to bypass all the rapids. It also had a useful current of about 1 mph in my favor, so I made good time without working too hard. My mind was reaching ahead to the massive Saint Lawrence, especially the part of the Saint

Lawrence known as Lake Saint-Pierre, a body of water 10 miles wide and 20 miles long. The storm back on Lake Champlain had spooked me, and I didn't want to be caught on big water that way again.

Though the Richelieu was a kayaker's picnic, it happened that I came closer to capsizing on it than anywhere else. At the town of Chambly, the river broadens to a small lake and then narrows back down. After crossing this lake, I was just about to enter the narrow part of the river when three speedboats came up the river and entered the lake together in a confused situation. In two boats with large families aboard, the drivers were clenching their teeth with concentration as they hit the waves of the lake, and didn't have time to slow down while passing me rather close.

Right behind them came a Jet Ski boat commanded by four boys, none older than 14, who were screaming with excitement and paying no attention to the outside world. They dashed past me 20 feet away with the throttle wide open. The three boat wakes combined to form a 5-foot cliff of water coming at me from the side. I didn't have time to swing around to face it. I hunkered down, braced my paddle against the water, and resigned myself to disaster. The wave slammed into me, drenching me from my head down, but the boat didn't capsize. I was angry at those idiot boys, but much encouraged to see how much my boat could take without tipping over.

Practically every town on the Richelieu is Saint something-or-other. The early settlers were pressing hard on the religion pedal when they founded this area. The river itself is named after Cardinal Richelieu, the prime minister under France's Henry XIII in 1624, and later famous as the persecutor of the protestant Huguenots. Each town along the river has a lovely church—Catholic churches, of course—with a graceful spire that can be seen from miles away.

At the town of Saint-Marc, I stopped at a little luncheonette near the riverbank. The proprietor, his daughter, and his wife knew almost no English. We put our heads together and made a game of figuring out what I should order, and decided on a strawberry milkshake, fried fish, and French fries. The daughter asked me how many pieces of fish I wanted. I had no idea what size they might be, so I didn't know how to reply meaningfully, until an idiom from my 46-year-old French popped into my head: "*J'ai beaucoup de faim*" (I have a lot of hunger). "Well, then," she said with a giggle, "you want three!"

For those whose picture of the world is shaped by headlines and TV news, such friendly camaraderie with the French-speaking Quebecois might come as a surprise. Many friends raised their eyebrows when I mentioned I had been traveling in Quebec. "Didn't they give you a hard time?" they asked. They were thinking of the anti-English policies of the government, especially the notoriously repressive language legislation. The Charter of the French Language, passed in 1977, mandates that school classes be taught in French and that all signs be only in French. This measure has been moderated by court decisions and subsequent legislation, but its thrust remains: English is officially hated.

The taboo against English flies in the face of common sense. Stop signs say only *Aret*, so, in theory, English-speaking motorists would drive right through them. A sign on a clothing shop in Sorel said "*On Parle Anglais Ici*": a deliciously irrational announcement, of no use to the helpless English speaker who desperately needed what was advertised, namely, "English spoken here." A government language police snoops about, levying fines up to $7,000 for the stray English word appearing in public signs. If the people of Quebec were as petty and intolerant as the bureaucracy acting in their name, it would indeed be correct to suppose that English-speaking visitors would be snubbed.

Fortunately, they aren't. The Charter of the French Language could have been passed on the moon insofar as the behavior of the Quebec people is concerned. Everywhere I went, I was warmly greeted and enthusiastically helped. In the scores of contacts I had with French speakers, I never saw the slightest sign of hostility toward, or anxiety about, the English language. The language issue did not create a barrier in my dealings; it produced a bond. We were human beings jointly struggling to communicate our ideas and our empathy using whatever words, sounds, and sign language we could invent. When lunch was successfully ordered, it was a cheerful victory for all of us.

At the Saint-Ours lock, the last lock coming down the Richelieu River, I found a useful camping situation at the picnic ground by the lock. The place even had a bathroom with hot running water, and, in a conjunction as rare as a solar eclipse, was left open all night by officialdom and yet was clean and sparkling, not trashed by vandals. Normally, picnic grounds are no-camping zones, but here I had a perfect justification for my presence: I was waiting to use the lock when it opened at 8:30 a.m. and would pay $12.50 for the service. As a paying customer, I had confidence that I would not be chased away.

Parked alongside me and also waiting to go through the lock was a towering, 50-foot, brand new cabin cruiser. Two Canadians had been hired to deliver it from Fort Lauderdale to a customer in Montreal—a two-week journey. I watched the men moor it for the night, using its maneuvering jets to edge it against the pier, for it was too big to be pulled by hand. The boat was made in China, and fitted out in Florida, so at least three nationalities of workers are benefiting.

One of the boatmen told me that the tide is huge at Quebec, about 20 feet, and gets less and less further up the river, until there isn't any by Lake Saint-Pierre. "The tide dies in Lac Saint Pierre," was the way he put it. I hoped that would be all that dies there. He invited me to share a pizza supper with them, but I saw his long-missed girlfriend had just arrived from Montreal and figured I'd be in the way.

THE SAINT LAWRENCE RIVER

The next day I reached Sorel, the city at the confluence of the Richelieu and Saint Lawrence rivers. I was startled to see the size of the ships docked along the waterfront. They seemed endlessly long as I paddled alongside them, and when I looked up, all I could see was a wall of steel extending to the sky. *If the Saint Lawrence is these guys' playground,* I thought, *what am I doing here?*

I made the right turn onto the Saint Lawrence and immediately caught a powerful following wind kicking up 3-foot waves. I found these rough conditions too nerve-racking an introduction to the Saint Lawrence, so I pulled into a marina for a rest, a walk around town, lunch at a local restaurant, and a nap in a park. Later in the afternoon, the wind and waves still hadn't relented, so at 5:00 p.m., I gritted my teeth and jumped onto the roller coaster. I gradually got used to the waves, but being on a river several miles wide continued to intimidate me.

After passing Sorel, the river broadens into many channels between low-lying islands called the *Iles de Sorel*. When the Saint Lawrence floods in April—remember, it's draining the Great Lakes and central North America—the river level is 4 to 8 feet higher than in June, and it carries a load of silt. When the water slows down in this widening of the river, the silt deposits and forms islands. The area is an unspoiled, uninhabited nature preserve, with abundant bird life.

Among these *Iles de Sorel*, I found a campsite that was awesome, in the old-fashioned sense of the word: magnificent and a little scary. It was an alluvial island that lay alongside the main ship channel, perfectly flat, about 5 feet above the water level, and densely covered with coarse grass 4 feet high. With the land flat and treeless, I had a sweeping 360-degree view. There were no buildings in sight in any direction across the miles of water, just flat islands and waving grass. Nobody could bother me—or rescue me if something went wrong; with the shallow water surrounding it, the island could be reached only by kayak.

Facing the ship channel, I enjoyed watching the monster vessels approach and pass. While I was opening a can of tuna fish for supper, I looked up and saw a container ship drawing toward me out of the sunset. Suddenly, the water level on the beach dropped alarmingly, exposing 50 feet of previously submerged beach. It was as if the entire Saint Lawrence was being drained away into a crack in the earth.

Fortunately, I knew what this was because I'd seen it once before on the Columbia River below Portland. I rushed to my kayak and heaved it up into the grass on top of the bank, tossed up all my belongings, and got myself and my can of tuna fish up there too. I waited. Sure enough, a 4-foot tidal wave came sweeping across the entire beach and smashed into the dirt bank on which I stood.

This is a rare kind of ship wake, by the way. Most freighters and tankers make waves no bigger than those of cabin cruisers. Perhaps the hull configuration of this ship accounts for it. The suction wave down on the Columbia also came from a container ship. It seems amazing that a boat can suck water away from a beach it hasn't yet reached, and a full minute in advance of the wave. It makes for a fair warning signal, like that loudly ticking clock of the crocodile in *Peter Pan.*

If this stupendous vista from the island had a drawback, it was that it was too spacious for a puny human being to absorb for long. After a time, I felt a touch of agoraphobia, and that feeling of forlornness, of being utterly cut off from the human race, a tiny atom lost in the vastness. But the glory of this campsite was that to escape the empty, windy panorama all I had to do was sit down. Instantly I was in my own cozy space, the tall, dense grass perfectly sheltering me from the roaring wind overhead. It was like going into a house and shutting the door. As darkness fell, I set up my tent in the grass, pushing the steel stakes into the soft loam and spreading my sleeping bag on the floor. I crawled in and zipped the tent closed, feeling perfectly sheltered from any conceivable threat of man or nature.

I may moan in these pages about the problems of finding decent campsites, but the truth is I wouldn't have it any other way. Part of the adventure of a kayak journey is the challenge of finding a place to spend the night, and not knowing what you're going to get. Dull indeed it would be to have prearranged, comfortable lodgings every night. Yes, sometimes the challenge of taking potluck turns out badly, and I spend an uncomfortable few hours. But other times I luck into a campsite that's so exhilarating it's a religious experience, a "lodging value" far superior to anything that could ever be purchased at the grandest hotel.

The next day, I tackled the dreaded Lake Saint-Pierre, 20 miles of open water. As I made my way through the nature preserve, I heard a multitude of bird songs, each distinctive and beautiful. I could also hear the thudding of the big ships coming down the channel several miles away, passing by at the rate of two or three an hour.

I headed down a side channel through the *Iles de Sorel* to reach the south shore of the lake, which I planned to hug while making the crossing. I expected to be able to camp on this shore about halfway across the lake.

After an hour's paddling, I reached the open water of Lake Saint-Pierre itself, and I didn't like what I saw. On my right, where I expected to find safety, there was no shore! The water extended for miles through reeds and marshes. Ahead of me, all I could see was water, since the far shore was out of sight below the horizon some 20 miles away. I was exactly where I didn't want to be: trapped way out in the middle of a huge lake.

I paddled east, hoping the border of reeds would give way to dry land. After several miles, I concluded that the entire south shore of the lake was marsh and reeds, mile after mile. I was paddling in water about 4 feet deep, and at least a mile from any true land. When I tried to paddle toward land I would just push into denser reeds until I couldn't go any further—but I would still be at least a half mile from dry land!

I assumed I was making progress to the east, but I was having trouble making sense of my position. I had only a large-scale road map of Quebec to go by, having outdistanced my detailed map of the *Iles de Sorel*. Several bays I expected to see didn't appear. Also, something was radically wrong with my GPS. It said I was 16.6 miles due east of Sorel, and that put me 8 miles inland. I may have been disoriented and rattled, but I knew my paddles were not striking the dirt of a farmer's field. My only reference for navigation was the occasional freighter marching across the lake in the channel 3 miles north of me.

I considered quitting and turning around, but rejected the idea, partly out of pride, but also from laziness. I would have a tough daylong slog back upriver to Sorel. Besides, the wind was light, so I was in no immediate danger. Clouds were gathering in the southwest, portending possible thunderstorm activity in the afternoon, but I had too much on my mind to worry about that danger as well. Considering the possibility of lightning, I muttered, *Strike and be damned!*

After several hours of paddling, I was granted a shred of encouragement. Far on the horizon ahead, a slender line of darker blue appeared lying above the surface of the lake: the far shore. This was not, after all, the ocean I was trapped on.

By lunchtime, I'd traveled about a third of the distance across the lake, skirting the reeds. I still had no way to reach dry land. To rest, I pulled up into the reeds and made a peanut butter sandwich while sitting in the boat. I tested the lake bottom with my paddle, and found only a foot of water and a fairly firm mud bottom. Gingerly, I got out of the kayak and walked around: no problem. My outlook improved. Instead of being on a lake, I could think of it as water-covered land. I couldn't camp there, but in theory I could walk out in case of a real emergency, assuming I could walk. I took off my clothes and gave myself a standing bath, figuring I might as well take advantage of the privacy that my isolation afforded.

I sat back down in the kayak and shared my predicament with the tape recorder:

> *I won't make it to the other side today. I'll have to overnight it, trying to sleep sitting up in the kayak. I'll be at the mercy of any storms that come up, especially lightning storms. If the wind comes up, I could really be in trouble. An east wind would block my progress and a south wind would drive me into the middle of the lake, into the ship channel. I feel like I'm stuck on this lake for the rest of my life. If I ever do make it out of here, we'll have to say the gods, or maybe The God, smiled on me. Judy says she prays for me every day; in fact she's put me on the prayer list of the First Lutheran Church.*

My kayak trips have been blessed many times by strokes of amazing, unexpected outside help, but none of these rescues was so improbable as my deliverance from—as the hobbits might call it—the Endless-Lake-Without-a-Shore. Fifteen minutes after I recorded my anguished entreaty, I looked up to notice that my isolation was not quite as complete as I thought. Off to the north, stood a boat with a flashing yellow light on top, like a police boat. As I began paddling again, the boat headed toward me, but not in the aggressive, menacing way the Bonner County Marine Sheriff bears down on canoeists to enforce life preserver regulations on Lake Pend Oreille back in Idaho. This boat politely angled toward my course. When he neared, he cut his motor and waited for me to paddle up.

Yves, the boat driver, was an employee of a private security company hired by the Canadian military. It turned out that I was paddling in the firing range of the army's 105-millimeter cannon. This was not quite as dangerous as it sounds. A backstop behind the target was supposed to stop projectiles, Yves said, but if it failed, the projectiles would come out to this area of the lake. He also told me that I had been under observation all morning from a watchtower halfway down the lake. (So much for my private bath: I'm probably on videotape and the Internet now.) The firing at the range was now stopped until this problem—er, me—was taken care of. Yves never indicated, either in manner or in words, that I didn't have a perfect right to be there. He was just laying out the facts, letting me come to my own conclusion—which was of course that his arrival was too good to be true!

"Well," I suggested, attempting to maintain a neutral, unconcerned tone, "would you like to take me over to the end of the lake?" He was delighted at the suggestion. We lifted the kayak onto his boat and sped to the marina in Nicolet at the east end of the lake.

Yves was studying English in hopes of getting a better job—he showed me his vocabulary list, which he keeps on the dash—but he didn't know the language yet. We mostly used French to communicate: in retrospect, it seems amazing that I was able to grasp the complex situation he was explaining. Apparently my brain was beginning to make a little sense of French words. At the dock in Nicolet, Yves asked in French, "Should we lift the kayak into the water?" I was thrilled to realize I understood him. He has two boys, ages 16 and 19. The 16-year-old was taking intensive English.

After I said goodbye to Yves, I walked ashore to spend a little time thanking my lucky stars, and, well, The God for such a speedy deliverance from Lake Saint-Pierre. The marina was closed; when I asked a workman how I could get some water, he took my bottle in the back door and filled it with ice water.

Resuming my trip down the Saint Lawrence from the marina at Nicolet, I had to grapple with an annoying north wind coming from the side, sloshing water into my cockpit and twisting me back and forth. It would have been nicer to travel on the north bank of the river, sheltered from the wind. My game plan, devised months before, was to make the worrisome crossing of the mile-wide Saint Lawrence at a narrow spot further down the river, but my spirits were high. Now suddenly seemed the best time to get on the north, Quebec City side of the Saint Lawrence. Looking closely up and down the river for freighters and seeing none, I struck out, angling across the river against wind and waves.

It was a healthy slog against an honest, but not menacing, 12-mph wind. When I reached the opposite side, just under the bridge at Trois-Rivières, I was exhausted, and more than ready to call it a day. I paddled 5 miles more, past Trois-Rivières and its interminable docks to a marina on the far side. Although it did have a lawn where I could probably camp, this marina was under the smokestack of a paper mill spewing stinking sulfur fumes. I refused to consider sleeping there, feeling that those fumes would undo in one evening what months of Judy's supplements were supposed to be doing for my immune system.

I pressed on further, and for once persistence paid immediate dividends. In just a few hundred yards I was out of the sulfur smoke and on a sandy beach in the town of Cap-de-la-Madeline. The beach was obviously private, belonging to the house on a cliff above. People were out on the lawn, which seemed promising. I climbed up a long, incredibly rickety wooden stairway—a liability lawyer's dream—and emerged on the lawn where a dozen people were sitting at a picnic table, eating and drinking. They eyed me with astonishment, like I was Banquo's ghost. As they explained later, they couldn't imagine how anyone could get to their beach except from the house. It was like having a complete stranger walk into your living room from the bedroom. The confusion was cleared up in a moment. It turned out that I had walked in on a birthday party and the honoree, Lizette, insisted on a congratulatory good luck hug from the tall, dark, handsome stranger (well, one out of four) who had arrived so mysteriously. They were interested in my trip; fortunately, Doris, who spoke good English, could interpret for everybody. They invited me to sleep on their beach, and directed me to a great restaurant just a few blocks away.

When I finally snuggled into my sleeping bag that night, I was almost too exhilarated by the events of the day to sleep, having lived several lifetimes in the space of 18 hours. I had covered 30.8 miles, 20.8 in the kayak and 10 in Yves's boat, and I was 412.9 miles from New York.

I rose late the next morning after a magnificent, well-earned sleep. Again, the sky was a crystal clear blue and the air was dry and cool, quite unlike New York City's muggy summer heat: I had paddled myself all the way into another climate zone. I felt especially buoyant because, now that I had traversed Lake Saint-Pierre and also crossed the Saint Lawrence to the Quebec side, my major worries of the trip were over.

I really had only one critical navigational task to attend to, and that was staying out of the shipping channel. This is not as easy as it sounds. Since the channel occasionally runs close to land, one can't assume that being only a few hundred yards from shore is safe. And I was often over a half mile out when cutting across indentations of the shoreline. So to be safe, one really needs to spot buoys and make sense of them to know where the big ships are heading. Unfortunately, the buoys are spaced miles apart, often invisible to a water-level kayaker. Therefore, there were times when I saw a ship heading in my direction and couldn't see any buoys—and therefore had no idea where the channel was.

What is a kayaker to do? Ships can't turn to avoid me—because turning would put them out of their channel. They're as unstoppable and implacable as freight trains, but more nerve-racking because they're going on invisible tracks. Imagine you're hiking in the forest and you hear a train whistle, but it's one of those trains that runs on invisible tracks. It can come blasting out of the trees right at you. What would you do? You wouldn't want to sit and wait, because you might be sitting in the middle of the "tracks." You want to run, but in which direction? You have no idea: you might run directly into the train's path. Now understand the panic I felt whenever I saw a ship but not any buoys.

The buoys on the left-hand side of the downriver ship channel are red, and therefore my objective was always to stay to the left of these buoys, which would put me out of the channel. Some of these red buoys have a conical top, and are known as "red nuns," because they recall the conical hat of an order of nuns. The buoys marking the far, right-hand side of the channel were "ashcans," green cylinders. My mantra, as I made my way down the left-hand side of the Saint Lawrence, was, "The red nun is my salvation." This wasn't a theological dogma meant to irritate Baptists, but a nautical rule of thumb. It meant that if I could see a red nun, then I knew where the channel was, and where my safety lay, namely to the left of her.

As I pulled away from Cap-de-la-Madeline that morning, I was paddling into a brilliant sun that blacked out all colors. I thought I could make out a red nun far ahead, and carefully maintained a course that kept me a hundred yards to the left of it. Eventually, I came close enough to see it clearly and I let out a shriek. It was not red, but green. It was the ashcan marking the *right* side of the channel, so I had been merrily paddling down the middle of the ship channel! Fortunately, my guardian angels aren't as error-prone as I am. No ships were coming, and I quickly hustled over to the left of the channel where I belonged.

Around noontime I chatted with a fully outfitted kayaker I met on the water near Batiscan, a friendly young man who taught welding at the state industrial school at Cap-de-la-Madeline. I asked him about kayaking skills and learned that he practices his Eskimo roll with his friends on a nearby lake when it warms up. I had to tell him that it was years since I even pretended I could roll. As I took note of each item of his gear, I felt increasingly outclassed.

His kayak was a long, low, sleek, yellow plastic 17-footer that looked ready for the Arctic Ocean. My high-riding, stubby, faded red canvas boat looked like a garbage scow in comparison. He was wearing a life jacket, I wasn't. He was wearing the mirrored sunglasses that airplane pilots use to project mystery and command. I had scratched Polaroid clip-ons. His airtight spray skirt was attached, so he was ready to right himself in the event of a capsize. I sat in an open cockpit. What really shook me was that he had a paddle tether rigged, an elegant multicolored braided strap made expressly for this purpose. It probably cost $39 in a kayaking supply catalog. The only time I've ever used a tether was in the Columbia rapids, thinking that if I went over, the paddle might spurt pretty far from the boat. My makeshift tether was the same scrap of rope I used for a mooring line.

I didn't have to ask this superbly outfitted kayaker if he was wearing regulation kayak booties. Thank goodness he didn't see the pink ladies' beach clogs I was using!

The only point of comparison in my favor was that he had started his trip in Batiscan, a mile away, and I started in New York 430 miles distant.

An hour after saying goodbye to the kayaker, I was sitting on the grass under a tree in Batiscan when a man came up to me.

"This is my property," he said, speaking English.

Oh, oh, I thought. *For the first time on the whole trip, I'm going to encounter hostility.*

"I'm sorry," I replied, starting to get up.

"No, no, you can stay here. It's fine," he said. "What it is, I'm a paramedic. When I saw you sitting down, I thought you might be ill. That's why I came over."

This exchange left the social scientist in me scratching my head. In the course of the trip I had met *only* friendly and helpful people, dozens and dozens of them. There are exceptions to every generalization about human behavior, right? So where were the exceptions to the rule that everyone treats a traveling stranger with courtesy?

A day later at Deschambault, I was pulling the kayak up on the mud-flats below some houses when I heard a shout. I thought it might be someone complaining about my right to land there. I looked around and saw a woman standing at the edge of her lawn looking at me. I wasn't sure she was the one who had shouted, but I figured I had better greet her and find out what was the matter.

I introduced myself, and we began conversing, haltingly, in French. (The shout, I soon learned, had nothing to do with me; it was a workman at a neighbor's house yelling to his partner on the roof.)

I guessed from hearing the word "*café*" and from her friendly attitude that she was inviting me for a cup of coffee, and I said "*oui.*" As I climbed up the rocks to her patio, her husband came out and greeted me, and we had a nice *petit dejeuner* (little lunch, that is, breakfast) together.

Claudette was a local artist whose specialty is making watercolor paintings of the area's churches. I had been taking a keen interest in these buildings with their high steeples ever since I entered Quebec. They are the only significant buildings in each village: many are practically cathedrals. Claudette had painted all 12 churches in her county, and had them printed up as color postcards for sale in shops. So she's a mini-publisher, just like me. I insisted on buying several of these exquisite cards from her. I promised to send her one of my self-published books when I got home.

Claudette and her husband go to Florida in the winter for 5 months every year (he's retired), but they live in a French Canadian community down there, so they don't get to practice much English.

Claudette brought out a jar of jam to put on toast. She made it herself, she said. "No soogar. No soogar because . . ." She hesitated, unable to find the English expression, then slid her hands down her ample thighs. Although the jam had no sweetener, I noticed that she had laden my toast with melted butter. I feared Claudette had an imperfect understanding of caloric inputs.

After breakfast and a trip to the village for provisions, I returned to the boat and found the tide had dropped, leaving me 50 yards from the water. I had to unload the kayak and then carry it across the mud to the water's edge. I began the work wearing the infamous clogs, but they stuck so badly in the mud that I kicked them off and did the job barefoot.

After leaving Deschambault, I found myself trapped in a river of rocks. As far as the eye could see, jagged boulders and bedrock outcroppings 20–30 feet apart stuck out of the water. I was completely hemmed in, threading my way around them in an easterly direction on pure faith that open water lay beyond. Some of the rocks jutted 5 or 6 feet above the water, some were at water level, others were slightly submerged. A strong current was sucking through the rocks, the combined effect of the river current and the falling tide. I watched for disturbances in the water surface to spot slightly covered rocks; being pulled against a half-submerged rock by the current might tip me. I put on my life jacket. The one positive aspect of this harrowing situation was that I didn't have to worry about ships, or even motorboats, running me down. Only kayaks could dare to be there.

For the kayaker from Idaho, the Saint Lawrence proved to be a charmed river, with every difficulty gently resolving itself into a blessing. My experience at Portneuf that afternoon was typical. I paddled into the boat basin, tied up, walked along the dock, and came upon a self-locking gate leading to land. I could go out, but I could not get back in without the combination. I hesitated a few moments, holding the gate open, hating to leave the kayak out of reach. The boat felt like a child in that respect, constantly cramping my style as a parent. However, I could see people in the restaurant on the hill, so I knew the marina was open and that they could give me the combination to get back in. I let the gate click shut behind me.

I reached the marina office, and found it closed (I later learned it was bankrupt and out of business). I went to the restaurant on the second floor of the building. They said they had nothing to do with the marina, and didn't know anything about the combination to the gate.

Yikes!

Since I could do nothing immediately about the problem, I decided to surrender to the Power of Now and have a late luncheon at the rather luxurious restaurant. I thought I was ordering something chicken, but the charming waitress brought out a superb dish of veal in a mushroom sauce that pleased me even more.

An hour later, I went back to the gate and found it propped open by a man who was messing with his boat. When Ivan heard about my trip he insisted I camp on the lawn and use the facilities of the sailing club to which he belonged. This would be a great blessing, since in addition to a hot shower, the club had a new washer and dryer to wash my clothes. He gave me the combination to the gate, a key to the yacht club facilities, and a letter from him explaining who I was, in case any other club member came by and questioned me. He spoke only French, but I think he explained that he was making this gesture "in recognition for your accomplishment." (Okay, this translation comes from someone who just ordered veal thinking it was chicken, but his body language helped me translate.)

The object of all my many days of paddling presented itself the next day in a most unexpected way. I had pushed along all morning in the bright sun, and finally cleared the point at Cap-Santé, where a long vista of the next section of the river opened up. About half a mile away, very tiny in my field of vision, a string of poles for holding fishing nets stuck out of the water. I had already seen many of these in Lake Saint-Pierre, and didn't take any special notice. After paddling 15 minutes, I noticed that the poles weren't getting any bigger, and I took a greater interest. Squinting carefully at the vertical lines, I saw they were a little straighter and more regular than fishnet poles would be. I gasped with delight. *Could it really be?* A few more minutes of paddling confirmed that these lines were not poles but the upright girders of the two bridges at Quebec, 25 miles away. I could see my destination!

With the help of the current I polished off 13 miles before noon, reaching the yacht basin and marina at Neuville. As I stepped out of my boat onto the dock, I was welcomed by Suzanne, a trim, middle-aged blond who gave me a hug. She pointed out the marina office where I could ask Simon, the manager, about mooring my kayak. "Simon take care of your little problems," she said with her charming French accent, "Suzanne take care of your big problems." That set my mind racing—as I suppose it was intended to. I found out later she and her husband have a sailboat moored at the marina.

I decided to overnight at Neuville, taking up the invitation of several members of the sailing club to camp on the lawn. Everyone told me that the tidal current is very strong, especially at the bridges, and that I couldn't paddle against it. I planned to set out early with the outgoing tide the next day. I was apprehensive about getting by the bridges in the current, wondering if there would be bad eddies by the bridge, and whether the pleasure boat traffic on a Sunday morning would be dense. And then, there was the problem of finding a hotel and getting the kayak to it. Of course I didn't have any reservation; I didn't even know the names of any hotels that might be near the water.

I had to practically slap myself out of my nervous funk. *Stop worrying!* I told myself. *"Sufficient unto the day thereof."*

I spent the rest of the day exploring Neuville. The plaques on some of the old buildings brought home just how long ago this part of Canada was settled. A girl's seminary was founded here in the early 17th century, only a few years after the Pilgrims bumped into Plymouth Rock.

While doing leg stretches on the lawn of the local church, I noticed cars driving up and people gathering outside the open church door. In the interest of adventure, I decided to attend the service, though not without the protestant's uneasiness at entering a Catholic house of worship. While of course we're great, teasing friends with the Catholics now, for the protestant there lingers about Catholicism an ancient memory of whips and chains that the passage of tolerant centuries has not entirely dispelled. Furthermore, I was in a foreign country, and who knew what old-time customs might survive in this corner of the world?

I was greeted at the door by a sweet lady who pinned a ribbon with a picture of a butterfly on my chest, and that somewhat put my mind at ease. The service, I learned, was to be a special, once-a-year service for *les malades,* the chronically sick and disabled. I took a seat in the sumptuously decorated sanctuary of this church, built in 1855, and waited for the service to begin.

Minibusses from nursing homes began arriving, and wheelchair-bound, elderly patients were wheeled up to the front. Except for two teenagers, who had obviously been recruited as helpers, everyone else at the service was well over 60, including the nine priests. I noticed all the men were dressed informally. No one wore a tie, many were in running shoes. I didn't feel out of place.

The service eventually got underway, with 40 wheelchair congregants arranged in front and 200 of the rest of us in the pews. Although the diction of the priests was clear and slow, I couldn't understand a word of either the liturgy or the messages. Apparently they were using words and syntax of a flowery, formal French.

A six-member choir, accompanied by organ, sung the hymns in unison, that is, without any harmony. The singing was forceful, bordering on screaming, suggesting that choir members were paid amateurs determined to earn their wages. The hymns were nothing like the square, chorale-like hymns we are used to (like "Oh God, Our Help in Ages Past"). They were lyrical with a wandering melody and slow harmonic rhythm, difficult to sing along with. The congregation barely joined in.

Toward the end of the service, the priests fanned out into the congregation, each with a tin of what looked like lip balm, and carried on an exchange with each and every congregant before applying the ointment.

My pulse rose as one of the elderly priests, accompanied by the sweet lady I had met before the service, came down my side of the aisle. He was asking each person a question and getting a reply, but I had no idea what was going on.

When he came to me, I stood up, as the others had been doing, and he asked me a question, "*Vous penance?*"

I tried to interpret the phrase, "Your penance." *Would this have something to do with sin, or punishment for sin?*

"Pardon?" I said, hoping he would elaborate. The elderly priest was fixed on carrying out his ritual, unaware of my discomfort.

"*Vous penance!*" he said again louder, impatiently. The eyes of the congregants began to turn in the direction of the protestant bee that had wandered into the Catholic hive.

Why is he asking me to do penance? Then I remembered that Catholics have a rite of confession and this could be some old-fashioned ritual where people are expected to publicly confess their sins. Was the priest demanding I confess my worst sexual transgressions in front of him and this nice lady and the entire congregation? *This is crazy!* I thought. *Even if I could recall such sins, I don't know enough*

French to describe them!

In desperation, I turned to the sweet lady, my one ally in a hostile land. "*Je ne comprend pas,*" I said, with pleading in my voice. She relayed to the priest that I didn't speak French and suggested he try another language.

Still stern and impatient he asked, "Vat ess yor nam!"

I understood him, but I was still paralyzed. Was I supposed to give him my full name, or my first name, or my nickname? I fell back on instant theology and decided God must know who I was no matter how I was called, so I told him, "Jeen," which I took to be "Jim" said with a French accent.

That satisfied him and he thereupon did big business with the lip balm, making the sign of the cross with it on the palm of each of my hands, and on my forehead, reciting all the while in French. Then he moved on, and I sat down, flushed and perspiring, my heart pounding. As my pulse slowed, I tried to guess what the question, "*Vous penance?*" meant. Apparently it was shorthand for, "In whose name do you make penance (seek absolution)?"

When the service was over, ushers rushed around the sanctuary with trays laden with candy bars and little cartons of Kool-Aid, urging all to partake. On the basis of this practice of eating in the sanctuary—and high-calorie junk food at that—I concluded that the Quebec Catholics are at least as reformed as American Catholics. I doubt that a church that distributes Kit Kats in front of the altar still maintains that we burn in hell for impure thoughts.

On the steps as I was leaving the church, I met the sweet lady again. She was handing out nicely gift-wrapped boxes the size of a pack of cigarettes, but heavier. She urged me to take one, and, still following the principle of when-in-Rome—albeit a little gun-shy now—I accepted the package. As I walked back to the marina, I tried to guess what the package might contain. I was pretty sure that it was a pocket-sized volume of religious writings, like a prayer book or a tiny copy of the Gospels.

When I opened it that evening, I discovered that I had underestimated Quebec's pace of religious reform (or deterioration, depending on your point of view). It was an elegant deck of playing cards!

I did it! I did it! I found myself saying this over and over to myself as I walked the streets of Quebec. Confounding all my worries, the concluding day of the trip went smoothly. Nature, man, woman, and guardian angels joined forces to give me a charming welcome to the city.

I set out from Neuville as soon as it was light, paddling hard because I knew I had to make Quebec on the outgoing tide. It would be absurd to get within a few miles of my destination and be caught by a tide shift that washed me back up the river. As I paddled along, the bridges grew bigger and bigger in my field of vision. I put my camera and my tape recorder in their Ziploc bags, ready for turbulence at the bridges.

In fact, there wasn't any. A 5-mph current pushed me along, but the river surface was calm and glassy. I would have believed I was in a millpond until I lifted my gaze and saw how fast the shore was slipping by. My worry about marine congestion was also unfounded. I was all alone on the water that Sunday morning.

The bridges stand 8 miles upriver from Quebec proper, so I didn't see any real sign of the city for some time. The first major landmark was a church with a towering steeple on a hill overlooking the water. Just as I came upon it, its bells started ringing energetically. I waved back, acknowledging their celebration of my arrival.

Other buildings appeared, several skyscrapers on the ridge to the north, and massive docks and warehouses along the river. Then, with delight I saw Quebec's signature monument, the Chateau Frontenac, the hotel built like a medieval castle, abounding in turrets and spires.

I entered the dock area totally at a loss. Because of the extreme high tides at Quebec, the harbor has concrete walls 40 feet high. You don't just walk off your boat onto land. I saw a lock to raise smaller pleasure boats up to a boat basin at street level, and thought I might take advantage of that. I waited patiently in front of the lock for several minutes, and when nothing happened, blew my silver whistle. Apparently the whistle had lost its magic powers, for the lock didn't open.

Then I spotted a floating landing stage at water level that was a mooring for sightseeing boats. I paddled over and climbed out onto the dock. That was a good first step, but how was I to lift the boat out of the water and get it up the 30-foot flight of stairs to the street?

I went up the stairs to explore. At the top a young man was waiting for me. Luk had been watching my futile paddling in the harbor below and wanted to talk with me about kayaks, since he was interested in buying one. So I had an eager helper. Together, we lifted the kayak from the water and carried it up the stairs to the sidewalk.

Then, another helper appeared, Marie, an attractive young woman who worked in the booking office of the sightseeing cruise line. (All young women in Quebec, I was soon to learn, are attractive; it is a city for breaking men's hearts.) When she learned my situation, she volunteered to call around to nearby hotels to find me a place. That took care of another big worry: for days I had been dreading that task, so difficult for an English-speaking stranger. Both Marie and Luk spoke good English.

In front of a crowd of curious Sunday afternoon bystanders, Luk and I took apart the kayak and crammed all the pieces into the carrying pack. Marie came out to report that she found a free room at the Hotel Belley, seven blocks away, which they would hold for me for a half hour. I thanked her profusely and, looking for some token of my appreciation, I gave her the pink Styrofoam clogs. As I handed them over I realized that such footwear would probably appall this stylish young woman.

"You don't have to wear them if you don't want to," I said.

"They're superb!" she replied, making a generous lie.

I began carrying the kayak pack but, at Luk's urging, soon surrendered it to him. The Hotel Belley was perfect: a small, reasonably priced hotel in the heart of Quebec's Old City. Above and beyond the call of duty, Luk carried the pack up the three flights of stairs to my room (the hotel had no elevator—one reason why it was reasonably priced).

With equipment safe and sound, I went out to one of the many restaurants for a late lunch. To distinguish myself from the American tourists around me, I ordered in French with confidence and élan, crossing my fingers under the table. The result quite surprised me, and would have provoked an expression of dismay were I not trying to maintain the pretense of competence. It was a kind of sausage made of a light, healthy, nonfatty ground meat that I suspected had more to do with the animal's intelligence or sexual powers than its ability to run or jump.

I spent the next days falling in love with Quebec as the most artistic and tasteful city I've ever visited. This love affair, the reader should know, began as a blind date. I knew nothing about Quebec before I came. When I first sketched out my itinerary, my thought was to end in Montreal. When I learned that the current in the Saint Lawrence was too strong to allow me to paddle upriver from the mouth of the Richelieu, making Montreal, to the west, unreachable, I moved my hand over to the right side of the map, and let my pencil fall on a city called Quebec. For all I knew, it was nothing more than paper mills and factories making asbestos shingles.

Well, they probably do make asbestos shingles in some other part of the city, but I had no contact with the commercial and industrial areas. The Quebec I experienced is called the Old City, the square mile or so of older buildings within and near the old walls (Quebec was a heavily fortified city in the days when the English were besieging it). This is the tourist heart of the city, with hotels and restaurants, but it doesn't feel touristy. Somehow the city absorbs its visitors, socializing them to its rhythms.

One thing I noticed as I walked the streets is that the city is quite clean. I took this cleanliness for granted at first because it was just like my hometown of Sandpoint, and I had to remind myself that I was in a large city and it therefore should be compared to places like, well, New York. Quebec achieves its remarkable standard of sanitation not by any strenuous effort. Some cities— Dublin, Ireland, for example—hire an army of sweepers who work throughout the day trying to pick up litter as it rains down (a losing battle in the case of Dublin). In Quebec, I saw no daytime litter collectors. I did see a sprayer truck out early one morning, but it was sweeping an already clean street. Quebec accomplishes its cleanliness through culture: people are simply too well behaved to throw down litter. I saw one pedestrian stoop down and put her cigarette carefully out in a tiny puddle of rainwater, then wrap it in a tissue and put it in her purse.

Another thing that reminded me of friendly village life was the way cars stopped for wayward pedestrians. I saw it happen many times: the pedestrian would start crossing in the middle of the block or against the light, see a car coming, and freeze in indecision; the car would stop and wave the pedestrian across. Were drivers making allowances because they knew many of these pedestrians were tourists on unfamiliar ground? But New York City has tourists too, and they are not indulged if they so much as put a toe off the curb at the wrong time. It is a difference in culture. In Quebec, the inhabitants are more relaxed, more inclined to be helpful.

Quebec is also a city of art galleries. The first thing I saw when I left the hotel after checking in was an art gallery, and I delayed having lunch to walk in and look around. The paintings were original and powerful, yet tasteful. I soon learned that artwork is not confined to the commercial galleries. There are serious pieces everywhere, in every restaurant and bistro. In my little Hotel Belley, paintings hung not just in the lobby, but also in hallways, stairways, and landings. None of this was schlock, the stuff usually turned out for hotels and bank lobbies. It was sincere, thought-provoking art.

I found myself caught up in the art trade. One morning I was enjoying the gallery located on the ground floor of the Chateau Frontenac when my eye fell on a painting that took my breath away. It was set on the floor, and, unlike all the other paintings, it was a raw unframed canvas. It seemed an orphan, a Cinderella of the gallery. The subject was a young girl out in the snow, bundled in coat, scarf, and mittens, surveying the winter morning with wonder and anticipation, and painted with a relaxed, unerring feel in design, balance, and line. I knew Judy would love it.

I continued walking around the gallery, but my mind was riveted on this painting. I was pretty certain its price was outside the range of what a Payne would ever feel justified paying for art. Finally, I went over to the manager. "Do I dare to ask what that painting costs?"

Sylvain, the son in this family gallery business, said the artist, Lucie Vezina, was new to the gallery. The painting had just come in last week, so it hadn't yet been framed and hung. He leafed through a book of records, and dug out the price: $1,400. That was Canadian, he pointed out. It would be around $1,100 US. As a gift for Judy, I thought I could just about justify it. I told Sylvain I would go to lunch and think about it.

At lunch, it quickly became clear that I was not weighing the pros and cons of anything. I had already decided: I had to have that painting! I started worrying that someone might buy it before I could get back. After all, it had been there only a few days. If it was as great a painting as I thought it was, the next customer in that store might snap it up.

I wolfed down my food and rushed back to the Chateau, relieved to find the little girl right where I left her. I made the purchase and arranged for it to be crated and shipped to Sandpoint.

In chatting with Sylvain, who spoke good English, it came out that I had kayaked my way from New York City, and he immediately asked, "Would you mind if the newspaper contacted you? I think they would be interested."

I said I had no objection, though I thought it unlikely any paper would pick up on my trip as a news story. I was puzzled that Sylvain thought it might be newsworthy.

An hour later, I was back at the Hotel Belley and the phone was ringing. It was a reporter and photographer from *Le Soleil* (*The Sun*), Quebec's main daily. We took the kayak down to the waterfront so the photographer could get a picture, and the reporter interviewed me for an hour. He had done some kayaking himself, and he knew the Saint Lawrence and places like Lake Saint-Pierre. His English was rather shaky, and I had to help him along, repeating many points using different words, gestures, and even using some French.

As we shook hands at the end of the interview, he said, adopting a rather formal tone, "It's is a great thing you did. I know I speak for others in saying we respect what you have accomplished."

The next morning I rose early and searched out a newsstand for a copy of *Le Soleil*. There I was, on page 6, grinning from behind my paddle: "From New York to Quebec in Kayak," said the headline. "Over 29 days, James Payne traversed the distance of 747 km just before his 65th birthday." The story seemed fairly accurate, insofar as I could make out the French. However, it did say the kayak cost $1,200 US, even though I clearly told the reporter $3,000.

After breakfast I explored the town, coming upon the Anglican cathedral where a sign announced a morning service at 8:30. Having participated in a Catholic service on this trip, I thought I should try brand B, and went in. There was just one person there, a man who worked in the administration of the Anglican church, the first native English speaker I had encountered in Quebec (excepting tourists). As soon as I mentioned I came by kayak to attend the service, he said, "I just read about you in the paper. I remember thinking as I read that, 'I wonder if he will show up at Holy Trinity?'"

The assistant priest—also a native English speaker—showed up, and the three of us read the service from The Book of Common Prayer. Although this weekday service was poorly attended (!) they said that the Sunday services—one in French, one in English—are doing well, with a thriving volunteer choir.

As a former president of the Sandpoint Mural Society, I was fascinated by the development of that art in Quebec. Most murals in other cities are pictures that belong on the wall of an art museum, such as a landscape or a portrait. These "picture" murals are somewhat jarring because even if they are fine paintings in themselves, they clash with their surroundings. The more elegant outdoor painting is an "environmental" mural, one that echoes or plays off its surroundings, and thus belongs to the scene. Well, Quebec has an environmental mural to beat the band. They've taken a five-story building and painted a complete urban scene in perspective so it blends into the street. You can't tell where the real street ends and the painted street begins, and, unless you look closely, you can't distinguish between the painted figures in the mural and the real people standing in front of the mural. The artists have peopled the scene with a whimsical mixture of historical figures dressed in their period garb and modern figures, including three boys playing street hockey. Visitors can't get enough of photographing each other interacting with the mural figures.

The public sculptures in Quebec reflected the same tastefulness seen in the galleries. Many were older, traditional pieces, and the newer ones exhibited flair and sophistication. There seemed to be none of those gross, abstract sculptures, found in many U.S. cities, which are often exercises in maximum ugliness. I'm thinking, for example, of the great, clanking mobile of Alexander Calder at the National Gallery, West Wing.

Late one afternoon I was conversing on this subject with the manager of an art gallery, praising the absence of ugly modern pieces of sculpture.

"Oh, but there is one," she said.

"Really?"

"Yes, it was a gift of the French government. We tried to stop it"—I gathered she was referring to the local arts community—"but the politicians wouldn't listen. They thought it would look bad to refuse it."

She took me out to the street and pointed where I should walk to find it. I agreed with her opinion. The work is a white cube 15 feet high with a smaller cube sitting on top of it, a pointless, meaningless monstrosity. The plaque said that it was a gift of the government of France to the City of Quebec. Well, that explained it. When one bureaucracy gives a present to another, this is exactly what I would expect it to look like.

Three days of sightseeing concluded, I headed to Quebec's small, lightly used airport, eager to return home. The kayak pack wouldn't fit in the trunk of the taxi, so we laid it along the back seat, pushing hard on the doors to squeeze it in, and I rode in the front. I explained to the driver—whose English was good—what the pack was and how it had reached Quebec.

"Did you really come from New York in a kayak?" he asked.

I nodded.

"Can I shake your hand?" And so he did, as we drove along the freeway to the airport.

There it was again, this open praise for my accomplishment. I can't avoid the conclusion that my journey revealed an unusual cultural trait: the Quebecois are more demonstrative than Americans when it comes to appreciating achievements—physical achievements anyway. I'd seen it throughout my journey in Quebec, starting with Vicki the lockkeeper at the first lock of the Chambly Canal, to Sylvain, the art gallery manager who felt my trip merited a news story, and the editor of *Le Soleil* who agreed with him. I met nothing like this enthusiasm anywhere in the United States. Along the Hudson and across Lake Champlain, many people reacted positively to my trip, pronouncing the journey "neat," "cool," or even "fascinating." But no one south of the border viewed it as an accomplishment meriting formal praise or a handshake.

In Quebec, I found out how it feels to be a hero, and I rather enjoyed the sensation.

In the boarding lounge at the airport I mentioned my trip to a fellow passenger, and he asked me, "So what was your overall impression?"

That vague question stumped me for a second, but then I realized I had a clear answer: how amazingly nice everyone was.

I don't mean this as a gushing compliment. I'm defending it as an empirical observation. My trip constituted, in effect, a survey of the state of human kindness, or the lack thereof, in the northeast corridor where I traveled.

In the course of the trip, I encountered some 70 situations where I asked people for help, or where people saw I needed some kind of assistance. In all 70 cases, the help was given—often more than I asked for. Seven times people went out of their way to drive me to places I needed to go, eight times I was given food to eat, six times people gave me a place to camp, twice I was invited to sleep in a home. Twice I was given laundry detergent, four times a shower, and Tylenol once. People let me park my kayak every time I asked. I was given water more than a dozen times, and directions and information about 30 times.

Then there were the interactions that involved people who were paid to do the helpful things they did for me. On the trip I found it difficult to distinguish between the two kinds of help, paid and unpaid. For one thing, the paid businesses and services were *help*. When we are at home in our own communities, we take for granted the commercial provision of goods and services, as if they were automatically our due. We drive up to the gas pump and fill the tank, so that we may continue to use our vehicle to fulfill our many needs and desires. After filling up, we never think of writing letters of appreciation saying, "Thank you, oil company, thank you, oil drillers, thank you, tanker crews."

On this trip, I didn't have this feeling of complacency. Always in a strange place, I felt vulnerable, and getting Fig Newtons, film, or needed superglue from a business often seemed a great blessing. Furthermore, the workers helping me were friendly. I suppose if they had been glum and hostile, as if saying, "I'm only doing this for the money," then I wouldn't be so impressed. But the clerks, waitresses, lockkeepers, taxi drivers, motel managers, and art gallery owners were cheerful and eager to help. The exchange of money was only an aspect of the interaction. In my eyes they were another hundred helpful acquaintances.

Finally, there is the much larger universe of people who were aware of my existence and who could have gone out of their way to harm or offend me. This group includes all the people who saw my tent and left me alone, and all the people who didn't steal or mess with my kayak when I left it. It includes the hundreds of boaters who steered around me.

Except for those inattentive kids in the Jet Ski, I had no negative experience with youngsters. Maybe we take this for granted, but you can't in other places. I recall reading an account of English hikers in Bhutan, who reported that the children in every village would pelt them with stones. It was the fun, accepted thing to do. On my entire trip, no one threw stones, or anything else, at me. Nor was I robbed, beaten, or threatened—even though I was a vulnerable, defenseless target.

Toward the end of my trip I was talking with my sister Dorothy on the phone, telling her how helpful everyone had been. My observation seemed to annoy her. "Now you just be careful," she said. "There are some bad people out there!"

Well of course there are, but we need to keep this danger in perspective. The picture we get from the media exaggerates evil. We seem to forget that the media does not present an unbiased, representative account of what happens in the world. The cameras are not pointed randomly; they are deliberately carried to scenes of mayhem. A thousand people can experience a happy, productive day while one person experiences tragedy: guess who you will see on the nightly news. The media gives us the thoroughly false impression that around every corner lurks an enemy seeking to do us harm. On my trip I went around many, many corners and I found no such enemy.

I do not mean this observation about the helpfulness of people to apply to the whole world. In fact, it clearly doesn't apply to many places where there are high proportions of violent, aggressive people.

Shortly after I returned home, I picked up Jeffrey Tayler's book *Facing the Congo,* about his attempt to go down Zaire's Congo River in a dugout canoe. He paints a chilling picture of a chaotic, impoverished society where most things a traveler needs cannot be had, for love or money. Almost everything he needed, from medicines to batteries, he had to take with him. Far from meeting with kindness, Tayler experienced almost constant aggression. He carried a shopping bag full of local currency so he could pay off the gangs of soldiers and police that threatened him at every turn. He had to hire two bodyguards to keep river pirates and hostile villagers at bay.

I was not traveling in Zaire or Bhutan. I am reporting how I was treated by the people along the Hudson, Champlain, Richelieu, and Saint Lawrence waterways. It's only one corner of the world, to be sure, but my experience may carry a broader lesson.

We hear over and over how people are supposed to be kind and help those in need. Like others, I have sometimes taken a cynical, hard-boiled view of these sentiments. Maybe Heaven is supposed to be that way, we say, but nothing like that can ever happen here on Earth, at least not in any regular, dependable way. My trip made me rethink this skepticism, and wonder whether Heaven on Earth might not be closer than we think. I did not encounter just one or two kind people and scores of indifferent or hostile ones. Seventy out of seventy people helped when the traveler needed help—a Good Samaritan batting average of 1000!

Yes, I was traveling through prosperous, cultured, long-settled communities. But perhaps this corner of the world demonstrates what the human race is capable of, what may eventually be achieved elsewhere, and everywhere, as we get on with the job of civilization.

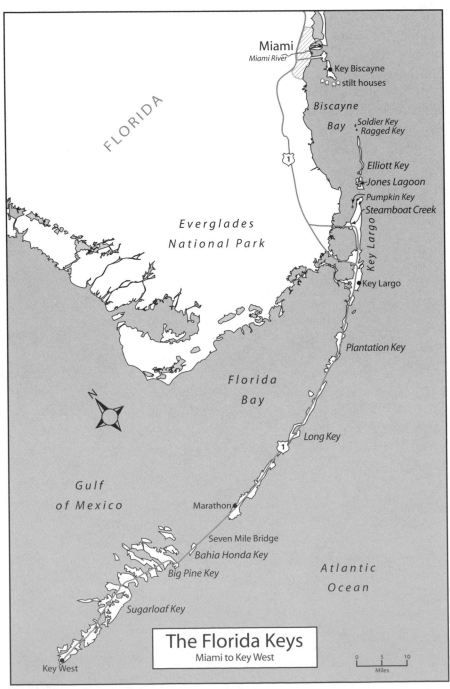

Miami
Miami River

FLORIDA

Key Biscayne
🏠🏠 stilt houses

Biscayne Bay

Soldier Key
Ragged Key

Everglades National Park

Elliott Key
Jones Lagoon
Pumpkin Key
Steamboat Creek

Key Largo

Key Largo

Plantation Key

Florida Bay

N

Long Key

Gulf of Mexico

Marathon

Seven Mile Bridge
Bahia Honda Key
Big Pine Key

Atlantic Ocean

Sugarloaf Key

The Florida Keys
Miami to Key West

0   5   10
Miles

Key West

Island size not to scale

6
Flirting with the Tropical Ocean

Miami, Florida to Key West (November 2005)

I WAS NOT TACKLING the Atlantic Ocean by design. I had not lain awake night after night longing to sail the high seas. I was afraid of the ocean. It is very large and very empty.

My original idea was to explore the southeast U. S. coast by paddling the Intracoastal Waterway in Florida. A trip there would, I felt, provide me with sheltered cruising, safe from big waves, and with frequent opportunities to find food and water. But as I studied the route, I saw that it was heavily built up, and likely to have few camping opportunities. Another negative would be the roaring engines and harassing wakes of powerboats in the narrow channels of the Intracoastal Waterway.

I went back to the map of Florida to look for a place with wider waters and less traffic, and my eye fell on the Florida Keys. The mystery and magic of that name was irresistible. I could voyage among tropical islands, starting at Miami and ending up in Key West, the island city connected to the mainland by an engineering marvel known as the Overseas Highway. The only problem was this appealing trip involved flirting with the Atlantic Ocean.

Oceans have breakers on their shores, so that setting out and landing requires going through a war zone of crashing surf that yanks, pounds, and smashes kayaks. I had read accounts of legendary ocean journeys by kayak, and noticed how frequently dangerous surf came into the picture. These voyagers were constantly picking their way through nasty breakers—getting twisted around, dumped over, rammed into sand, and on occasion even pitchpoled, that is, being flipped end over end.

In his book *Southern Exposure,* Chris Duff details one notable disaster during his circumnavigation of New Zealand's South Island in 2000. In trying to land during a storm, he was overturned twice while approaching the shore. He was able to recover both times with Eskimo rolls, but a big wave at the beach caught his boat and smashed it open like a pea pod. The next day he was rescued by helicopter. Determination runs in the sea kayaker's genes, however. Duff found a local fiberglass boatbuilder to reconstruct his kayak and went on to complete the circumnavigation.

Scary tales of ocean surf had about led me to give up the idea of this wonderful trip to Key West when I made an interesting discovery. Pouring over the maritime charts, I noticed that the soundings are very shallow. The Florida Keys are low islands that sit on coral reef, a shallow platform of limestone. In many places, the water is only 3–4 feet deep. In other places charts show large patches in green where the water is so shallow that the land is exposed in the lowest tides. For a kayaker, one benefit of these shallow depths is they keep powerboats away. They have to follow marked channels to avoid running aground, whereas I could go anywhere I liked.

The other benefit of the shallow water is that it kills the surf. Breakers are created as the ocean floor rises and lifts the swells higher and higher until they form breaking waves. In the Keys, the ocean floor rises at the edge of the reef, 3–5 miles from land. This is where swells destroy themselves in a churning of surf. So unless local winds are unusually strong, there isn't any surf crashing against the land.

The absence of significant surf made the trip in the Keys doable, but it did not end all dangers. For one thing, I was facing the novel flora and fauna of the tropics. I knew about the animals of the

Northeast and the Northwest, where my other kayak trips took place. In the Keys, I would be dealing with a string of novel threats, including coral snakes, water moccasins, crocodiles, sharks, barracuda, and stingrays. Also lurking in the forests was a poisonwood tree, which I didn't know how to identify—and I resolved not to hug any trees until I could.

But I wasn't going to let amorphous worry stop me. A few days before I left Sandpoint, I was chatting with some older friends about my proposed trip.

When Peggy heard me say I was to kayak the Florida Keys alone, she said, "Why you can't!" She was alarmed and adamant.

"Why not?" I asked.

"Because something might happen. You could get killed!"

"Hey, we're all going to die sometime."

"That's what I tell her," piped up Lee, her husband. "She won't even let me go hunting any more. I tell her it's better to die out there in the woods than in Life Care looking at the ceiling."

Turning to me, Peggy said, "I suppose you're right." Somehow, though, I didn't think Lee was going to get to die in the woods.

The first challenge in a kayak expedition is to find a suitable accommodation to serve as a staging point. On the Florida trip, this task involved more than the usual uncertainties. My first doubts about the Miami River Inn came from its price: $89. How could it be so cheap when all of Miami's other centrally located hotels wanted over $200? And shouldn't being on the National Register of Historic Buildings—it was built in 1906 when Miami hardly existed—add to the price?

I ignored this little alarm bell of doubt, however, because I was thrilled with the inn's location. It was situated on a little estuary, the Miami River, which runs through the middle of the city and empties into Biscayne Bay. That made it the ideal place to start my trip from Miami to Key West, enabling me to enjoy the thrill of setting out in the heart of an urban area and escaping to the freedom of open water.

More doubts about the inn surfaced when the taxi driver taking me from the Miami airport said he had never heard of it. But then, he was Haitian—still learning his way around, I figured. It was a dark and stormy night—really. The rain made it hard to see and added a Hitchcock touch of suspense to finding this mysterious lodging. Relying on my map of the city, I directed the driver toward the spot where the inn was supposed to be. Soon I understood what was wrong. When the Miami River Inn was built back at the turn of the century, it no doubt stood in a wide-open field, just a quarter mile from Henry Flagler's magnificent Breakers Hotel. But the city had grown past it, and literally over it, with elevated highways crisscrossing the area. Below these highway superstructures was urban blight: warehouses, parking lots, junkyards, the Miami River (which had become a ship channel crossed by a half dozen drawbridges) and—somewhere—the Miami River Inn.

We spent a half hour driving over and around where the inn was supposed to be, without finding a way to get to it. It seemed like one of those "You can't get to it from here" jokes.

The neighborhood was rough, with homeless and drunk people lounging under girders of the expressways. The cab driver, Hari, was getting nervous.

"You no walk here!" he said, pounding the steering wheel. "No walk 'round: bad people, bad people!"

We stopped at a liquor store to ask directions. I went to the locked door and waited. After deciding I was more likely to buy booze than to steal it, the Cuban manager buzzed me in. When I asked him how to get to the Miami River Inn, he chuckled.

"Verry trickee, verry trickee," he said, rubbing his hands with sinister glee.

Using the directions he gave us, we made our way to a two-story wooden frame building with no lights and no sign. The area looked especially seedy because Hurricane Wilma, which had come through the week before, had swirled broken palm fronds and trash over the sidewalks. Hari was emphatic about the dangers of the neighborhood, and was eager to take me to a proper hotel. "You no want. You no want here!"

He pointed to two women standing on a balcony. "Those whor'. Bad place, bad place!" he said, shaking his head vigorously. As I got out of the car, Hari said he would wait to take me to a regular hotel, assuming that I would soon share his sensible opinion that only murder and microskirts awaited me here.

I asked directions from the so-called whores. They were nice young women as it happened—Hari's imagination was running away—and they pointed me to a path that led around to the office. The front door was locked; through the window I could see the dark and unattended lobby. I rang the bell. After several minutes, a small, balding man opened the door. Carlos, the Cuban manager and factotum of the place, turned on a naked lightbulb that threw long, dark shadows across the lobby. Carlos was neatly dressed and spoke precise English, obviously a cultured person.

"Do you want to register?" he asked.

I glanced around, trying to find some basis for making a quick decision and my eyes fell on the hardwood floor, which was spotless and lovingly polished to high luster: this was not how drug dealers or traffickers in stolen body parts would treat their floors. I concluded that the Miami River Inn was a safe place to stay and a legitimate hotel that somebody cared about, even if its business had declined to the vanishing point. I signed the register. As it turned out, I was the only guest that night: at least no rowdy parties would disturb my slumber.

Forgetting the neighborhood, the inn was a charming time capsule, with antique furniture and old-fashioned lamps, rugs, and vases, and a hand-carved wooden banister running up the stairs. There was not an ounce of plastic or aluminum in my room. The plumbing was delightfully antiquated. The sink had an "H" on both faucets: after running both for a long time, it seemed the one where cold should be was slightly warmer. I slept in a gorgeous Empire-style mahogany double bed, a piece of furniture fashioned before Miami—named in 1896—came into existence.

Two mornings later, after a day of rounding up supplies in Miami, I let myself out of the deserted lobby of the Miami River Inn and hobbled and staggered with the overloaded kayak pack two blocks to the Jose Marti Park alongside the Miami River. In a few minutes, the kayak was assembled and ready to launch.

I was surprisingly nervous. I took deep breaths and repeatedly thrust my shoulders back to dispel the butterflies. Apprehension is normal at the beginning of a kayak trip, but it was especially sharp this day because I was to venture for the first time on the vast salty ocean.

A freighter was coming down the Miami River as I lifted the kayak into the water, and it seemed polite, as well as prudent, to allow him to pass before I got underway. The Miami River isn't wide enough for really huge ships; this was a pocket freighter, only 200 feet long, but its walls of steel stretched to the sky from where I sat. After it passed, I followed in its wake, almost keeping up with it. One by one, drawbridges heaved up to make way for the freighter, their bells ringing incessantly like old-fashioned alarm clocks. The bridges stayed raised, as if for me, and it made me feel quite important to hold up hundreds of cars. A sign on the side of one bridge announced a $100 fine for needlessly causing the bridge to be opened. *Catch me if you can,* I thought.

Soon I was in downtown Miami, craning my neck toward towering condos, and waving at pedestrians on the streets above. The horns of traffic echoed off the shipping canal's concrete walls, but there was no congestion where I sat. In a few minutes I reached the mouth of the river, turned south into Biscayne Bay, and found a 15-mph wind at my back, whipping up medium waves and speeding me along.

I had planned to hug the west shore of Biscayne Bay for safety, but seeing how much extra distance that would add, I boldly pushed on a straight course for the bay bridge. After an hour, I was cruising past the multimillion-dollar waterfront homes on Key Biscayne. I stopped to ask for water from a houseboy who was hosing down a 60-foot cabin cruiser. I only wanted to fill my bottle from his hose, but he insisted on bringing out two chilled bottles from the house. Trail magic was working in this part of the world also.

Next I came upon stilt houses, about a dozen homes standing on 20-foot pilings in South Biscayne Bay. They seemed extremely vulnerable standing out in the ocean, but of course the wave-killing shallow water is their unseen protection. Hurricane Wilma's winds had torn off sections of shingles, however. These vacation houses have no utilities, including no sewage disposal. Paddling under them and looking up I could see their sewer pipes simply emptied into the water below (I ducked as necessary).

Leaving the protection of Key Biscayne, I now had nothing but ocean on my left. This was a situation I had worried about for many months. Friends put it to me simply: "What if you get blown out to sea?" For the longest time I had no answer to this question.

A tragic kayak disaster took place in 1993, in Lyme Bay on the southwest coast of England, near Exmouth where Judy and I were living at the time. A group of teenagers had been taken for what was supposed to be a simple kayak trip across Lyme Bay, but a strong inland wind blew them out to sea and capsized them. They were rescued later in the day, but chill water had done its work; four of them died of hypothermia.

In the Keys, it would take a freak wind to drive me away from land and capsize me, but there was a chance of it happening. I could end up captured by the Gulf Stream, drifted at 4.47 miles per hour toward the land of roast beef and Yorkshire pudding. What could I do to mitigate this danger?

I explored several approaches. I devised a system for using my life jacket as a paddle float, so that I could reenter the boat if I happened to capsize. I practiced on the lake and found that it worked in calm water, but I doubted I would have success with it in stormy conditions—which would be when I was likely to need it. I considered bringing a cell phone, but I just couldn't bring myself to compromise my sense of independence. Ditto for using a shortwave radio. I looked into buying a desalinator. On the Internet I saw a unit for $695 that worked on reverse osmosis and weighed only 2.5 pounds. However, making water with it was a slow and tedious process; two minutes of pumping would produce only one ounce of fresh water. It occurred to me that in pumping the thing I could lose more in sweat than I recovered in water. The manufacturer's ad tried to make a joke out of the slow yield: "Hey, when you're on a life raft, you only have time to kill anyway." I decided against the desalinator on the grounds that having this expensive, unused item kicking around in the bottom of my kayak would get on my nerves.

After expending much brainpower on techniques for overcoming a castaway crisis without finding many answers, I reversed my approach and thought about what accepting such a crisis might mean. Of course I would make every effort not to be pushed out to sea, but if worst came to worst, what would happen? I would die, expiring slowly through dehydration, perhaps having some interesting visions on the way out. The idea didn't seem too scary a possibility as I turned it over in my mind. After all, death is not a question of whether but how. I agreed with my friend Lee: compared to watching the ceiling tiles in a nursing home, I'd take a dry tongue and hallucinations about celestial virgins any day.

After leaving the shelter of Key Biscayne and paddling toward that open horizon, it wasn't the philosophy of life and death that concerned me, but the practical question of navigation. I wanted to head for Soldier Key, but in which direction was it? Here the GPS, used only as a toy and a conversation piece on my other kayak trips, became essential. Dialing the coordinates for Soldier Key, I let it tell me which way to head. In fact, it pointed me 90 degrees to the left of what my instinct told me, and into what appeared to be empty Atlantic Ocean. But I trusted it, and sure enough after a while I could make out a tiny sliver of purple on the horizon that eventually proved to be Soldier Key.

As I paddled along, a huge fish leaped far out of the water about a quarter mile away and came crashing down against the water. A half hour later, the same thing happened again, but this fish was closer, only about 200 yards away. The fish was black and white, and I could clearly hear the splash of it hitting the water. Some minutes later I almost jumped out of my skin when one of these monsters came crashing down just 15 feet behind me. That set me to thinking. Were these beasts smart enough not to come crashing down on my kayak? I wanted to trust Mother Nature's creatures to know what they're doing and have a due reverence for human life, but I had just finished reading *Adrift*, a tale of survival by young sailor Steven Callahan, whose boat was destroyed by a whale that surfaced right under it. I put on my life jacket—for an hour or so.

Later, I learned that the fish was an eagle ray. These 200-pound monsters do not jump out of the water while chasing fish to eat, as I had supposed. Rather, they seek the shock of falling back into the water to dislodge parasites in their gills—the equivalent of a dog scratching fleas.

I stopped for the night at Ragged Key, a small, uninhabited island with a spot of sand on which to pitch my tent. In the distance, 17 miles north, Miami had shrunk to a tiny clump of skyscrapers. There was no moon that night, but Venus was so bright it created a shimmering path across the water, just as the moon does.

Eating my supper in the dark—a peanut butter sandwich and beef jerky—I felt a nibbling on my barefoot toe. It was one of the hermit crabs I had seen dragging themselves around the beach when I came ashore. They're a bit creepy, looking like large spiders, but innocuous and innately polite. This one was not biting me, not breaking the skin. He was just inquiring to see if I was dead or not, because if I was, he and his friends would be pleased to eat me. I declined the invitation.

I started the next day realizing that my drinking water supply was getting critically low. I had only 2 quarts left and no place to resupply until the town of Key Largo, 35 miles and at least two days away. How inept of me! I knew I would face having only saltwater all around, but still I made no adequate preparations. I had become too complacent after all my years paddling in freshwater. Now that $695 desalinator didn't seem so silly after all.

A few hours later, guardian angels had figured out a solution to my problem. On Elliott Key, I pulled out of the glaring sun for a few minutes of rest in the deserted campground. A ranger, whose house was on the property, came by. When I explained my plight to him, he pointed out that I was 30 feet away from a faucet of freshwater from the island's desalinization plant. "It runs on biodiesel," he announced proudly. After I'd filled all my bottles, the ranger came by again and gave me half a case of bottled water—seven bottles. So now I was weighed down by fresh water and was pondering throwing some of it away, but I didn't.

The backdrop for my trip was the devastation of Hurricane Wilma, which had passed through the Keys the week before I arrived. In Miami, the streets were piled with broken branches, palm fronds, and ripped plywood. Out along the Keys, the leaves of the trees along many sections of the shore were brown, as if they had suffered a deep freeze. Locals disagreed about the cause. Some blamed the salty spray lashed up by Wilma's winds, others said it was the great velocity of the drops of rainwater hitting the leaves, and others attributed the damage to the high winds that shook the leaf stems. The leaves would regenerate: two weeks later in Key West, I saw the new growth beginning.

Using my detailed chart, I took a route that threaded me through narrow passages into Jones Lagoon, a lake surrounded on all sides by mangroves. I expected to find the water muddy and stinky, but it was crystal clear, because no wave action stirred up the mud. Every twig and leaf on the bottom stood out clearly in the 8-foot depth. Schools of minnows swam about, all darting collectively as one, as if they were wired together and controlled by a single central computer. A thin, tube-like needlefish, about an inch thick and a foot long, hovered motionless for a few moments, then suddenly disappeared as if by magic, its great speed making it quicker than the eye.

As I glided down the channel, I noticed the mangrove trees lining it. I had supposed they live on dry land with their branches overhanging the water. But no, these trees live in the saltwater of the ocean: that's what they drink. A close look at their limbs revealed they have two kinds of branches. One is the normal kind, reaching skyward and producing leaves. The other grows out of a leaning limb's underside and is a straight, budless and leafless stick that heads directly down to the water, becoming a root to anchor the mass of trees into the limestone. These trees have no individual trunks, just masses of branches and roots extending into depths of water to about 6 feet.

When approaching land from the water, I found these mangroves often barred my passage to dry land.

Halfway down the channel, I pulled the boat into the shade under mangrove branches to rest and eat lunch. Mangroves blocked wind and waves, making this spot secluded and perfectly still.

Suddenly I heard a thrashing sound in the water 100 feet away. It was the same sound that coots make back home on Lake Pend Oreille when my approaching kayak scares a flock of them into flight. When they take off, these ducks paddle the water furiously with their feet to gain speed, creating a waterfall sound. But I could see no birds, or anything else on the surface. The sound died away, then broke out again, closer. Something large and energetic was headed my way, but still I could not see the creature. Then the water right next to the kayak churned. Finally, I saw what was making the commotion: a school of minnows darting out of the water en masse, pursued by snappers a foot long. All around the kayak, the furious battle took place, with bigger fish thumping into my kayak's sides, and some of the minnows leaping all the way into the cockpit. Eventually the hullabaloo subsided and all was perfectly quiet again.

The carnage made me wonder why these minnows congregate in large schools, seemingly making themselves inviting targets for bigger fish to feast on. Why don't they lead a solitary life, hanging around mangrove roots alone where they wouldn't be noticed? Maybe the answer lies in their coordination as a school. Individually, they might not be able to spot a predator fish in time. But a school of 1,000 has 2,000 eyes, so when one sees a predator, they all flee together.

My trip through Jones Lagoon led me from the Atlantic Ocean to the Florida Bay/Gulf of Mexico side of the Keys, an innocent-seeming change in route, but one that proved to be an underlying cause of the most dangerous camping experience in my life. On the Atlantic side of the Keys, the wave action in heavy storms keeps mangroves back and leaves occasional spots of sand, like the one I camped on at

Ragged Key. But in the sheltered water west of Key Largo, the mangroves grow solidly all along the shore, providing no campsites.

As the afternoon lengthened, I eyed a small island called Pumpkin Key, as a possible camping site. I paddled around to the leeward side and discovered a mansion and many outbuildings, as well as a yacht moored at the dock complex. Off to one side lay a small beach where I landed the kayak. I walked up to one of the buildings and shouted hello, but no one came. A tractor sat in front of the house, with a pile of leaves half loaded in its wagon.

From one of the smaller houses on the property, a black lab came out, barking furiously. I spoke kindly to it, but that only made it more hysterical. I followed the tactic of not looking in its eyes and walking calmly away, a surefire technique for getting a dog to calm down in the past.

To my astonishment, it bit me on the ankle! With a surge of adrenalin, I turned and screamed at it, raising my arm as if to strike and staring fiercely into its eyes. The dog stared back, still snarling. But it did not bite again. I took a few steps back, keeping eye contact, and it also retreated, keeping eye contact, but not barking any longer, satisfied with making its point. As I collected my wits, I realized that the bite was surprisingly soft; it hadn't broken the skin. It dawned on me that the dog was an extremely adept guard dog, trained to scare people without hurting them, the kind of guard dog a millionaire would have.

Down at the dock, a motorboat arrived from the Key Largo mainland, a quarter mile away. I went to meet the major domo of the estate and another employee. I explained my situation, not mentioning the dog bite in order not to complicate things. He was nice, but said that the whole island was private property, and as caretaker, he couldn't give me permission to camp. He said he thought I might find a place to camp where the bridge to Key Largo crosses a channel known as Steamboat Creek.

I pushed off, my pulse still pounding from the encounter with the dog. The waves were alarmingly high, but I didn't give a damn. I slashed at them with abandon, muttering imprecations against the filthy rich with their vicious self-protectiveness. *If the Count of*

Pumpkin Island came to my front yard and I wasn't at home, I kept thinking, *I wouldn't have a dog there to bite him.* I paddled two straight hours to the Steamboat Creek channel, arriving just as the sun was setting. I had made 20.5 miles on the day and was bushed.

I came to the bridge that carries traffic over the channel to Key Largo. In a parking lot beside the bridge was a patch of dirt where I could set up my tent, the only open space in miles of mangrove swamp. The parking lot was strewn with litter, despite the trash barrels—a warning that the visitors to this spot were not middle-class environmentalists.

A dozen men were fishing from the bridge. Since they had a full view of where I wanted to erect my tent, it seemed best to introduce myself and allay suspicions. They were Cuban manual workers enjoying a busman's holiday, not serious fishermen. They urged me to try my hand at fishing with one of their poles, which I did. After a few minutes, I excused myself and went to set up my tent.

At the campsite a strong smell of rotten eggs, hydrogen sulfide, seeped from the mangrove swamp. The ravenous mosquitoes drove me inside the tent as soon as I set it up. I ate a peanut butter sandwich cramped inside, lying on one elbow.

I hoped the coming of darkness would send the fishermen home, but nightfall didn't interrupt their revels, and they continued yelling to each other about what they were catching and not catching. One excited lad ran to his truck, his feet flopping heavily on the dirt, to grab a flashlight to shine on the fish. Cars kept entering and leaving the parking lot. A heavy rain shower fell, adding to the hot and humid air in the tent. Traffic on the highway did not drop off as I had hoped. Trucks kept roaring back and forth across the bridge. Wearily staring at the ceiling of my tent, I wondered how I would ever get to sleep.

With so much activity in the parking lot, I had long ceased trying to keep track of what was going on. My tent, the reader should be reminded, was a dark olive color, chosen to reduce my visibility as a commando camper. On this occasion, however, that color choice nearly killed me. At around 9 p.m., I was suddenly aware of a crunching sound of tires coming closer and closer! I unzipped the tent and peered out. A pickup truck with a boat trailer was backing toward my tent; the trailer had already passed me. The driver obviously hadn't seen my dark green tent in the darkness, and it was pure luck that he hadn't driven the boat trailer right over my head! Its wheels stood a foot from my nose.

I screamed and the driver stopped. People got out of the truck. They were Cubans, dressed in yellow oilskins—serious shrimp fishermen who had just launched their boat for an evening's work and were now parking the truck and trailer. We sorted it out. I wasn't angry: it really was my fault for having the unnoticeable tent. They pulled the trailer a few feet away and parked their truck, and I crawled back inside the tent to await developments. I wasn't sure which emotion was stronger: fright at nearly being driven over, or elation at being missed.

Soon the fishermen went roaring away down Steamboat Creek. There was no question of allowing myself to go to sleep, since I knew they had to come roaring back at some unknown time later in the night, and then maneuver their boat trailer across the parking lot, perhaps remembering where I was camped, but perhaps not.

An hour passed. Just as a degree of peace and quiet had descended, I heard a heavy, urgent hammering—five or six angry blows—from the far side of the parking lot. While my brain was struggling to imagine what it could possibly be, I heard a massive explosion and crash at the Cubans' truck, just 15 feet from my tent. I froze. It sounded like a shotgun blast shattering glass. After a few seconds, I quietly unzipped my tent flap an inch to take a peek. I couldn't see much, just that the truck door was open and someone was rummaging about the front seat.

A robbery was taking place! As I added up the sounds, it seemed that two men were robbing two vehicles, and that they were armed. They obviously did not know I was there. But what would happen if the robber spotted my tent after he was done? I would be a witness, and don't crooks kill witnesses? I remember thinking: *This is not funny. This is not just an outlandish experience to recount to friends later. This is plain, damn, terrible.*

Whenever I camp in an uncertain, threatening situation, I lay out my defensive resources neatly by my head, and I had done so this evening. I carried a little flashlight, a cartridge of mace about the size of lipstick, and my Leatherman tool with the knife blade opened—not exactly the Arsenal of Democracy, but they help me feel I'm not completely defenseless. I bought the mace two years before for the New York trip, and had never tested it. Even if it worked, and briefly immobilized the crook, what would come next? I couldn't run into the impenetrable mangrove swamp. My only escape route was the highway, and I couldn't outrun anyone with my bad hip. And besides there were two of them, and they were armed. Now I was very, very grateful that I had bought an inconspicuous dark green tent. All I could do was freeze and pray they didn't notice me.

The crook rummaged in the cab of the truck for an interminable time while I stared at the roof of my tent, breathing quiet shallow breaths. Finally, I heard footsteps walk away to the other side of the parking lot. A door slammed and a vehicle drove away, and all was silent.

I let many minutes pass before I felt it was safe to conclude that the crooks had truly departed. I began breathing a little easier, but I knew my troubles weren't over, because the fishermen were due back, and they would be shocked and angry, and could well blame the robbery on me. I thought of packing up and fleeing in my kayak even in the dark, but that would just make me look guilty. I stayed put.

An hour later they returned. I stepped out of my tent to meet them and to explain what I had heard. It's a good thing I speak Spanish because they spoke nothing else. They—a young man, and his wife and father—had escaped on their boat from Cuba just 3 years earlier. They struck me as salt of the earth, working hard to make good.

They seemed to understand right away that I couldn't have been the perpetrator and were quite calm about it. I told them I didn't see anything to identify the crooks. They did a lot of investigating, walking up and down the parking lot, looking in all the trash cans. Finally the young man came back to me.

"I'm new in this country so I don't understand how financial bodies work. Perhaps you could tell me: Can checks that aren't signed be used?"

I told him no. That was all the crook had taken from the truck: his checkbook! Their explorations convinced them that one crook had parked at the other side of the lot when they arrived, and he used a big chunk of coral, not a shotgun, to smash the window. So the robbery had been carried out by a lone jerk dopehead—which made more sense than the theory of a deliberate attack by two robbers. He said they had insurance for the truck window. I urged him to report it to the police, but he said it wouldn't do any good. I wondered what his immigration status was.

After an hour of pondering the robbery, the fishermen went back up the channel in their boat to catch more shrimp, returned later, and finally drove off. Now the parking lot was completely quiet. I had no idea what time it was, and didn't see any point in digging out the GPS to find out because I knew I was a prisoner until daylight.

I had no intention of sleeping. I had suffered two very dangerous crises that night, the truck almost running over me and the robbery, and I was feeling deeply superstitious. I thought, *A third danger is yet to come!* I lay with my eyes wide open staring at the roof of my tent, ears cocked for the slightest sound. One worry I had had from the beginning was crocodiles. As I said, the parking lot was virtually a garbage dump, and I was sure fishermen had been regularly leaving fish guts all around. Bears will come to camp garbage; wouldn't crocodiles of the mangrove swamp come to feast on the garbage here? I heard a bloodcurdling howling off in the mangroves, but it was actually too scary to be scary. It sounded like an overblown jungle sound effect in a B movie. Probably a bird; a crocodile would come silently.

As I lay in this posture of dread, a thought flashed into my mind: *I already had my third danger today!* The dog bite! And—with the beautiful symmetry that nature sometimes contrives, outdoing art—that event was also a case of lucky bad luck. In each of the three episodes, I had come within inches of a nasty accident (within millimeters, in the case of the dog's teeth), and emerged unscathed. Now my superstition about threes gave me confidence. My breathing relaxed. I now felt that the forces of the cosmos were aligned in my favor and the cycle of misfortunes was complete.

And it was. Though I stayed alert, nothing molested me further, and with the first hint of gray dawn I packed my gear, shoved off, and paddled up Steamboat Creek, not pausing to eat even a nut until I was well out of sight of the bridge.

The frights of the previous night wore off as I made my way along the northwest side of Key Largo. I had to cross several wide bays and sounds, which left me rather far from land in uncomfortably high seas most of the time. The wind remained at my back, coming from the northeast. I soon learned that any shoaling of the bottom, going from 15 feet to, say, 6 or 8 feet deep, caused the waves to rear up, producing breaking waves that could dump water into the kayak. But such overspill was only a cupful or two when it happened.

Though the breeze was moderately strong—around 15 mph—this Florida wind was much more consistent than winds on the inland lakes and rivers I had traveled before. On the Columbia, the Hudson, and Lake Champlain, wind was gusty and irregular, easily doubling in speed in a few minutes. This made any wind a cause for anxiety, since I always feared that it could easily get much worse in a few moments. Along the Keys, wind speed stays about the same all day long, so I came to trust it like a friend.

On this day, I had only one encounter with marine life. In the middle of the 5-mile crossing of Barnes Sound I saw a black fin about 300 yards ahead, moving slowly back and forth across my course like a sentry guarding a gate. *What did this shark want?* I wondered. Was it jealously patrolling its territory or hunting for food? Then the fin disappeared below the surface. I put on my life jacket and continued paddling. What else could I do? A few minutes later, crossing the spot where I'd seen the fin patrolling, I heard a loud breathing sound just behind me, and turned my head just in time to see the water close over a porpoise 9 feet long. I felt much better knowing it was not a shark, although I suppose either beast could turn me and my kayak into egg foo yong if it was so minded.

In the late afternoon, I reached Popp's Motel, right on the water, having logged a very creditable 19.9 miles on no sleep whatsoever. I had accomplished 57 miles from Miami and decided to treat myself to a two-night stay.

On my free day, a helpful man I met in the café that morning drove me to a Winn-Dixie supermarket for food. I returned on the bus, free of charge—fares having been suspended as a hurricane relief measure.

In the afternoon, I helped Linda Popp with the cleanup of her motel grounds after the devastation of Hurricane Wilma. I made it my project to clean up piles of seaweed that the wind had driven onto the boat ramp. Using a trash barrel and a golf cart, I trucked the whole mess up alongside US Highway 1 to a pile of debris that was already as big as a house. It took me 30 trips to do the job. My pile was matched by an endless row of other piles of organic debris, and other piles of ruined furniture and appliances.

The disorder left by the hurricane was depressing for locals. For the most part, homes and businesses were intact, but there was a great deal of less dramatic damage—torn shingles, ruined gardens, broken tree limbs, flooded appliances—that made people feel that all comfort had gone out of their lives. On one of the trips from the boat ramp to the highway, Linda boarded the golf cart and, being a high-spirited Idaho visitor, I took her on wild detour across the lawn, swerving around palms and plowing through low-hanging limbs. She giggled, then said, "You know, that's the first time I've laughed since Wilma."

While I was cleaning the boat ramp, a motel customer came down to chat. He was an insurance adjuster specializing in floral nurseries, and reported that the Miami area was so mobbed by people in his trade that this was the nearest vacant motel he could find. *Well,* I thought, *I know one hotel, or inn, in the Miami area that's not full of insurance adjusters.*

My next big stop was Marathon, a key with quite a substantial town—including an airport. Here I girded my loins for the crossing at Seven Mile Bridge. As the name of the bridge implies, seven miles of open water separate Marathon Key from Little Duck Key. Bridging this stretch was the greatest engineering challenge in the construction of the railway that first connected the Keys and Key West to the mainland. Built by hotel magnate Henry Flagler and completed in 1912, the railroad was something of a wonder of the world at the time and a godsend for the people of Key West. It was really philanthropy disguised as a business, for the railroad couldn't even cover its operating expenses, let alone repay the $25 million investment to build it. When the railroad was wrecked by the hurricane of 1935, the line was sold to the state for a pittance, and a highway was constructed on the bridges and embankments where the tracks had been.

I'd been worried for months about crossing so much open water, since it presented the danger of being blown out to sea or drifted out by the current. I was made aware of the strength of the current on the previous day when I made the 2-mile crossing at Long Key Viaduct. I had intended to paddle on the Gulf of Mexico side of the viaduct, but found the current too strong to let me maintain that position. It sucked me under the bridge and out into the Atlantic by about a half mile as I made the crossing. This current, by the way, was a combination of the tidal current coming from the Gulf of Mexico and the beginning of the Gulf Stream, powered by the Mississippi River. Under the Long Key Viaduct the current moved at about 4 mph, and lessened as the water broadened below the bridge.

With the lesson of the Long Key Viaduct in mind, I decided to tackle the Seven Mile Bridge by crossing from the "upstream" side, that is, the Gulf of Mexico, and hold as much upstream distance as possible, to cushion against the current that wanted to drag me into the Atlantic. I had hardly left Marathon behind when this strategy proved unworkable. I came upon a shoal area too shallow to cross, so I had to drop down into the Atlantic, letting the current drag me between the pillars of the bridge. Being on the wrong side of the bridge at the outset made me nervous, and I paddled with great seriousness, splitting my course between compensating for the drift of the current and crossing to the other side. The ocean surface was curiously inconsistent. In some spots, the water was almost calm while in other places the waves were steep, and coming from different directions at once. For the first time in the trip, I rigged my spray skirt to ward off the splash of the waves.

After an hour of steady paddling, I paused for a few seconds to suck on a little tube of glucose "goo" for an energy boost. I was nearly a half mile out to sea and the bridge looked far away. I paddled harder. After another hour, I was even further out in the Atlantic, but I was closing in on the other side and saw I would be able to make up the distance back to the mainland after completing the crossing.

As it happened, my open-water crossing was cut to only 5 miles because I made use of a stopping point, Molasses Key, a tiny island that lies a half mile south of the bridge. When I arrived on this key, I found three men in tennis sneakers walking around in the shallows, collecting something from the rocks. They explained that they were wholesale aquarium suppliers gathering little crabs they called blue legs, which are used to clean saltwater aquariums. They ship them all over the United States. At first I felt sorry for the crabs, but after the men told me about their grisly methods of acquiring real estate, they lost my sympathy. The blue legs commandeer one-inch clamshells by killing and eating the shells' rightful owners. It seemed fitting punishment for this barbaric behavior that they should be sent off to clean aquariums in Akron and Newark for the rest of their lives.

I had purchased a bird identification book in Marathon, and took pleasure in trying to identify some of the winged creatures I was seeing. I learned to recognize three kinds of egrets—great, snowy, and cattle—as well as the great blue heron, and the white ibis with its long, curved beak. My favorite birds were the brown pelicans. Watching them fish is endlessly fascinating. They swoop down and skim just inches above the water, wings absolutely motionless, holding that position for hundreds of yards, like a Pan Am Clipper coming in for a water landing. If one spots a school of fish, he doesn't dive directly into the water. Instead, he makes a steep turning climb to about 20 feet and then from that altitude plunges, smashing headfirst into the water with a crash that would break the neck of any lesser creature.

As I learned by paddling across the areas where they were fishing, they eat fish less than 3 inches long. I doubt they aim at a specific minnow when they dive. I think they plunge into the middle of a school, and maybe catch several at once. After a successful dive, they spend a few moments on the water making big gulping motions, transferring the fish from their bills to their stomachs. When they miss, they take wing immediately. Using this behavior as a clue, it appeared they were catching fish nine times out of ten tries—a success rate any human fishermen would envy.

Once, I saw white pelicans, only five of them, flying high in a perfect "V." Perhaps they were completing their fall migration from the lakes of Manitoba in Canada.

The evening after clearing the Seven Mile Bridge I camped on the beach at Bahia Honda Key. This is the premier beach in the Keys, and in normal times you need reservations a year in advance to camp there. However, because of hurricane damage and debris, the campground was officially closed—as were all other campgrounds and beaches in the Keys. I camped at the extreme north end, far away from the park entrance, and never saw a soul. I had complete privacy for my yoga practice, and to take my first—and last—swim in the ocean.

Travel posters had given me a vision of swimming every day in warm, aquatinted, crystal tropical waters, perhaps surrounded by bikini-clad maidens from the same travel posters. Alas, everything about this fantasy proved bogus. The seawater throughout the Keys was cloudy, having been stirred up by the hurricane. In most places I couldn't see more than 4 or 5 feet down; the water at Bahia Honda looked like piña colada mix. There was no basking in warmth: the water was downright chilly, and I was soon shivering in the evening breeze. To add to the disagreeable beach experience, the sea bottom shelved very slowly. To reach a good swimming depth, I would have had to walk out from shore for a quarter mile over rough limestone pebbles. I gave myself a quick splash and a rinse, then dog-paddled for a few feet with shortened strokes, trying not to scrape my knuckles on the stony bottom, and crossed swimming off my list of activities.

The colorful red and orange sky didn't last long, evidence that in the tropics it gets dark quickly after sunset. I think it's because the sun, following a high arc, dives straight down below the horizon. Further north, the sun angles down, and remains close to the horizon longer after it sets.

After the daylight disappeared, I watched a bright, orange Mars, unusually close to the Earth at the time, chase a nearly full moon up the eastern sky.

A new Florida Keys begins after the Seven Mile Bridge. The upper Keys are narrow islands, generally less than a quarter mile wide, with condos, motels, and restaurants crowded alongside the Overseas Highway. South of the Seven Mile Bridge, the land opens out, with islands several miles wide and mostly uninhabited, empty acres of palmetto and stubby slash pine. One aim of my visit to Big Pine Key was to see a key deer, the diminutive native species that make Big Pine Key their principal stamping ground.

I had been keen to set my eyes on these deer for years, to resolve the puzzle of the miniature deer I encountered that night on the Columbia River trip. My theory was that the deer I saw was a miniature that had escaped from a nearby ranch. A far-fetched idea, I grant you, but preferable to accepting the hypothesis that I dreamed the whole thing up. When I heard about the tiny key deer, I thought it possible that this was the creature I had seen, and I wanted to see one to confirm this theory.

Making my way toward Big Pine Key, I ran aground for the first and only time on the trip. I tried to make it through a shallow channel, but after a half mile it shoaled to 3 inches and my paddle blades were striking coral on every stroke. I returned down the channel to ask directions at a house alongside the water. There I met George and Karen, tropical island pioneers.

They welcomed me as if I were a neighbor—the kayaker magic of instant familiarity was at work again—and told me all about their unusual lifestyle. They live on Cook Island, a spit of land too small to be dignified as a "key," and their only link to civilization—Little Torch Key six miles away—is a motorboat. Karen makes and paints clay bird figures that are sold in a gift shop in North Carolina; rows of them were laid out in the sun to dry.

They have a cistern to collect rainwater, which George drinks; Karen prefers bottled water from the supermarket. For electricity, they have solar panels and a wind generator (recently blown down by Hurricane Wilma). They also had a septic system with a drain field. This "drain field" involved Styrofoam, and the pipes had been floated out of the ground by the flooding from the hurricane. George was in the middle of trying to rebury them. I put "drain field" in quotes, because on this island, and in the Keys in general, there's very little true soil. The ground is mostly solid limestone, so sewage from most systems drains pretty much into the ocean. The current building code for new construction bans drain fields and requires a sealed, anaerobic septic system—which is very expensive.

George and Karen built their house two decades ago, without any permits or regulation. Lately, much to George's annoyance, government officials have been coming around imposing requirements. Recently, he had to raise his house 3 feet, above a possible storm surge. Without that, he said, his house would have been flooded by Wilma.

"So is this a case where government regulation was helpful?" I asked.

George did a long double take as he digested such an alien concept. Finally he said, "In this case, yes."

While we were chatting, we heard a clinking noise from beside the house. It was a key deer! It was rattling the empty water bowl Karen had put out for it. Even though it is against the law, many residents feed and water the deer: Bambi is just too adorable to be denied. I was surprised to see one out on this little island but George said the deer swim from island to island—quite an accomplishment given the tiny feet they have for paddling.

So, was this the deer I saw on the Columbia? I'm afraid I have to answer that it was not. The key deer are not all that small. They stand about 3 feet high, and should probably be thought of as just smallish ordinary whitetail deer. The deer I saw, or thought I saw, on the Columbia was about 2 feet high: a true miniature deer. So where does this leave me? Puzzled for the rest of my life, I guess, and forced to concede that sometimes there are things that just can't be explained.

I stayed at Parmer's Resort on Little Torch Key, which lies next to Big Pine Key. Parmer's is an unpretentious motel complex with a 1960s feel. The rooms have no phones: the motel information sheet proudly announces the existence of a "courtesy phone" in the laundry room, that is, one pay phone for 70 guests. Cell phones have bypassed this absurdity today, but I can't imagine how the residents managed 20 years ago.

The morning after checking in to Parmer's, I hiked along the Overseas Highway to Big Pine Key where I rented a bicycle to explore this the largest of the lower Keys. Miles from anywhere, I came across the remarkable little No Name Pub. Inside, it feels like a tavern in an Idaho mining town, with a low ceiling and small windows, cozy and tight. However, as soon as my eyes adjusted to the dim light, I saw that the bar was unlike any I've ever seen or heard of. The walls and ceiling were papered with dollar bills, every square inch covered. I watched a customer add to the treasure, writing her name on a dollar bill and tacking one end of it to the wall with the staple gun the management provides.

My social scientist brain was thoroughly befuddled by the scene. In the first place, why would visitors freely part with their dollar bills? Surely this act does not buy immortality or any kind of fame. Were they seeking some kind of thrill in throwing money away? And how do customers manage to behave normally in this money cocoon, sipping beer and nibbling French fries as if nothing unusual were afoot? I could only stand with my mouth agape.

The biggest puzzle is what keeps the money there, safely fluttering in the breeze of the air conditioner week after week? There's not even a sign saying, "Please don't pick the money." What happened to that great engine of human mischief, greed? Why doesn't this spread of freely fluttering currency drive emotionally unstable customers berserk, to lunge at the money with panting breath? Why don't more calculating customers surreptitiously filch one or two bills at a time when the bartender isn't looking, so that the currency gradually disappears, leaving bare walls in the end?

Somebody needs to do a sociological study of the No Name Pub, and find out what hormone or enzyme is at work keeping people from grabbing money when it's lying right in front of them. And then distribute this substance to legislatures and corporate boardrooms around the country.

My three-day visit to Big Pine introduced me to the pressures behind the crushing real estate squeeze in the Keys. It's an attractive place for snowbirds, being warm all the time (as mainland Florida is not), but the demand for new housing is choked off by many restrictions on new construction. The area has been declared critical wildlife habitat by the feds; many locals also resist new development. In Big Pine, the local government was discussing an ordinance to prohibit the building of any kind of chain—McDonalds, Pizza Hut, and so on. There's practically a freeze on building permits, with only 200 a year for the entire Keys, which makes for something like a 10-year delay between applying for a building permit and getting one. Real estate prices are sky-high. A simple 1,500-square-foot home, not on the water, costs $750,000. Empty lots are also expensive—around $150,000—even though, given the dearth of building permits, you can't build on them, and they don't have water or sewer.

As a tourist destination, the Keys seem to attract a laid-back clientele, visitors for whom luxury, comfort, and idleness are paramount. The Keys are not a playground for the energetic. They offer no mountains for hikers and mountain bikers, and no cliffs for rock climbers. There isn't even surf for surfers, because the big swells are broken at the edge of the reef 5 miles from land. I didn't see any serious kayakers on my 2-week journey, just tourists put on kayaks for brief, chaperoned visits to the reef. Fishermen there are aplenty, but most of them fish from luxury cabin cruisers, seated in padded fishing chairs. I never saw anybody fishing from a human-powered craft like a row-boat. The Keys are a place for taking life easy—and for wallowing in wealth. One massive cabin cruiser was christened "Poverty Sucks," its owner seemingly saying he was a shallow materialist and proud of it.

Picture postcards for sale in drug stores depict dangerously obese people on a sunny beach along with the caption, "Welcome to Florida." I struggled to grasp the subtext. Were they saying, "If you are overweight, Florida is the place for you," or, "Come to Florida and we'll help you put on the pounds?"

I struck up a conversation with a man and his wife in a restaurant. As an unthreatening traveling stranger, I was taken into their confidence as they explained the pattern of their lives. They come to the Keys twice a year, like clockwork, in April and November for 2-week stays. They have breakfast on the balcony, lunch on the balcony, and dine out in the evening. After being a chef for many years, he now works for a restaurant supply company in Ohio.

"When I took the job," he said, "I told them I had three things that were important to me in life. One was my grandchildren, one was going to the Florida Keys for 2 weeks in the fall and 2 weeks in the spring, and the third was Beefeater gin."

His wife turned to me, "You notice, he left me out of it."

He heard her remark and thought about it for a second, but he did not amend his statement.

On the next day, Saturday, I spotted a stuffed key deer on display at a wildlife interpretive center in a shopping mall, and went inside to get a closer look. (The animal was the same medium size as the one I had seen on Cook Island.) I couldn't resist teasing the volunteer at the desk: "Why did you shoot this poor, defenseless deer just to stuff it?"

It flustered her into earnest defensiveness. Of course it hadn't been shot, she said, it was an automobile fatality—about 80 key deer are killed by cars every year. I wanted a photo of it and needed a human being in the picture to provide a sense of scale, so I asked her if she would crouch down and put her arm around the deer's neck. She did, and I was just about to snap this charming scene when she abruptly stood up.

"I can't do this!" she said.

"Why ever not?"

"Because you're not supposed to pet key deer, or approach them in any way. If this picture got out in the newspaper, people might think I was petting a live deer."

So all I got was a picture of a distraught woman walking away from a key deer.

That afternoon, my bicycle wanderings took me to a Lutheran church where I found some volunteers at work. It was called Lord of the Sea Lutheran, and unfortunately the Lord of the sea had just paid them a very personal and challenging visit. The storm surge from Wilma flooded 3 feet deep into the sanctuary, trashing the electronic organ, soaking chairs and pews, and ruining hymnbooks and Bibles. Husband and wife Ben and Maggie, along with their friend Ruth, had been working for days on the cleanup. "You have no idea how dirty that water was," said Maggie. "It picks up all the filth and pollution from the land as it advances." I joined Ben in wiping off rust and silt from a set of folding chairs.

I asked him about the new church building that stood 30 feet away, a wonderful new building raised 10 feet in the air on sturdy concrete pilings. Everything in it would have escaped water damage from Wilma. But nothing was in it! Why was it unoccupied? Ben was furious as he explained the problem they had been having with the county government. Though the building had been completed for over a year, they still couldn't get an occupancy permit because one obscure environmental requirement was unfilled. They were required to plant additional pine trees to make up for the trees lost by the construction—this on an island of 70 square miles of scrub pines. This nit-picking regulation cost them the organ and the heartbreaking mess of the church. Recalling George and Karen, apparently the lesson is that regulation giveth and regulation taketh away.

The next morning, Sunday, I stopped at the Methodist church and bumped into one of the choir members getting ready for rehearsal. I mentioned that I sang in my choir at home, and she invited me to sing with them. In the position of chorister, I donned a robe made of heavy blue velvet, 5 pounds of billowing authority that transformed me into a Nordic king. These robes, used nationwide in the Methodist church, were designed for choristers in frigid New England; in a land of palmetto swamps and 100-percent humidity only the church's powerful air conditioning saved us from heat prostration.

Afterward, I was hiking back to Parmer's along the Overseas Highway when a car stopped to give me a lift. It was Ben and Maggie from the Lutheran church, even more surprised at the coincidence of our meeting than I was.

"I was just talking about you in our church service a few minutes ago," Ben said.

"My goodness, what about?"

"I got up in front of the congregation and told them that yesterday we had an example of how the Lord works in mysterious ways. Here I was with all these chairs to clean, and just about ready to give up and go home. And just that minute walks in out of nowhere a fellow from Idaho, of all places, who traveled all the way from Miami by kayak, if you can believe that, and he helps me clean the chairs and we got every last one of them done. Not in a million years could I have imagined that. I tell you, the Lord works in mysterious ways!"

I didn't know what to make of that, except that if a scruffy tourist killing time on Big Pine is an agent of the Divine, then anybody can be.

Sunday afternoon I began my final push for Key West, less than 30 miles away. The wind had picked up in recent days, and soon after setting out I was battling high waves that angled across my route. In these conditions, the rudder is necessary to maintain course. I was struggling along in open water a mile off Sugarloaf

Key when suddenly my rudder pedals went limp and the boat slewed sideways across the waves. I craned my neck around to see what was going on at the stern. The rudder was gone! Looking more closely, I saw the rudder assembly flopping uselessly underwater, dangling by the control cables. The whole mechanism had popped off the rudderpost.

The rudder mounts on a slender metal shaft, and this shaft is held in place by a tiny stainless steel retaining clip about the size of a paper clip. I'd never had trouble with that clip before, but all my experience was in freshwater. Perhaps the saltwater corroded the clip away, allowing the rudder assembly to pop out of the rudderpost when hit by a big wave.

It took me the better part of an hour to make it to shore, using more paddling energy to keep the boat pointed in the right direction than in making distance. The struggle proved that a working rudder was imperative if I was ever to make it to Key West. There wasn't a shore to land on, just a mass of mangrove trees extending out into the water. I had to hold onto branches and walk on mangrove roots to clamber around to access the rudder assembly. The shoreline was infested with no-see-ums, tiny biting flies about the size of a pinhead that drove me crazy as I grappled with the problem.

The shaft that holds the rudder, a steel rod 5 inches long and 3/16 inch in diameter, had gone to Davey Jones' Locker. My first thought was that I would have to improvise a substitute. I thought of carving a slender shaft out of dense wood, using the knife of my Leatherman, but I doubted that a wooden shaft that thin would be strong enough to take the stress.

Trying to be systematic, I asked, *Payne, what metal items do you have in your equipment? Think!* In the circumstances, the question was ridiculous. To save weight, I'd reduced my baggage to bare essentials, even cutting off the handle of my toothbrush. There wasn't a stray aluminum pull tab in the boat. And even assuming that I had any iron among my minimal possessions, what were the chances that it would be a 3/16-inch steel rod?

Fortunately, I didn't stop to realize that the question was absurd. I took it seriously and began an inventory. As I mentally unpacked my belongings, I realized that I did have some metal, in the form of the little steel pegs that anchor my tent! I dug them out, and, amazingly, they were exactly 3/16 inch in diameter, and one of them served perfectly to mount the rudder! Later, when I made it to a beach to camp, I wrapped a clump of dental floss on the bottom of the shaft to serve as a nut to keep the shaft from being popped out by a big wave. It worked fine all the way to Key West.

If you don't think guardian angels were working overtime on the rudder challenge, consider the sequel. The following spring, I unpacked the kayak and looked around my shop for a rod or bolt that would serve as a rudder shaft. I had several brass rods but all were either too thin or too thick. I had hundreds of bolts and nails but they were too short. So I went to Merwin's hardware store and bought a long bolt that I thought would do the trick. The first time out it bent, rendering the rudder inoperable. (Guess what would have happened to a whittled wooden rudder shaft!) In the end, I had to buy a piece of cold-rolled 3/16-inch rod from a steel supply company to make a serviceable rudder shaft.

In other words, if I had been the compulsive type of guy who prepares for every possible danger and malfunction and had taken my entire shop plus the local hardware store along with me on the kayak trip "just in case," I still would have been out of luck when the rudder failed!

The next day, with the rudder repaired and a night's rest, I paddled the last 16 miles to Key West nearly all in one sitting, not because I favored a stinging bottom but because I couldn't find any good place to stop without going out of my way. The waves were the highest I had seen on the whole trip, and kept increasing as I approached the city, frequently breaking into white water and drenching me. A Jet Ski party of young tourists came whizzing by: one girl was thrown off her machine by a big wave and the rest of the group came back to rescue her. The guide came over and asked me if I needed help. I couldn't decide whether to feel appreciative or insulted.

My destination was South Beach, which was within walking distance of the Abaco Guest House, where I had made a reservation. I had to maneuver out to sea a number of times to clear docks and jetties, which meant going against and sideways to the waves, getting many lapfuls of seawater in the process. At several points, I was tempted to pull ashore and flag a taxi for the rest of the trip, but I persevered all the way to South Beach.

At the beach I faced a one-foot surf—well, perhaps it was only 8 inches, but still, it let me share the aura of legendary surf-busting sea kayakers like Chris Duff and Paul Caffyn. The main challenge in coming ashore was to avoid hitting toddlers playing in the waves on the crowded beach. Finally, I skidded onto the sand with gallons of water in the bottom of my boat, thoroughly drenched and somewhat shaken. I persuaded a bikini-clad maiden to take my picture (Florida does have these after all).

The swimmers on the beach were impressed when I told them I had traveled from Miami in my little boat. I was pleased that I had accomplished every inch of the 154-mile trip under my own steam. I had spent 10 days on the water and I was nearly a week ahead of schedule, thanks to the generally following wind.

I found Key West a worthy destination, a town with real character, full of older houses with balconies and balustrades, and unusual tropical trees. It's the second oldest city in Florida (after St. Augustine), and was apparently the wealthiest city in the entire nation in the 1800s, when it thrived on collecting cargo from ships that ran aground on the reef. By the early 20th century, ships had adopted steam power and better navigational methods, and the shipwreck business—and Key West—declined. The hurricane of 1935 wrecked the railroad and cut off communication with the mainland for three years, leaving the city still more depressed, perhaps the poorest in the entire nation.

A new era dawned in 1938 when the Overseas Highway was completed. It connected the town to legions of Americans who were curious, bored, or just chilly, and placed Key West in the eye of a storm of tourism ever since.

Though commercially successful, the city has retained a cosmo-politan and zany feel, with roosters freely roaming the streets. It's a myth, by the way, that they announce the dawn. Key West roosters have no conception of time. You will hear the first crowing at about one in the morning, and they continue screeching until about noon.

I turned my six-day stay into a working vacation, writing in the mornings, and visiting museums and places of interest in the after-noons. I also attended yoga sessions at a local studio, and joined one of the standard reef cruises that puts customers on kayaks (not exactly a new thrill for one customer, but I didn't mention why).

Key West attracts honeymooners and second honeymooners, so one sees lots of couples holding hands, and almost no children. Two giant cruise ships arrived while I was there, disgorging thousands of resolute shoppers, but the town seemed to absorb them without strain. Tourists buzz around town on motor scooters, and one after-noon I did too. T-shirts are a major industry. Most of these souvenirs say, simply, "Key West," but other slogans appear, some veering on the gross, some clever. On the back of one T, I read, "If you can read this, the bitch fell off"—obviously to be worn by a motorcyclist. Another said in big, bold letters, "Nobody knows I'm a lesbian." Another: "Please tell your boobs to stop staring at my eyeballs."

Key West celebrates writer Ernest Hemingway, who was a local resident for eight years back in the 1930s, fighting and drinking his way to literary distinction at Sloppy Joe's Bar, now a major tour-ist attraction. I took a tour of his mansion, a handsome structure on spacious grounds, to see how he lived and worked. One of the first things that caught my eye were Hemingway's collection of Spanish birthing chairs—low, three-legged wooden stools with nar-row wooden backs and handles to hold on to. Hemingway liked to sit in them, said the guide, because they afforded some relief for his painful back.

Hemingway's writing studio was on the second floor of a nearby carriage house and he had a skywalk built to connect his bedroom to the studio so he could get there as fast as possible in the morning to write. The guide claimed that he worked hard at his writing, but I wondered. During the trip I read his *To Have and Have Not*, which is set in Key West, and found it to be a pointless tale characterized by senseless violence and jaded sex. The guide also mentioned that Hemingway was well known for being a heavy drinker, which led me to speculate that perhaps the alcohol content of his blood, more so than the skyway to his studio, shaped this literary product.

After attending a local Methodist church service on Sunday, I took the Greyhound bus back to Miami, passing again at warp speed the landscape that had taken me nearly two weeks to traverse in the kayak. We flashed past Little Torch and Big Pine keys and then soared up onto the Seven Mile Bridge where I eagerly scanned the broad waters for kayakers, but saw none. As we motored along Key Largo, I was surprised to see that the towering piles of hurricane debris alongside the highway, including the one I contributed to in front of Popp's Motel, had all been removed. I wondered where all the mess went to.

In just a few hours I was back in Miami, and took a taxi to . . . the Miami River Inn!

Yes, I know, it looks like codependency, but it was the devil I knew, and besides the funky place has charm. I did have to put up with some miscues, however. To start with, my room key didn't work in the lock, and Carlos couldn't find any that did. So after opening my door with his passkey, we just decided I wouldn't lock it for the two days I was there.

To avoid carrying the kayak pack up the stairs, with some misgiving I allowed Carlos to lock it in a side room on the first floor. When I came down the morning of my flight, the front desk was empty and my shouts brought no one. Out on the porch, a young woman with a baby had been waiting for an hour to show her child to grandparents staying in one of the rooms. I brought her inside and we scoured the materials behind the front desk until we deduced the room number of the grandparents. (I refused her offer of a tip.) Once she was taken care of, I started taking keys off the rack behind the counter and trying each one on the room that held my kayak. None worked. I was starting to panic that I would miss my flight when Carlos appeared at last, carrying bananas and muffins for the continental breakfast.

In conclusion, if you want a place to stay in Miami that both *has* character and *builds* character, there's no better place than the Miami River Inn.

On the plane ride home, seated in a window seat, I spotted an irresistible sight as we flew over the Mississippi River. The river wound back and forth in lazy loops, and I spied long strips of brown on the inside of every curve. These brown strips wouldn't have had any meaning to anyone else on the flight, but for me they were stupendous, and I watched them intensely for as long as they remained in view. They were sandbars, exposed at the lower river level in the fall.

In all my kayak journeys, the one great, persistent worry has been finding a decent camping spot at the end of each day. This is a universal problem for all who travel rough. Robert Louis Stevenson noted it in his 1878 memoir on hiking in France, *Travels with a Donkey in the Cevennes:* "There is nothing more harassing to an easy mind," he said, "than the necessity of reaching shelter by dusk."

On a kayak trip, this mental "harassing" begins in the early afternoon as the brain mulls all the scenarios and strategies involved in devising a safe, private, level, legal, and tranquil place to camp, a place unthreatened by suspicious landowners, police, security guards, rednecks, paper mills, superhighways, brambles, poison ivy, poisonwood, dogs, bears, tarantulas, crocodiles, and clandestine lovers.

It was obvious that these sandbars would be the perfect kayaking camping spot, free from all above-named hazards. They are perfectly private: no one would know, or care, that you were out there. No one could reach you by land. The one possible bother might be mosquitoes, but in October, which would be the best time to kayak down the Mississippi, they should be nearly all gone. Best of all, the sandbars are a continuous chain, giving the kayaker complete flexibility. There would be no need to stop early in case no other campsite could be found, and no being forced to paddle in the dark, wondering where you will rest your weary head. If I decided to stop at 3:37 p.m., I would have a perfect campsite, guaranteed, by 3:37:10.

Now you understand why the veteran of Steamboat Creek and countless other camping agonies had his eyes glued to the window. From 37,000 feet, with perfectly reckless enthusiasm, I believed I was seeing the kayaker's camping paradise. To enjoy it, all I had to do was paddle down the Mississippi River.

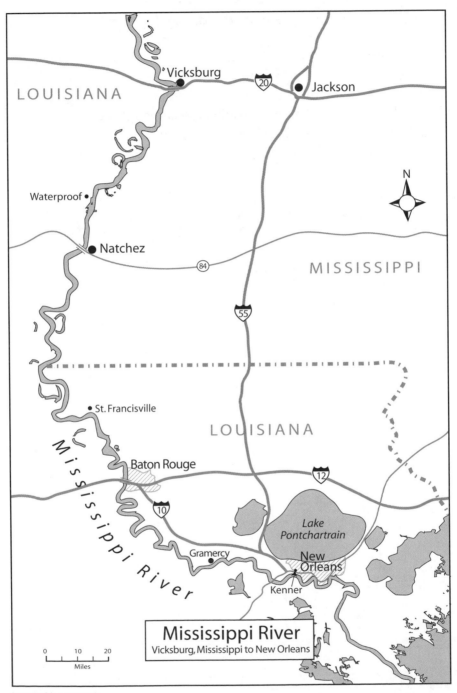

Mississippi River
Vicksburg, Mississippi to New Orleans

0   10   20
Miles

River width not to scale

7

A Scary Piece of Cake

THE MISSISSIPPI RIVER
Vicksburg, Mississippi to New Orleans, Louisiana (October 2006)

"YOU GOIN' OUT ON THAT THING?"

The fisherman had watched me assemble my kayak at the launching spot on Vicksburg's Yazoo River, the big black pack transformed, like a molting caterpillar, into a faded red canvas kayak 12 feet long. The curious observer could now grasp that it was a vessel meant to carry a human passenger over the waters.

"Sure," I replied. "I'm going to New Orleans."

"You're a bold one," said the fisherman. His tone was grim.

As soon as I was well into the Yazoo, muddy and swollen because of recent heavy rains, I used my GPS to clock the current. I noted with satisfaction that it was slightly less than 6 mph—nowhere near the 12 mph that people in town, speaking with energy and alarm, warned me it would be.

A black man stood on a tied-up barge, watching me as my kayak shot out of the Yazoo into the Mississippi. His greeting also struck a serious note.

"You got more nerve than I do," he yelled.

"I'm going to New Orleans!" I shouted back.

"You be careful," he said. "I seen trees in that river go under and never come back up."

On my earlier trips, such cautions would have plunged me into panic, because at the start of those journeys my brain was overflowing with things to worry about. This time, I basked in self-assurance. As I figured it, the Mississippi was a benign body of water: no rapids, no great width to permit large waves, no grizzly bears or other menacing creatures patrolling its banks. Its shores afforded clean and level sandbars for safe and private camping, and its current would scoot me down to New Orleans without requiring much effort on my part.

Furthermore, I was now a seasoned kayaker, with years of experience under my belt, unlikely to be frightened by difficult conditions. As I made my way down the Yazoo, the water swirled about, yanking me off course and spinning me around, creating a feeling of being out of control. That sensation used to alarm me, but it was old hat now. I knew the river was only playing with me.

So when locals gravely commented on my nerve and boldness, and told me of racing 12-mph currents, I laughed it off as the uninformed twitter of nervous Nellies. As one sign of my nonchalance, I left my camera and tape recorder lying open to the elements when I entered the Mississippi from the Yazoo. At the beginning of other trips, these items were tightly sealed in Ziploc bags in anticipation of disaster.

In fact, in the first days of the trip my biggest worry was that nothing would happen, that it wouldn't be interesting or challenging. I wondered, *Is this how youth is lost, through too much experience taking away the surprise and fear that is the soul of adventure?*

Having read so much about the majesty of the Mississippi, I expected a stupendously wide river, but on entering it I found it tamely narrow, only one-quarter mile wide at Vicksburg. Seeking to explore a sandbank on the opposite side, I crossed the water with just a few paddle strokes. It is true that the river narrows at this spot, constricted by the bedrock outcroppings on which the city of Vicksburg stands. But elsewhere, it spans only one-half to three-quarters of a mile, and I found myself crossing it many times a day without a second thought.

When I chose Vicksburg, Mississippi, as my jumping-off point, I knew nothing about the town, except that it stood 350 river miles from New Orleans. Starting there would provide me with the 12-day trip I projected. As I explored the town for two days before setting out on the river, I discovered it is a city where they take their history personally.

For northerners, the Civil War is an ancient tale, hardly more real than the stories of the brothers Grimm, but for inhabitants of Vicksburg it happened yesterday. In the shuttle from the Jackson airport, we passed a military monument on the outskirts of Vicksburg and I remarked on it.

"Was there a battle here or something?" I asked.

Logan, the driver, practically slapped my wrist.

"You mean you don't *know* about the siege of Vicksburg?" she said. "They had us surrounded. We were completely cut off!"

"Really?"

"We were starving! We lived in caves to escape the shelling! We held out for 71 days before we had to surrender, on the Fourth of July." Her tone emphasized the irony that this travesty should have occurred on Independence Day.

This young woman with her sugary Mississippi accent was born well over a hundred years after the last cannon sounded at Vicksburg, yet she spoke as though she had crawled out of those caves just a few days before learning to drive this van.

The next afternoon, I touched that ancient bombardment with my fingertips. At Cedar Grove, an antebellum mansion in the center of town, a cannonball came right through the front door—you can still see the patched-over splintered hole. The shot followed an angled path through the parlor doorway, passed above the (now) antique French Pleyel piano, and embedded itself in the wall. The iron sphere, 2 inches in diameter, has been polished smooth by caresses of countless visitors. Squinting with one eye, I lined up its trajectory and determined that if someone had been playing the piano at that moment, the cannonball would have blown a hole right through her bouffant hairdo. It is doubtful that music was being performed during that time, however. Cedar Grove was hit 41 times in the course of the siege, and that sensible pianist was no doubt cowering in the Vicksburg caves along with the rest of her family and Logan the van driver.

One reason why Vicksburgers are so engrossed with their Civil War history is that their 71-day resistance is something to be proud of. Other southern cities on the Mississippi did not do as well. Natchez and New Orleans surrendered to Union forces without a fight, a fact that chauvinists in these cities would prefer to forget.

Across the street from the Cedar Grove mansion stands another old house, Belle of the Bends, where I stayed for the two days I was in Vicksburg. These old mansion bed-and-breakfast establishments are the most remarkable lodging value in America. The idea of sleeping in any mansion is a dream, but make that an old mansion with ornate fixtures, carvings, and period antiques, and you have a fairy tale come true. My room at the Belle of the Bends had a four-poster bed, antique armoire, and ceilings high enough for a volleyball game.

If you want to see a period room in a museum, you pay $10 to get in, the room is roped off so you can only peer at it from the hall, and you can't so much as lay a finger on the surface of a Chippendale dining chair. Stay at an old mansion bed-and-breakfast—for about the same as a Holiday Inn will cost—and you live for a day or two in that priceless setting. You walk on the antique carpets, you sleep in the antique bed, and you can put your feet up on the antique chair (though I hope you won't).

What makes this lodging miracle possible is an amazing class of philanthropic entrepreneurs who supply huge investments of money, time, and organizational skills that running an old mansion as a bed-and-breakfast requires. Before she and her husband Dan bought Belle of the Bends, Mary Ahern managed a medical practice in Denver. She is busy every minute of the day, beginning with making a five-course breakfast for guests (starting with a strawberry parfait), dealing with calls and emails for reservations, serving as chambermaid and housekeeper, handling shopping and laundry, and showing the house to tourists who knock on the door. Then there is upkeep of the building. I noticed the exterior paint was peeling in spots and mentioned it to Dan (who left an engineering job in Denver). He said the first estimate they got for painting the place with all its balconies and balustrades was $44,000. Divide that into the $110-per-night room charge and you get a feel for the hopeless economics of running this kind of place.

Do the Aherns feel burdened putting so much work into a questionable economic venture? "I've been waiting 31 years for this," says Mary. Running an old mansion as a B&B is a dream for people like her. Well, thank goodness for dreams. All around America, idealists like Mary and Dan are putting grand old mansions to public use and, at the same time, saving them from the wrecking ball. There ought to be some kind of medal for this achievement.

The Mississippi may have God's fishes swimming in it, but the creature that dominates its waters today is the barge tow. I saw the first one 15 minutes after entering the river, had counted five within the next 2 hours, and thereafter decided an enumeration was as pointless as trying to count clouds passing in the sky. Since these monsters were the only moving things in my environment, I got to know them intimately. They were objects of interest and admiration at first; darker feelings developed later.

The basic unit of a tow is a rectangular steel barge, typically 35 feet wide and 200 feet long. Lashed together in rows and columns, the set of barges provides a graphic application of our school multiplication tables. The biggest tow I saw was 5 barges wide by 7 long: I leave it to the reader to calculate how many barges there were altogether. The entire tow was over one-quarter mile long.

The tops of the barges are covered with closely fitting curved roof sections, so it is not possible to tell what cargo they carry. This would be revealed to me in the stretch of the river below Baton Rouge, when the covers come off and the barges are unloaded at docks or directly into oceangoing ships.

The mass of tied-together barges is called a tow, but it is not towed. It is pushed by the towboat, an oversized blunt-nosed tugboat usually four stories high, with many staterooms to house crew members who live aboard. The largest towboats have three 16-cylinder,

3,200-horsepower diesel engines, three funnels to pour out the coal-black exhaust, and three propellers to explode the water behind. This screaming, thudding workhorse makes an exciting sight when passing by, except that the show lasts too long. Big tows creep upstream at little more than 2 mph, which means they can blast your eardrums for a half hour. Crew members are required to wear ear protection when they venture outside their cabins, and I often wished I had brought some for myself when tows passed, especially when I was trying to sleep at night. When one drew alongside my tent it sounded like someone had parked and forgotten a working 50-kilowatt generator.

For the longest time I couldn't figure out how the towboats turn the barge train to follow curves in the river. Then one day, when I got dangerously close to one, I learned they have side thrusters. To turn the barge train to the left, the tug moves sideways to the right.

On that first day setting out down the river, I saw no danger in the barge tows. I understood where their channel ran and where I needed to be, a feeling of confidence that contrasted with my insecurity on other waterways, especially on the Saint Lawrence River, where I seldom knew where my safety lay when I saw a ship approaching. At one point that first afternoon on the Mississippi, I was headed straight at a barge tow that was coming directly at me. Instead of paddling in fright toward the nearest shore—my response in yesteryear—I continued paddling directly at the tow, no more concerned than if it had been a pelican. I had identified the red nun buoys, understood their pattern, and knew how my course would put me just to the left of the tow when he reached me. And that's the way it happened, with my kayak shaving past his steel walls 50 yards away.

It was satisfying to feel competent about my navigational abilities, but, I noted wistfully, along with this mastery came a loss of excitement. It was another sign that the overexperienced kayaker was in for a boring journey.

The mood of competence and control lasted a day and a half. I spent an uneventful night camping on a broad sandbar never visited by human beings, and the next morning got underway again in fine weather. For some reason, no barges were running for several hours, so I put myself in the middle of the river to take advantage of its current. I could see no sign of man, no structure on either side of the river, just a continuous band of trees. My visual field was the flat sweep of tan water below and the soaring sphere of blue, cloudless sky above. It crossed my mind that I was seeing more of the sky than practically anyone else in the state of Mississippi, because their view of it would be blocked by nearby trees and buildings.

I took advantage of this Tom Sawyer moment to slouch back in the kayak and open a book about the Mississippi River, for a few minutes of lazy reading. For many months I had looked forward to reading the book because it was supposed to be a literary masterpiece. When I saw the first sentence of the first chapter I was dismayed. Appalled, actually. Here is that memorable lead sentence:

"The Mississippi is well worth reading about."

As an exemplar of literary style, this sentence commits practically every possible error and crime. It is passive, not active. It contains one of those famous weak adverbs ("well") that editors keep telling writers to purge. It ends in a preposition, a notorious faux pas. It is embarrassingly short, suggesting a Dick-and-Jane mentality, not the sophistication of a writer capable of winning the Booker Prize. Worst of all, it is bland. Publishers tell us the lead sentence of a book ought to grab the reader's attention with a powerful, suspense-filled image, something like, "Trapped beneath 20 feet of muddy, miasmic Mississippi water that was choking me like the failed marriage I could not leave, I was running out of air." (Okay, this needs work, but you get the idea.)

This lead sentence I'm deconstructing as a deplorable example of literary style is the opening line of the celebrated classic, *Life on the Mississippi*, written by that giant of American literature, Mark Twain. At first, I didn't know what to think. Was the man overrated, or was I missing something? I read further into the book, prepared to carp and criticize, but I was soon caught up in the subject itself and forgot about words and style. Even though the book begins with seemingly dull facts—statistics about the river's length and depth, and not a word about anybody's failing marriage—it is interesting! What makes it interesting is the author is obviously engrossed by his subject. He is not a hack grinding out words for money, or a poseur trying to look literary with elaborate language. He is an explorer arriving breathless from a far-off land, eager to tell listeners about the exciting things he's found out. That's the message of that first, seemingly lame, sentence: Boy, have I got something to tell you!

As I read *Life on the Mississippi* that morning, I wondered if this isn't the lesson of Mark Twain for would-be writers: Engaging writing isn't a matter of style, but of enthusiasm. If a writer isn't fired up about his subject, fancy phraseology and convoluted sentences won't help.

And so the morning progressed, without a cloud in the sky, literally and metaphorically. I did a bit of reading, a bit of paddling, and plenty of daydreaming. At noon, I pulled over to the bank and walked up to the overhanging trees to have lunch and a nap in the shade. An hour later, I was back on the river, and I then noticed a few clouds in the west. By 3:00, the clouds had become very dense and black. Now being a prudent elder statesman of kayaking, I thought the wise plan would be to find a good camping place, unload the boat, and set up the tent before the rain hit.

I began paddling with swift, strong strokes to reach a distant beach. Suddenly, the boat stopped moving. I was aground, stuck on sand that lay just a few inches below the surface. I jabbed the paddle into the sandy bottom to push myself back into deeper water, but the blade plunged down through the sand and gave me no purchase. I thought of getting out and towing the kayak, but it occurred to me that this might be quicksand, and if I got my feet stuck, getting back into the kayak might be difficult or impossible. I put the paddle aside and used my hands to push off the sand. This inched the boat free, but within seconds I was aground again. The whole area was a maze of shallows hidden by opaque muddy water.

Soon the rain arrived and I was no nearer dry land. I rigged the cockpit rain cover, which keeps out most water in an ordinary rain, and put on my rain jacket, which keeps me mostly dry in an ordinary rain, and felt cozy and contented, watching raindrops make their romantic little concentric circles on the coffee-colored water.

The poetry lasted but a few seconds. A roaring sound came from across the river, and I lifted my gaze to see a curtain of rain rushing at me. It hit me like a locomotive. This was not rain by any human definition. It was all the fire hoses in town spewing at me, and slashing the surface of the river into a noisy boil. Within minutes, I was in a desperate situation.

If an ordinary rain is a romantic, cozy event in a kayak, one might wonder why a rain 20 times as hard should be life threatening. Isn't water, water? Before that afternoon, I wouldn't have been able to answer this question. Now I can, precisely.

First, the heavy rain created a roaring noise that drowned out all other sound, including the sound of any barge coming toward me. Further, it cut visibility down to a few feet, so I could not see said barges. And it drenched my glasses, so that I had to take them off, further impairing my vision.

This might not have mattered if there had been a definite shore to land on, but I was trapped in shallows and concealed sandbars. Not being able to get ashore was a cruel irony. What lured me onto the Mississippi in the first place was my seeing, from the airplane returning from my Key West trip, what looked like immediately accessible sandy beaches all along the river. "A beach wherever and whenever you desire," was the huckster's promise made at 37,000 feet. Well, now that I was at river level, this proved to be extremely fraudulent advertising because of the concealed sandbars. I could not make my way past them to reach the shore, and I could not make progress across them. I had only two options: stop paddling and wait the storm out hunched in my kayak, or move toward the middle of the river and paddle down the barge channel.

I tried stopping, and this might have worked if the rainstorm had been brief—which, given its intensity, the laws of meteorology practically required. But it was not brief. God had turned on the faucet and forgotten all about it. As the minutes passed, the volume of water began to overwhelm my systems for keeping dry and warm. I can give a statistical measure of what I was up against. When it rains, the rain cover over the cockpit collects water in a little pool between my knees, and when a cupful of water collects, I carefully lift it from below and tip it over the side. In an ordinary rain, it takes a half hour for a cupful to collect. In this deluge, the rain cover was filling every 30 seconds!

The avalanche of water pouring from the heavens found ways through every crack and chink of my rain protection. It came through my rain jacket at the neck; it slopped onto my stomach from the rain cover and trickled down my pants; it sprayed onto my legs through the gap at the coaming; it poured onto my shoes through the one-inch hole that takes the sailing mast. Within a few minutes I was soaked. I was wearing only a thin T-shirt under the rain jacket—remember it was a lovely sunny day before all this began—so as the cold rain beat against my jacket, it drained warmth from my torso. Soon I was shivering and feeling painfully cold, like someone had injected me with poison that would turn my body to stone if I didn't work it out of my system. I had to paddle to keep up my body temperature, and that meant I had to go out into the barge channel.

This hammering rain continued for several hours, forcing me into a drawn-out game of where's-the-barge. I paddled along in the gloom, expecting to see steel walls emerge in front of me any second. A red nun would appear from time to time, and I would know for those few seconds that I was safe, but I could not embrace her. Each time I had to say adieu and plunge away into the curtain of roaring rain.

Weeks later, after I returned from the trip, I asked my doctor why I seemed to be so vulnerable to hypothermia. He gave a jolly laugh and pointed at his own potbelly: "You don't have any protection, like us guys do. If you were thrown into 40-degree water, your core temperature would start falling in seconds. For me, my core temperature would be maintained for around a minute."

He also mentioned that the head loses 50 percent of the body's heat if it isn't thermally protected, and of course mine wasn't. Only the thin nylon hood of the rain jacket covered it.

Another point that occurred to me many days later concerned the life jacket. It was lying right at my feet, yet, amazingly, it never occurred to me to put it on. I knew that it provided warmth, for I had used it as an extra covering on cold mornings back home. Hypothermia is notorious for causing irrational behavior, so perhaps I can blame the tunnel vision on that. Surely if ever a life jacket made sense for safety, it was during this deaf and blind groping for barges in the shipping channel.

Fortunately, no barges confronted me. After a painfully long time, the sky began to lighten and the rain lost some of its fury. I found a shore where I could land and drew the kayak onto the sand. I pulled out the tent and set it up—not an easy job, for it was still raining and my shivering had graduated into large-scale shudders, making my arms jerk like a marionette's as I tried to insert the tubes of the tent into their proper holes. When the tent was finally set up, I pulled the Blue Miracle from the duffel bag and flopped it onto the tent floor, stripped off my pants, and slid into it. I zipped the tent closed, zipped up the sleeping bag, and within twenty seconds I had stopped shivering.

I now knew I was going to survive, but I still had some chores. First, I had to get out of my wet T-shirt, a complicated job since the tent is too low to sit up in. I writhed and squirmed, and wrestled with myself like a tormented soul, aware that a video of this ridiculously frustrating exercise would be hilarious. Once that was off, I could really warm up, since the Blue Miracle was dry, despite being wetted on the inside and on the outside.

I turned my attention to the sandbar on which I had taken refuge. I had read that sandbars on the Mississippi can disappear overnight, and it seemed this one was a possible candidate for such a Houdini act. The water fell off steeply at the edge and a strong current swept against the sand. A red nun marking the channel just 40 feet from shore indicated the depth of the water swirling against the bank. Questionable as the site might have been, there was no way I was going back on the river in the rain that night to find a better camping spot. The best I could do was lug the kayak across the sand and clip its mooring line to the tent. That way, if the river took the sandbank, the expedition would be held together, one sodden mass drifting to New Orleans. I didn't even want to think about hypothermia in such a catastrophe.

Propped on one elbow, I stoked a peanut butter sandwich into my empty stomach, and then lay back to reflect on my astounding reversal of fortune. In a matter of minutes, I went from drifting along a sunny river, calmly practicing literary criticism, to playing a dangerous game of barge roulette in a state of hypothermia. What especially disturbed me was the realization that I had been lucky in a number of ways. No barges came during the time I was in the channel. There was no lightning, which was unusual for a storm of this magnitude, and there had been no wind along with the storm. My mind was not easy as I drifted off into a shallow sleep, the rain still pelting the tent. If I could be plunged into a life-threatening situation in these relatively benign conditions, what other dangers did the Mississippi have in store for me?

The next morning I encountered another one. Overnight, the rain stopped, giving me overcast skies and a strong north wind that pushed me along down the river. I was 19 miles from Natchez where I hoped for a meal in a warm restaurant and a chance to see human beings again. My fresh water was used up so I made my first brew of *eau d' Mississippi* while underway, dipping my bottle into the river and then dropping two iodine tablets in it. Mark Twain reported that old timers on the river believed that the mud in Mississippi water had health-giving powers; I hoped they were right.

I was making my way through the choppy water when I hit what I never expected to see on the lower Mississippi: rapids! Apparently the bottom was shallow and irregular at that point, and the current accelerated over it, creating turbulence. In calm conditions, the disturbance might have been modest, but just as I hit the stretch, steep towboat wakes swept in. The result was a set of tossing, bouncing waves just as vigorous—and just as nerve-racking—as the rapids I braved years earlier on the Columbia River at the U. S. border. *Hey, dammit,* I thought. *I've already paid my dues in this stuff.* As on the Columbia, the stable Klepper kept upright, but it was a white-knuckle moment, and further expanded the list of dangers to worry about.

At the boat ramp at Natchez, a police car was parked on the street above, the officer observing my struggle to land against the wind. After I dragged the boat onto the concrete, he drove the car down and got out.

I was staggering a little, as I do when I get out of the kayak after many hours, stiff and shaky.

"Are you all right?" His tone was so serious and official that I thought he had spotted something amiss. I carefully counted my arms and legs before I answered.

"I think so."

When he found out I came from Vicksburg, he asked, "Is anybody checking on you?" He made it sound like a legal requirement.

"What do you mean?"

"Does anybody know where you're supposed to be, when you're supposed to arrive places?"

I told him no.

"Do you have a cell phone?"

Again, I said no.

He gave me a look of disapproval. He seemed to want to arrest me, or at least report me somewhere, but couldn't figure out what crime I was committing. "Well, you be careful there," he said as he turned back to his patrol car. "This is a dangerous river. There're whirlpools."

Three days earlier I laughed up my sleeve at these kinds of warnings. Now I wondered if the nervous Nellies were right.

I walked up to the park—Natchez, like Vicksburg, stands on a bluff overlooking the river—where I met John Kent, a retired executive from Conoco. He had just moved back to his hometown of Natchez after working many years in Indonesia. When I asked him for directions to the supermarket, he insisted on driving me there, and on driving me back to the waterfront after I made my purchases. That kind deed spared my hip a 4-mile walk.

Near Natchez, less than a mile off the Mississippi, lies a town called Waterproof. When I first spotted it on my map, I thought it seemed a good place to be if you lived in the ever-flooding Mississippi Valley. I mentioned it to John and he laughed. He told me when he was growing up, newsmen from all over the state used to visit it during floods and take pictures of inundated houses and drowned automobiles just so they could print wisecrack headlines, like "Not Quite Waterproof," and "Waterproof Leaks Again." So, ironically, the town became famous as a place of inundation. Town fathers might just as well have named it "Flood City."

The Mississippi had more lessons to teach me in the stretch after Natchez. As before, I was lulled into complacency by an easy beginning. A cold, dry air mass that properly belonged in Idaho pushed into the area, making for a crisp, sunny fall day. At sunset, I found a broad sandy beach to camp on and set up the tent well away from the water. The night was unusually cold, not quite freezing, but close to it, yet my Slumberjack tent and the Blue Miracle—also made by Slumberjack—kept me adequately warm. I felt I should start a new religion, worshipping the god of Slumberjack.

In the morning, I peeked out of my tent to look across the river. A shower of dewdrops fell on my face as I pushed back the fly. The orange sunlight lit up the trees on the opposite bank. Birds began twittering in the trees behind me, but in weak voice, singing only out of obligation. Like me, they were conserving energy against the cold. I heard a splashing sound, the front barge of a long tow coming up the river, its empty barges glowing richly red in the rising sun as they slid past. The towboat was so far away I hadn't heard its engine.

Wearing every stitch of clothing I carried, I slipped out of the tent to inspect my beach. In the sand were fresh tracks of a raccoon that visited me during the night. The tracks showed he came out of the trees and walked across the beach to within one foot of my tent, then spun around and hastened away when he realized a human being was guarding the peanut butter.

The forests around the river teemed with wildlife. I saw deer, often at quite close range because they were too puzzled by my kayak to be afraid. At one campsite, I found a deer stamping ground, a dirt patch that had been churned up by male deer to attract females during the fall mating ritual. On the river itself, I frequently saw a peculiar kind of jumping fish, about a foot long. It leaped four or five times, one right after the other. I couldn't decide whether it was pursuing minnows, or trying to escape being eaten by a larger fish.

White pelicans were the standout wildlife on the trip. The Mississippi is the main flyway for their migration from the lakes of Canada to the Gulf Coast, so I saw them many times. One evening I camped near a flock of 200 resting in the shallow water of a cove. Just at sunset, they took wing in convoys of 20 or 30, headed southeast. I assumed they were resuming their migration and planned to fly all night. This theory was exploded the next morning when, exactly at sunrise, the same number of birds came flying back in the opposite direction and returned to the same cove. My new theory was that they spent the night in the trees, to be safe from coyotes.

In flight, white pelicans are spectacular. These are big birds, mind you, with wingspans of over six feet, all white except for the handsome jet black that outlines the leading edge of their wings. They are highly social, closely attuned to one another. To feed, they work together to herd fish into shallow water where they can prey on them. In flight, this social instinct leads them to pay close attention to one another, in a split second closing up any gap that develops between one bird and the next. The observer sees a line of birds that is alive, squirming like a snake slithering through the grass. Compared to this highly sensitive social behavior, Canada geese are individualists. When a gap develops in their formation, the laggard practically takes a smoke break before he bothers to pull himself back into position.

Speaking of coyotes, I could well understand the pelicans' anxiety about them. I began hearing their nighttime yipping and howling in the stretch after Natchez, and it always made me uneasy.

On my Columbia River trip, I enjoyed hearing coyotes. Their howling came from one definite place, and the performance lasted just 10 or 15 seconds and was not repeated thereafter. From this carefully organized sound I inferred a well-disciplined, well-adjusted group of animals, each of whom knew its place in the group, and groups that knew their place in the natural order—the first law of which, I liked to suppose, was never, ever to attack man.

The howling of the coyotes of the Mississippi did not have this reassuring quality. It was disorganized, with the barking coming from all over the forest, and coming from lone animals, not groups. And the yapping continued off and on for many hours. As I lay awake listening to this confused howling, I got a picture of a broken coyote social structure, of animals without moral standards, self-discipline, or common sense. "Hey, man," they seemed to be saying, "we're so crazy we might even attack a bulldozer."

Back on the river that chilly morning, I began to suffer from a sensory deprivation that would grow increasingly oppressive as the days passed. The panorama of the river was emphatically simple: a big sky, a broad stretch of water, and bands of trees on each side. There were no buildings along the banks, no houses, no villages, no stores, no farms, and no mountains or hills. Just water, sky, trees, water, sky, trees—mile after mile. On several occasions I explored the forest along the edge. In a very few steps, the vegetation became nearly impenetrable, with trees and bushes growing close together, and vines, especially the hated kudzu, wrapped around everything. The common trees along the river are tulip poplar, sycamore, and especially, black willow. This fast-growing, spindly tree sprouts like grass along the banks, creating a wall of vivid green foliage. I also saw several thorn locust trees, attractive with their lacy leaves, but guarded by the inch-and-a-half thorns that grow on every branch and twig. These are the trees you tell your children to go climb when you're fed up with them.

One other feature in the monotonous vista along the river needs to be noted: the levees. These mounds of earth about 20 feet high run along one bank or the other and are covered with some hard material to keep the river from eroding them at high water. Levees come in three flavors of facing: an amorphous black surface that looks like asphalt but isn't; mats of rectangular brown concrete blocks held together by wires, and—the facing of choice today—crushed rock, whitish-gray in color. That's about all I can say about the levees. Perhaps Hollywood will make a feature film about them some day.

Although the emptiness of the riverbanks made for an occasional moment of sublime isolation, it weighed on me. The barges were as impersonal as freight trains, and I saw practically no other boats. I might have seen one ordinary powerboat of fishermen a day, and at such a distance that I could not make out the figures in them. I started to sing out loud just to use my voice, but this proved a poor substitute for talking with people.

Paddling became so boring that any departure from the framework of water, sky, and trees became a major event in my life. Passing by the Three River outlet channel, I heard a highly amplified electronic tone sounding every 20 seconds, piercing the silence for miles around. I listened to it carefully for the several hours it was in earshot. It was a musical note, quite pure, its pitch E above middle C. I racked my brains to imagine what function playing this tone all day long could possibly serve. The only theory I came up with was to enable the locals seated on their porch steps to tune their guitars.

My need for sociability became so strong that it influenced my decisions. When I came to the ferry that connects Route 10 to St. Francisville, I pulled over to the landing just to find someone to talk to. I walked up to a line of cars waiting for the ferry and approached the first one, an older, two-tone brown Pontiac LeMans driven by a middle-aged black woman.

When she rolled down the window I noticed that she had incredibly long white artificial nails attached to the ends of her fingers. I had never seen fingernails of this size and heft, and my mind was racing to understand how she could function wearing them. It seemed impossible that she could pick up a pencil, for example. When she changed her grip on the steering wheel, it sounded like a pony prancing on a tile floor. These nails were an inch and a half long. I realize this is the figure I just gave for the length of the thorns on the locust tree, but I'm not just throwing numbers around. I measured both very carefully.

Struggling to keep a straight face, I asked her my prepared conversation-starting question: Did she think they let foot passengers on the ferry? She wasn't sure.

Then I asked her about a café anywhere near. She said she thought there was one about a mile away.

That completed the interaction. As an exploration of the human condition in the post-industrial age it may have fallen short, but it helped fill my need for human contact.

Back in the middle of the river several hours later, I spotted a white figure walking briskly along the shore, perhaps a half mile away. I swung the boat around to paddle over to greet this person. I planned to start the conversation by asking about that E above middle C being played up the river. I couldn't make out either arms or legs, because this person was wearing a white smock. This observation led to the idea that he or she was probably an artist, and had finished a day in the studio and was now clearing out the cobwebs with a brisk walk along the river. After weighing the matter, I concluded that the figure was probably a woman, on the grounds that a woman was more likely to wear a smock, and also because women like to walk for exercise more than men. I was in the middle of trying to estimate her age when this figure leapt up and flew into the air. It was an egret.

Okay, okay, how could anyone be so dumb? Well, I did have one excuse. Nature had contrived a delightful trick of perspective. The egret, which was one-quarter the size of a human being, was walking on a sandbar one-quarter of the distance to the shore, a sandbar I could not see because it was covered by a few inches of water. All I could see was water all the way to the shore, so my eye insisted I was seeing an erect form four times as tall on the shore, which could only be a human being. Even granting the optical illusion, this bird shouldn't have tricked me for so long. An artist walking along the shore of the Mississippi! In a smock! Obviously, I was so eager for human contact that my imagination was willing to overlook quite a few differences in anatomy.

On the river I was totally out of touch with the world. In Natchez, I called Judy from a bar. After I told her where I was, I asked her how things were going back home. At just that moment the singer in the bar began her amplified yowling, and even putting a finger in my other ear, I still couldn't hear a word Judy said. For all I knew, she was telling me about another 9/11.

After leaving Natchez, I began to have serious doubts about my physical ability to handle the trip. The hypothermia episode indicated my lack of reserve: just a few hours of heavy rain had practically wiped me out. On the second night out after Natchez I suffered another troubling incident.

I had developed a yearning for a bath. I had been on the river five nights and each time I lifted my arm, I felt reproached. I knew this impulse for washing was purely cultural, that bathing brought no health benefits and involved risks of chilling the body, but . . . well, let's just say I felt I couldn't live with myself unless I got some kind of bath. So after carrying out the interminable list of camping chores to establish myself for the night, I walked into the river and did a quick body wash, dried myself with a sock, and raced back to my sleeping bag. This time the Blue Miracle failed. I couldn't get warm, even after I breathed into the bag for a time. My feet and fingers were stone cold. Reasoning that I had a calorie deficit, on account of skimping on food, I gave myself a shot of glucose by squirting a dollop of honey into my mouth. After a half hour, I warmed up to normal.

The experience led to a night of soul-searching about my vulnerabilities. Obviously, my stamina was marginal, and that put a different light on my number-one fear, the danger of capsizing. Until now, I always operated on the assumption that capsizing was not the end of the world, because I would be able either to tow the boat to shore, or to right it, half full of water, and paddle to shore. Now I knew I probably could not withstand the cold in such a crisis—remember this water was coming from Minnesota in October. The safe solution would be to wear a wet suit, but of course I didn't have one (and, if the truth be told, couldn't bear the idea of spending my kayaking life in one).

I once asked an opera singer, a woman of much experience with many vocal challenges, what she does if she has to sneeze in the middle of a song.

She said, "It just can't happen."

"But . . . it could happen?"

"It just can . . . not . . . happen."

That had to be my answer to capsizing, but I was not reassured by it. Not sneezing might be a matter of sheer mental control, but I didn't believe that willpower would be sufficient to tame the waters of the Mississippi if they wanted me.

And what about other physical systems? Each day I had to carry the kayak well away from the water to make sure it was out of the barge wakes. My back had given me problems various times in the past. If a vertebra slipped out while I trying to lug the kayak, where would that leave me? And then I could get other injuries, or get sick with a fever or a stomach problem. A person with good stamina could persevere even if injured or ill, but could I? I was beginning to see that I might have bitten off more than I could chew with this solo trip down the Mississippi. When I planned the trip, I thought it would be a piece of cake; now I saw it was sustained by the slender thread of my limited physical abilities.

Just as I'm having these discouraging thoughts, the coyotes start their crazy barking, reminding me that I am in a wild land, cut off from other human beings. *This is not a good place to get appendicitis,* I told myself. If any one of a dozen things went seriously wrong, I might be unable to bushwhack through miles of brush and vines to reach help.

Dark thoughts brought me to another issue I had to face frankly. The cell phone epitomizes the apron strings that I wish to cut while on kayak adventures. As the reader will recall, I have been emphatic in my arguments against carrying one. Now, as I was toting up dangers and noting my possible helplessness, intellectual honesty forced me to reconsider. No true believer ever felt more dismay on seeing heresy suddenly made plausible. I wrestled and squirmed, finding my formerly unanswerable arguments against cell phones falling flat. Finally I muttered my grudging conclusion into the recorder: *I'm not saying I'm in favor of a cell phone, but at just this moment I'm on the fence.* These were the words of a defeated debater, just one too set in his ways to concede.

Although I regained my body warmth, I didn't sleep that night. I was camped close to the channel, and a parade of barges came through with their incessant roaring. As soon as one drew out of range, another took its place. I can't blame my insomnia entirely on the barges. My hip was hurting too, no matter what position I shifted to: that a hip replacement was scheduled two weeks after my return did me no good at the moment. The little bivouac tent added to my woes. With the roof just inches from my nose, I had little room for movement. On this trip I would often declare that it felt like solitary confinement, and just as often correct myself for making an inadequate simile. In solitary confinement you can sit up, stand up, and walk around. The bivouac tent was a coffin.

The fact was that on this trip I was not sleeping well, averaging no more than three hours of sleep a night. I seemed to be able to paddle with adequate strength each day, but I was concerned that my sleep deficit would catch up with me in one way or another.

I brought that night's many restless hours of reviewing my situation down to a single conclusion, which I shared with the tape recorder. I reproduce it here verbatim to establish a documentary record to put against my subsequent behavior:

> *I can summarize this entire discussion by saying that if some-one of my age and in my condition proposed to kayak the Missis-sippi River alone, I would advise him against it. I would tell him that there are just too many things that can go wrong.*

One glory of travel is that each day is a new spin of the roulette wheel, and glum moments can be replaced by elevating visions. As dawn crept in the next morning, I peeked out at the river. Barges had disappeared and the land was magically quiet, the stillness broken only by hooting owls. It was hard to believe that just two or three hours earlier barges were crashing through my campsite like the bulls of Pamplona. The light strengthened and I was blessed with another breathtaking dawn on the Mississippi. High cirrus clouds, rose-tinted in the sun's first rays, traced across the deep blue sky. The glassy surface of the river was graced by wisps of fog that trailed off into the sky. *God, I love life*, was my prayer.

That morning I participated in a paddling mystery. I invite Agatha Christie fans among my readers to solve the crime.

I came to an island and took the minor channel to the right around it. Before committing, I checked for current, because I didn't want to find, 3 miles later, that I had paddled to a dead end. As a reference point, I used a red nun stranded on the sand to my left. After lining it up for a few moments while I drifted, I concluded a good current was running through the side channel, so I paddled merrily down it under the now-overcast sky. After a mile, I took my mid-morning break, snacking on a few nuts and working on a Sudoku puzzle.

Ten minutes later it was time to get paddling again. I noticed that the light breeze I had been paddling against was now behind me, but this wasn't unusual. Light winds are fickle, and can change direction in a short time. When I reached the end of the channel and joined the river, it didn't look at all like the map said. Was the map wrong? For my trips, I buy the state map book put out by the DeLorme Company, which has a scale of 3 miles to the inch, and I cut out the pages that apply to my journey. These maps have good resolution, but they are not maritime maps. Another thing didn't fit: the current was against me. I could tell because there was another stranded red nun at the mouth of the channel to my right, and I could see that when I stopped paddling, I drifted back into the channel. My brain invented an elaborate theory to explain how, temporarily, the current at the mouth of a channel might run upstream.

I am sure my readers, who are far cleverer than I, have solved the mystery from the clues given, but I was still befuddled until a barge appeared *from my right, where there was only supposed to be land*. Finally, I realized that I had paddled backward, ending up at the mouth of the channel where I started an hour earlier, right alongside the same stranded red nun. The solution to the mystery? While I was studying my Sudoku, the boat had rotated 180 degrees, so it was pointing upstream when I picked up the paddle, and I simply accepted this direction as correct.

I was supremely embarrassed. I mean, how difficult a navigational challenge can it be to go down the Mississippi River? Even a wood chip with no brain at all can do it, yet I managed to get it wrong.

As with the artist/bird mistake, I have a partial excuse, rooted in the mental mechanisms we rely on to function in the physical world. In all my other kayak journeys I never had to consciously ask what was the right direction to paddle when resuming after a rest. The structures on the shore, and the land formations—bays, hills, mountains—were automatic locators. So I always trusted my unconscious brain to know the correct direction. On that morning, I still trusted it. I assumed it had done whatever it needed to do to head me in the right direction. But, of course, the poor thing was befuddled and paralyzed by the Mississippi's repetitive environment of water-sky-trees devoid of landmarks for reference. If you close your eyes and spin around on the lower Mississippi, vision cannot say whether you are headed up the river or down. Of course, if the sun were out, that would provide orientation, but as I noted in the presentation of clues, it was overcast that morning.

In addition to dramatizing the monotony and featurelessness of the river, this "Wrong Way" Corrigan experience also points up the importance of having a companion. I'm sure the blunder would not have occurred, or been prolonged so long, if I had been comparing notes with a comrade.

That afternoon, I had another, far graver, paddling mishap. I made personal, horrific acquaintance with high-energy towboat prop wash—despite full knowledge that this would be an insane thing to do.

My days on the river had taught me that towboats generate two kinds of wakes. One set of waves comes from the blunt hulls of the barges as they push through the water. These hull waves are low and smooth, no problem for a kayaker, even when barges pass quite close.

The waves generated behind the towboat by the prop wash are something else entirely. The towboat is attempting to move a virtually immovable object. A tow of loaded barges draws 10 feet of water and covers 5 acres. To move this mass, the towboat engines are opened flat out, sending thousands of horsepower through the propellers into the water.

The water cannot accept all this energy in an orderly way. It explodes behind the towboat in a volcano 10 feet high. This volcano subsides and then reemerges 30 feet further back, in another smaller eruption, and then again further back, and so forth. So what you see behind the towboat is a string of 10 or 12 eruptions of descending height.

Beyond the region of explosions, the water begins to get a grip on itself and organizes the energy into the form that is familiar to it: waves. These waves are steep swells about 6 feet deep from trough to crest, and they persist for more than a mile behind the towboat that caused them. But here's the oddity: these swells do not move away from the towboat, in the direction the water was originally propelled. Instead, they surge toward the boat, as if they were trying to catch up with it. Whenever I paddled through these swells, they made me think of an angry burgher running through town in his nightshirt, futilely chasing the miscreant who disturbed his slumber.

So I knew all about the danger of towboat prop wash; nevertheless, on that afternoon I became trapped in it. After the evidence I have given of my incompetence on other occasions, you might think that I was to blame for this crisis, but it is not so. I was not trying to dare anybody, nor being inattentive. I was wholly in the right, doing everything a wise and courteous kayaker should do.

Two tows were heading down the river, rather close to the left bank, and I was to the left of them, heading in the same direction. The first tow, somewhat ahead of me, stopped his engines. Instinct and experience told me that the best move was to get away from this traffic by crossing in front of the second tow and gaining the middle of the river. But I knew if I did that, the second tow would blow his horn at me: the pilots get antsy whenever anyone is in their path, even if you're far enough away to be clear in plenty of time. I'd already been rebuked on this score earlier in the day.

So, out of courtesy, I continued along the left side and started to draw alongside the barges of the stopped tow. Then I noticed that this string of barges was drifting left, toward me. Had this towboat's engines quit because of a breakdown? In such a case, the tow would continue to drift toward shore and could crush me against the bank. I turned around and paddled vigorously back up the river.

In a few minutes, I was alongside the towboat again. Just then he started a smallish engine and I saw water bubbling underneath him amidships. He began moving sideways toward me, quite rapidly. I put two and two together: he had a side thruster and was using it to move to the left so that he could propel the tow away from the bank. Any second now he was going to turn on his main engines and blow me out of the water! I got in three paddle strokes fleeing his stern before those engines did indeed come on full blast.

I have been scared many times on my kayak trips, but this was only the second time I was terrified (the other was the robbery at Steamboat Creek, p. 218). I had entered the aquatic equivalent of an astronomer's black hole, where ordinary principles of physics are suspended. Rapids and wind waves have some order, so that in facing them a kayaker can prepare for and react to the buffeting. This turbulence was out-of-this-world, high-energy, randomly exploding water. In the maelstrom I saw only one feature the English language has a word for. A whirlpool, 3 feet deep and 4 feet across, appeared 10 feet from my bow. But this was no ordinary whirlpool, the kind that forms at your bathtub drain with the water lazily circling around. It was a steep, muscular structure capable of wrestling man-size objects to the river's bottom.

I didn't paddle much in the middle of this turbulence, feeling that motion on my part would only add to my instability. I just slumped low and tried to balance and brace, though I didn't know what I was bracing against. By all rights I should have overturned, but somehow the amazing, stable Klepper kept upright. After perhaps 20 seconds, the violence of the water abated as I was driven further from the towboat, and I paddled free of the prop wash. I struck out directly across the path of the oncoming second tow, seeking the open water in the middle of the river. If he blew his horn at me, he was going to get the finger. He didn't: I suspect he had watched my crisis and understood what I was up to. As my breathing returned to normal I thought, *It seems I'm a cat with nine lives on this river and I'm using them up at a dangerously rapid rate.*

As I paddled on, I noticed I had not been wearing my life jacket during this crisis. This struck me as fairly shocking, and it led me to reexamine my long-standing opposition to wearing a life jacket. All of my old reasons for shunning the device—discomfort, bravado, the desire to flaunt authority—now seemed less than persuasive, and I resolved henceforth to wear it. Since this was about the eighth time in my kayak travels that I had been caught in a dangerous situation with the life jacket off, we have a gauge of what it takes to overcome a juvenile's boneheadedness when it comes to his own safety.

I wondered if the towboat pilot who nearly killed me with his prop wash had seen me. My guess is that he did, but that he had to act to save his tow, which was drifting into the bank. If you asked him what a kayaker should have done in that situation, I believe he would agree with me and say that I had done nothing wrong. But he would not feel guilty about nearly killing me. He would say that kayakers don't belong on the river. Towboats need the entire river, from shore to shore. Sometimes, when they need to push the tow away from the bank, they even need the shore, too, driving their prop wash 10 or 20 feet up onto dry land and thus sweeping to destruction any small children who might be standing there clutching their teddy bears. Therefore, in his opinion, small craft, especially human-propelled craft, should be banned. In other words, Tom Sawyer adventures on the Mississippi River should be illegal.

Well, I thought, *he knows where he can shove that.*

Another cloud gathering over the expedition as the days progressed was a food shortage. This crisis had its roots in diverse factors, including unsatisfactory suppliers, the wilderness conditions, and vagaries of the current. No doubt, driver error also contributed to the problem.

Difficulties with food supply began in Vicksburg when I attempted to shop for wholesome foods in the only store I could walk to, a supermarket called County Market. It should have been called Carbohydrate Inc. The selections on its shelves reflected the eating habits that give the state of Mississippi the highest obesity rate in the nation. The bread section was dominated by white bread, huge loaves at 91 cents each, the astoundingly low price made possible by making this bread from thin air. The company putting this stuff out must have been ashamed of the nutritional content label: it said zero for just about all categories. A few loaves purported to be whole wheat, but they felt as puffy and fluffy as the white bread, and appeared to be the same thing all over again with a little brown coloring added. If you sat on a loaf, you would be left with a pancake sticking to your behind.

The search for edible protein ran up against obstacles at every turn. The store had no real energy bars, the high-protein snacks I have come to depend on for my trips, just sugary breakfast cereal bars, Pop-Tarts and such. I asked about beef jerky, which I hoped to make a mainstay of my diet. One employee had never heard of the stuff. Another, a wizard of a stock clerk who deserves to be made manager, knew that behind register 9 was a little can containing tiny strips of processed beef. There were three left in the display container and I grabbed all three. Just after I withdrew my hand, a young black woman reached into the container to get some, and of course it was empty. I felt such pity on her, trying to find protein in this starch-laden store, that I gave her one of mine. I suppose a true Christian would have given her all three.

In desperation, I bought two cans of sardines, a reliable if unsavory source of protein. Several days later, when I opened the first one, I found I made a mistake. I expected twin rows of delicately tiny fish, but what I got was three big fish with their heads chopped off. They smelled and tasted slightly off, and their vertebrae crunched as I bit down. I also think I saw a part of a fish's eye floating in the oil. *Not unless I'm starving to death,* I said to myself, *will I consider opening that second can.*

Starvation was closer than I imagined. In addition to not being able to buy the right foods, I failed to buy enough, in both Vicksburg and Natchez. My thinking was stuck on the assumption that I would find villages along the way, with stores and restaurants to supplement my needs. This was a false assumption in this realm of water-sky-trees. The shores of the Mississippi have no shops or services; I had to rely entirely on my own inadequate food supplies.

Contributing to the problem of running out of food was an incorrect estimate of the current. My plan wasn't to paddle to New Orleans. I wasn't going to be a hard-driving, hard-core kayaker, but a Huckleberry Finn, letting the river do most of the work. I had seen the figure of 3 mph given as the river's speed, and made my plans on that basis. Once on the river, I learned this estimate was much too high. There were spots where this speed was reached, and even exceeded. Coming under the bridge at Vicksburg, for example, the speed was 4.2 mph.

And on the outside of curves, the current was generally 3 mph or more. But there were also many wide, straight sections where the current dropped under 2 mph, and shallows and inside curves had almost no current at all.

I did my best to take advantage of what current there was by staying in the boat to accomplish various chores. I brushed my teeth while drifting, and shaved, and also read. I even washed my underwear while underway, and hung it out to dry on the deck. I made lunch while sailing—well, if you call a lowly peanut butter sandwich lunch. And I napped several times, not intentionally, because I knew it was dangerous with barges about, but because my sleep deficit sometimes wouldn't let me keep my eyes open.

Despite these efforts to keep moving, I fell behind my schedule. When I pulled into camp on my sixth night, the negative algebra of food supply hit me squarely. I should have been in Baton Rouge that night, yet I was one, and possibly two more days away, and had just scraps of food left. I implemented a severe rationing: only one piece of bread with peanut butter per meal. In between these "meals," I would allow myself a few nuts and pieces of dried plums to kill hunger pains. After laying out this plan I licked the inside of the peanut butter lid: I didn't consider that cheating, since its food value hadn't been included in the rationing program. My groping fingers kept encountering that second can of sardines at the bottom of the food bag, but I still refused to consider it part of the food supply. So perhaps I wasn't as desperate as I thought.

To escape the nighttime distraction of barges and their incessant pounding, I came up with the plan of pitching camp on the far side of an island, well away from the maritime channel. In a well-ordered world, this bright idea should have given me a peaceful night's sleep, but Nature rewarded me with bitter gall. An angry southeast wind blew strongly all night long, turning my tent into a shuddering, flapping hell. The wind also blew small particles of sand off the beach onto the tent. They then rained down through the mosquito netting onto everything, including into my eyes as I lay on my back staring at the roof—a real visit from the sandman. The sand and the wind noise left me with a second sleepless night in a row.

When I turned in, I had harbored hope that I might make the 24 miles to Baton Rouge the next day if I paddled hard and conditions were favorable. As morning came, the southeast wind, coming straight up the river against me, dashed this expectation. I was in for a day of futile clawing against wind and waves.

There being no point in listening to the Stockhausen tent-flapping symphony more than necessary, I got underway before first light, hunkering down against the spitting waves. Fatigue, hunger, and loneliness had brought my spirits to a low ebb. I didn't expect to reach any destination that day, and could only look forward to another nasty, solitary, and brutish camping experience that night. I paddled simply because it was the only activity open to me; if there had been daytime TV to watch, I would have sat and watched it.

The river in this section had large, wide bends 4 or 5 miles, or 3,000 paddle strokes, apart, a perfect definition of monotony. My world consisted of nothing but going from one bend under a low gray sky to the next, which, when achieved several hours later, revealed I was 3,000 more paddle strokes from the next bend. I paddled continuously, since stopping meant being blown back up the river. The conditions reminded me of that day on the Columbia by Hood River, Oregon, where I accomplished a total of 3.6 miles against the wind. Hardly any barges were on the river that morning; I wondered if they had tied up to avoid some especially threatening weather they knew about and I didn't.

So went the day, a display of sheer, dull persistence. Rain began in the late morning and grew heavier as the day progressed. I made only one stop, at a terrace with smooth-looking grass that looked like it might be a lawn of a house or estate where I could get help. I climbed up and found the flat grass was just an accident of nature. There was nothing but wild, impenetrable forest as far as I could see.

More than once, it crossed my mind that now would be a perfect time for a miracle, one of those improbable rescues that had happened so many times on my other journeys. It was not difficult to imagine the needed deliverance. It would be a large cabin cruiser, toasty warm inside, with mahogany paneling and polished brass fittings, commanded by literary and artistic people charmed to be able to rescue a bedraggled former college professor from the Mississippi's grip. After a leisurely meal and delightful conversation, they would convey me to Baton Rouge, and, using their cell phone, call a taxi to meet me at the marina and take me to a motel. I carefully scanned the gray, empty waters for this approaching craft, but it refused to appear.

All morning I had avoided consulting my map, not wanting to discourage myself by documenting my slow progress. Finally, in the early afternoon, I could bear the uncertainty no longer and pulled it out. I was surprised to discover I had covered 17 miles. Apparently, getting up before the birds, and my tortoise-like persistence—along with a little help from the current—had paid off. I had covered most of the distance to Baton Rouge and could be there in just a few more hours! Many obstacles still stood in the way of a hot shower at a motel, but I now knew that overcoming them was just a matter of more persistence.

The map showed that the campus of Southern University lay on the river at the north end of Baton Rouge, and I decided to take out there, figuring it was a good place to enlist aid because it would have young people who would be interested in my trip. This school, I was to learn, was founded in 1880, in the days of segregation as an all-black university. After all the social changes and the mountain of 20th-century civil rights legislation, it still remains more or less an all-black university.

I had hoped to find a dock or some kind of ramp for the rowing crews that I assumed the school would have, but as I pulled closer, I could see no access from the land to the water, just the familiar wall of black willows. After beaching the kayak, I plunged through the trees and walked up a steep, grassy bank to the campus. The first building I encountered was the student union cafeteria and snack bar—just the place I needed after subsisting on half a peanut butter sandwich for the day.

As I wolfed down my double meat, double cheese cheeseburger and fries, I sized up the male students at the other tables, evaluating them as possible assistants to help me carry the kayak up from the river. It was not a promising field. None of them had greeted me or made eye contact, and their faces projected an attitude of suspicion.

All the boys were wearing baggy trousers with the crotch at the knees. I felt that if I approached them they would not be curious about my trip, but uncomprehending and possibly hostile.

After I finished eating, I found the manager. I started by apologizing for my appearance.

"Don't mind that. You're not as bad as what's in here all the time," he said, indicating the students. He had a point: they were as disheveled as I was after a week in the Mississippi's rains.

I explained my problem and offered $20 to a helper if he could find one. I assumed he would recruit one of the students, but instead he came back with a middle-aged cafeteria worker. Robert was everything the kids were not: well groomed, cheerful, helpful, and interested in the outside world. I pointed out to him that his shiny black shoes were going to get wet in the grass, but he said he didn't mind. As we carried the kayak up to the campus, he asked me a half dozen questions about my trip.

I couldn't miss the tragedy the contrast represented. Robert, at age 50, had a youngster's eager inquisitiveness. The kids in the cafeteria seemed prematurely old, as if something—whether video games, television, cultural propaganda, or something else, I couldn't guess—had robbed them of youth and its natural curiosity. I wished there was some way Southern University could get its students to regain an open, positive attitude, for it seemed to me that would do more to help them thrive and enjoy life than years of book learning. Maybe Robert should teach a class in it.

At the top of the embankment stood the university president's mansion with an empty three-bay carport, and Robert suggested we put the kayak in there. This was a brilliant move since it kept me out of the heavy rain that came later that afternoon while I took the kayak apart and repacked my gear. During my labors, the mansion's housekeeper came out and asked me if I needed any help. When she learned my situation she went back in and brought two bottles of water for me.

As I was finishing the job, a police car drove up, driven by a campus security officer curious to know who was squatting in the president's carport. I explained myself, and the cop—a very overweight white man—offered to call a taxi for me. So that part of my rescue fantasy back on the river came true after all. While we waited for it, I listened to him rail against the university administration. He told of a scandal, reported in the local newspapers, about top administrators who were using precious university funds on vacation junkets for themselves, while the students' needs were neglected. Their dorms looked like slums, he said.

The taxi came and we struggled together to lift my sinister-looking humongous black pack into the trunk. I asked the driver, a young black man with a crew cut, "You know what's in here?"

"I don't have the slightest idea."

"It's the body of the president of the university," I said. The cop who had been criticizing administrators laughed hysterically.

"See, that's it all the time," said the driver, laughing too. "The cops are the last to know what's goin' on." The cop laughed at that, as well.

During the trip to the motel, I asked Anthony, the driver, about his attitude toward the Mississippi River. The absence of any boat ramp or dock at the university added to my impression that locals on the lower Mississippi disliked the river. One indication of this aversion was the lack of interest in real estate overlooking the river. Of course, levees and the threat of flooding prevented building on the edge in most places, but even where there are bluffs, such as at Vicksburg and Natchez, they are not built upon heavily with luxurious dwellings as lakefront or oceanfront property is elsewhere. The locals don't seem eager to have a view of the Mississippi.

So when I asked Anthony if he ever swam in the Mississippi, I was not surprised he found the suggestion preposterous.

"I don't swim in it, I don't eat anythin' that comes from it. I don't want nothin' to do with that river!"

It isn't hard to explain why locals turn their backs on the river. With its mud, it looks dirty, and with the heavy barge traffic, it resembles a railroad line. Currents and waves make boating rather treacherous, and swimming even more so. And, of course, the river's floods are a source of tragedy and terror. It is not a body of water people are likely to view as a pet.

Anthony dropped me off at La Quinta, my dream come true.

In filling out the registration form for me, the desk clerk asked me how I arrived, by personal car, or rental car, or plane, or what?

I told her, "I am the only person who arrived in Baton Rouge today by kayak."

It took her a while to digest this. When she finally grasped that it meant paddling on the muddy water of the Mississippi, she was incredulous. "You *like* doin' dat?"

In short order I had taken a hot shower, changed into dry clothes, and feasted on pork ribs served in a restaurant across the street. Then I hit the king-sized bed and stretched out in its comfortable embrace, safe, secure and overjoyed at my deliverance from starvation, hypothermia, and appendicitis on the Mississippi River.

I had a beautiful sleep on La Quinta's mattress, my first decent night's sleep since leaving Vicksburg, and awoke in fine spirits, my strength and mental equilibrium restored. I was well prepared to decide the important question facing me, which was, should I continue the kayak trip?

It made all kinds of sense to skip the rest of the river and take the packed-up kayak in a cab to New Orleans where I could enjoy myself as a tourist. All the close calls I had experienced were a warning; it seemed foolhardy to push my luck by challenging the river further. I had come 216 miles on the river from Vicksburg, so I could say I had met the Mississippi River. A few more days on the river wouldn't prove anything. Furthermore, past Baton Rouge the river becomes a channel for oceangoing ships as well as barges, and its banks are crowded with docks, refineries, and heavy industry. There is very little scenic about it, and much dangerous to a little kayak. About the only reason to paddle to New Orleans was the feeling that self-respect demanded I complete the trip as originally advertised.

I planned to spend several days in Baton Rouge, so I didn't need to decide the question just then, but on that first morning I was leaning toward ending the trip. I was perfectly aware that I was thinking like an adult, that I was focusing on what would be safe and practical. But if my perspectives had changed, I could do nothing about it. There is no point in pretending to be a kid if you aren't.

I took a cab to downtown Baton Rouge to look around. I visited the State Library and various museums, and took in local attractions, including the Old Louisiana State Capitol building that Mark Twain hated so fulsomely, because of its imitative Gothic architecture. By the middle of the afternoon my wanderings had brought me to the top of the city's levee, where I had a commanding view of the river.

That's where I had an epiphany.

An oceangoing freighter was coming up the river, a strong and stately monster, its complicated booms and derricks jutting out in the brilliant afternoon sun. Instantly, I felt I wanted to be closer to it, to travel the waters it traveled, to follow that gleaming river around the far-off bend to the adventure that lay beyond. At first this thought was simply an idle idea, a pipe dream anyone standing on that levee might have. Then I realized I was not a landlubber daydreaming about a fantasy I couldn't accomplish, as if I were visiting Baton Rouge for a conference or a job interview. I had a kayak back in my motel room and could be out on the river whenever I chose. The entire decision-making process, if you can call it that, took less than three seconds: I absolutely, positively had to be out on the river again, and nothing anyone could say would change my mind.

Then I remembered the solemn advice a wise and experienced person had uttered into the tape recorder.

Hey, what is this? I said to myself. *Just a few days ago, you were declaring it to be your mature, considered opinion that you should not be on this river, because of all the dangers, lack of stamina, blah, blah, blah, and now you're throwing that advice to the winds. What's the matter with you?*

At the moment, I had no explanation for the wild inconsistency. Later, I figured it out. *Youth does not listen to the voice of experience!* That's not just a generalization; it's a definition. If a boy says, "Okay, Mom, putting on my hat is a good idea because, as you say, my head might get cold out there in the snow," he is not a child. He is an adult in a child's skin. For better or for worse, my blowing off the advice of the old fogy on the tape recorder showed that I was still a kid.

Because I wanted to use my reservations for the B&B and airline in New Orleans, I needed to catch up some distance. So when I decamped from La Quinta the next day, I took a taxi to the town of Gramercy, 40 miles down the river from Baton Rouge. I managed to persuade the cab driver to explore a little until we found an access road that took us over the levee, so we could unload the kayak pack close to the river. The mosquitoes in the area were voracious, driving me to distraction as I assembled the kayak. I had encountered hardly any insects on the river prior to this time, but these beasts made up for it. It was nearly noon in blazing sunlight—the only time in decades of camping that I can recall mosquitoes attacking without quarter in the open sun.

An oceangoing freighter was anchored right in front of me as I got underway. I paddled right up to its bulbous nose—it was empty, riding high in the water—and then passed alongside its massive anchor chain, its steel links so thick I could not grip my hand even halfway around them. It was exciting to be on the water again.

Late that afternoon, my search for youth took a remarkable turn.

I had pulled the kayak onto a spot of beach and was making preparations for camping when I chanced to look out over the water. There was a kayak! I was dumbfounded by the improbability of it. We were probably the only two kayaks within a hundred miles. What thread of fate brought us together?

The kayaker came straight for my beach.

"Hello," he said when he was still 30 yards out.

"Hello yourself," I said. "Come on in."

He beached his boat and got out. This was Isaac, a young man who had set his boat into the water near his home in Emigrant, Montana, back in July, and had spent the past 89 days traveling down the Yellowstone, Missouri, and Mississippi.

But for the taboo against hugging strangers, we would have hugged. We both had suffered the Mississippi's endless loneliness, and we were eager for companionship. He had undergone an odyssey of endurance, dragging his (hard-shell) kayak around dams on the Missouri, fighting contrary winds on its lakes, dodging barges, and suffering rainstorms. He carried a huge supply of freeze-dried food, and had camped all the way. His mother made a trip by pickup truck from Montana to resupply him in the middle of the trip.

I plied him with questions, eager to know his background. He had dropped out of high school, feeling insecure in the face of the bois-terous competition of boorish teens and intimidated by their risky behavior. The Mississippi trip, he said, was helping him overcome his shyness: the loneliness was forcing him to interact with strang-ers when he got a chance. He hadn't given up on education. He had just finished his high school requirements through a home-schooling program using the Internet.

He was a carpenter, building houses with his father, and they fin-ished a house at the time he completed his high school work. To him, it seemed the right time for a coming-of-age adventure. He had cel-ebrated his 22nd birthday on the river.

That meant, I noted with a stab, that I was over three times his age. Then it occurred to me that our meeting afforded a good oppor-tunity to explore the meaning of youth. I would be able to note, point by point, the differences between a 67-year-old with youthful lean-ings and the genuine article. I began to contrast our situations.

If starting out on a trip minimally prepared is a youthful trait, Isaac ran to form. He had not bothered with research or taking les-sons. He did hardly more than buy a kayak, take it to a launching spot near his hometown, and push it into the Yellowstone River. He had only a Louisiana state road map, which showed no detail of the river, such as islands, and gave no useful information about the location of villages and points of interest. He didn't have a GPS. He used no sunblock (he reported that his nose peeled every day of the trip), he had no sunglasses to ward off the water's fierce glare, and wore only a baseball cap, not a wide-brimmed hat that would have protected his ears and neck. I suspected that the baseball cap was a stubborn choice of style, however, and would not come off even with a chisel. When we went to a fancy restaurant several days later in New Orleans, he kept it firmly on his head throughout the meal.

He didn't know about adjusting the paddle into a feathering position, to reduce wind resistance. His paddles were set in the square position, so that each time he moved the blade forward it was flat against any oncoming wind. When you're paddling thousands of strokes against the wind, that adds a lot of work.

He never wore his life jacket, but I could hardly call him out on this point. I figured he needed another four or five close calls without it before he would see the light.

The equipment comparison did not go all in my favor. Isaac had a one-person tent he could sit up in, and it didn't weigh much more than mine. When I saw it, I kicked myself for putting up with my cramped coffin of a bivouac tent for so many years.

We compared notes and found we had shared many of the same experiences. He, too, deliberately used his voice to break the lonely monotony, singing "Row, Row, Row Your Boat," and other nursery rhymes. The coyotes bothered him, too. One night, one ran right against the side of his tent and then ran away, confirming my idea that they were a bit loco. He also had seen the fish that makes repeated jumps. His theory was that they were playing: perhaps only a genuine kid would think of that explanation.

As we chatted, we agreed to camp together that night, and continue on to New Orleans together. He told me his mother and sister were driving down from Montana to meet him at the end of the journey and take him back home.

We had several hours of daylight left and I talked Isaac into hiking over the levee in search of some humanity. The first thing we came upon was a field of Louisiana sugarcane, with stalks growing 15 feet high. I pulled out my knife and showed Isaac how to cut it off at the bottom and trim it to suck the juice. He found the plant so fascinating that he cut a whole armload of it to bring home, a piece for each member of his family.

Beyond the field, we came to a tract of middle-class houses, with a boy holding a football in front of one. We walked over to greet him, his father came out, and soon Isaac was playing catch with the boy while I chatted with the dad. We made a good team.

Back at the beach, Isaac lit a fire of driftwood to heat water for his freeze-dried meal. He pressed me to have one too, since he had more than he needed now that the trip was nearly over. I shared some of my home-dried plums with him. I thought of offering him that second can of sardines, but I thought it best not to risk our nascent friend-ship with such a problematic gift.

The next day our challenge was to dodge barge and ship traf-fic. The Mississippi River below Baton Rouge is one of the nation's great commercial transshipment points, and we found ourselves right in the middle of it. Coal, crushed rock, lumber, and shipping containers were passing from water to land, or land to water. Barges laden with sweet-smelling grain that had come down the river were being unloaded, sometimes directly into ships, in other places into grain elevators for storage on shore. Tankers coming up the river from Venezuela were unloading petroleum at refineries, and the refineries were filling barges with distillates to be sent up the river. The petroleum loading docks displayed the now-familiar post-9/11 huffing and puffing about security. Signs announced that this or that facility was designated "MARSEC Security Level-1," ominous lan-guage sufficient to reassure bureaucrats, no doubt, but laughable to kayakers, since these facilities were completely accessible to us from the water.

No red nuns adorned this stretch of the river because the channel is the whole river: it belongs to maritime traffic from shore to shore. Parked along the edges were rows and rows of barges waiting to be assembled into tows. Tugboats worked among these barges, pulling one from one place and pushing it somewhere else, as in a railroad switching yard. The middle of the river was taken by ships, which were quieter and faster than barge tows. Some of them went over 15 mph and could sneak up behind you in just a minute. Amid all these massive comings and goings, two kayaks were rabbits trying to cross a Los Angeles freeway.

At least we had our two heads to put together to figure out the best strategy for surviving in this moving maze. In general, Isaac seemed to have the better grasp of what was happening, so I tended to defer to his suggestions. He also had a young neck that could swivel around and check traffic behind us. That was a great boon, since any time I wanted to see behind I had to slow down and turn my boat. Here, indeed, is a reliable difference between the two types of youngsters.

We made our way thoughtfully down the river. In a typical moment, we were paddling near the middle of the river when a tugboat rushed out from the bank on the far right side, crossing the river. We slowed to let him cross well in front of us. When the tug reached the line of barges on our left, he stopped and the pilot came out of the wheelhouse, yelled something at us, and pointed vigorously up the river.

"Did you get that?" I asked Isaac.

"I think he's saying there's a tanker coming down the river and we're in his path. I've been keeping an eye on him."

"So we should drop over to the left?"

"Yea, I think so."

Sometimes it seemed that the tugs were deliberately trying to wipe us out. In one case, a tug came out from shore with a barge heading toward us. We dodged past it, then it turned around, barge and all, and headed back at us. We joked about what they were saying on their radios about us.

"Dang it, Billy Bob, you let them kayakers git clean away! Yo' way out a' practice, boy."

In the mid-afternoon, we went looking for a plantation. My map showed a number of these quite close to the river and I had set my heart on seeing one, and Isaac was willing to depart from his hard-driving style in order to accommodate me. And besides, I told him, maybe we could find a phone to call his mother on her cell phone.

We beached the kayaks under some trees where we thought they would be unnoticed and unmolested, and made our way over the levee to an industrial park. We walked into the front office of a firm called ABC. I greeted the secretary and explained our background. She was hesitant, put off by my rough appearance.

Was there any store where we could buy things?

She eyed me warily. No, nothing within walking distance.

I explained our need for a phone. Did she know of one nearby?

Again suspicion. No, not that she knew of. I was floundering, obviously failing to establish rapport.

Then Isaac piped up, asking the question I was too timid to ask. "Well, then, could we use *your* phone?"

I could have hugged him for having the guts to make the direct request for help. I assumed he would be turned down, and resolved to commend him for transcending his Montana shyness, even if in failure.

But he didn't fail. "Well, yes," said Pam. "You can use the phone here in the conference room."

A demonstration of the charm of youth at work. It gave me a sinking feeling to realize I lacked charisma, but I felt good knowing our expedition had a secret weapon for dealing with the opposite sex.

Pam led us into the big conference room, and Isaac struck up a conversation while I used my phone card. I spent five minutes unsuccessfully attempting to reach Isaac's mother—failing, we learned later, because Isaac had the wrong number for her cell phone. During this time another secretary, Debbie, joined Pam, and by the time I hung up for good, Isaac had worked his magic. The ladies had taken him— and by extension, me—under their wings and were eager to help us on our journey.

I mentioned that Isaac didn't have sunglasses, and they found a brand new pair for him. The firm managed job-training services for employers and somehow wound up with lots of complimentary products. They gave us a brand-new thermal-insulated tote bag, and bottles of cold water to go in it. I asked if they had any safety pins: both of our tents had failed zippers and the mosquitoes were penetrating at will. Pam couldn't find any, but she came up with something better: an entire box of spring binder clips. To help with mosquitoes, Debbie gave us her bottle of scented Avon mosquito repellent. I feared it would serve as no more than an appetizer for the fierce Louisiana mosquitoes, but we were touched by the gesture.

The manager came by and heard our story (to avoid confusion, we told people we came down from Montana together, so I got to bask in the limelight of Isaac's achievement). He thought our trip newsworthy enough to put in the company newsletter, and took us out on the lawn to stand in front of the company sign while he took a picture of us with the ladies. He already had his headline, "Kayakers come all the way from Montana to visit ABC Services."

Laden with goodies and good cheer, we made our way back to the boats, which remained safely hidden in the trees. We never did find the plantation.

As the afternoon progressed, we could see that finding a decent camping spot that night would be difficult, though we never imagined how difficult. The shoreline afforded no more sandy beaches but was mostly taken up with moored barges, docks, piers, and industrial facilities. The open bits of shore in between were lined with large jagged rocks dumped there to halt erosion. This presented an almost impossible landing place for me, because even after I empty the kayak, I cannot safely carry it over uneven, slippery rocks.

Fortunately, there were two of us to carry it ashore, and Isaac's hard-shell kayak could be dragged over anything. But we still had to find clear, flat ground beyond the rocks to pitch our tents, and that wasn't easy. After rejecting a number of spots, we finally settled on a park next to the water in Kenner, a suburb of New Orleans. The park was a public place, with many people walking and riding along the path atop the levee, but at least it had level, grassy ground for our tents.

We hauled the boats out of the water, and I took a load of bags from my kayak to the edge of the grass. It was sunset and we decided to go into town to look for a phone. There seemed little danger leaving our things lying out in plain view, since we didn't plan to be gone long. After we made it to the street and learned that a phone was quite a few blocks away, I gave Isaac my phone card and told him to go make his call while I went back to watch our stuff. We hadn't been away from it more than 10 minutes.

Well, 10 minutes was too long. We had been robbed. My food bag and my clothes bag had been opened, items strewn around, and some things taken.

The theft stirred in me a wave of deep dismay, not because of any physical loss it involved but because it challenged an article of faith. When I began my kayak trips, I had an underlying confidence in the goodness of people. I suppose this was part of my youthful outlook: children are inclined to trust strangers. Friends and family members argued against my kayak trips on the grounds that the world is full of bad guys who might put my life in danger. I pooh-poohed their fears as exaggerated, a result of watching too much of TV's hyperbolic coverage of crime.

My first trips confirmed this confidence in a benign world. On the Potomac, on the Columbia, and on the trip to Quebec I met only helpful people, scores and scores of them, and was never threatened by anyone. A warning note sounded on the trip to Key West, when I came frighteningly close to a robbery; but since I was a bystander, not the object of aggression, the crime did not hit me where I lived. But now I was the victim, and I felt a distinct shift in my attitude. This one act of aggression did not overturn my optimistic view. I still believed most people are helpful and can be trusted. But a guardedness entered my outlook, and I suddenly felt much older.

In practical terms, the theft suggested we were camping in a dangerous place. We had been warned about crime in New Orleans by just about everyone we had talked to, but had shrugged it off. Now this brazen robbery suggested that here in Kenner we might have stumbled into a hot spot of mayhem. It was only a petty thief who took my stuff, but now that one bad guy knew about us, I reasoned, he might tell much badder guys who might come back later in the night. It seemed imperative that, difficult as it might be, we relocate our campsite.

Though disheartening and sinister interpretations could be placed on the robbery, it was itself a comic-opera theft. A magpie could hardly have done less damage with its idiosyncratic selection of things to take and leave. Out of my clothes bag, the thief left my red fleece sweater and my rain jacket, both rather costly items and extremely important to a kayaker who lived on the edge of hypothermia. Instead, he took the plastic Ziploc bag in which I carried my toothbrush, toothpaste, floss, nail file, and comb. Perhaps today a better-groomed thief with whiter teeth is walking the streets of Kenner.

In dealing with the food bag, the thief eschewed the Ziploc bag of priceless homegrown, home-dried plums, and instead took an apple, a jar of peanut butter that was almost empty, and, glory of glories, that abominable can of sardines. I had visions of him eating it, gagging and in this way learning the lesson that crime does not pay.

It was fully dark when Isaac returned, bubbling with enthusiasm about arrangements for the conclusion of our journey. He had reached his father in Montana, got the correct number of his mother's cell phone, and spoke with her. She and Mercedes, his sister, were already in New Orleans, and would meet us the following day at Jackson Square at 12:30 p.m.

"Well, that's the good news," I said after I heard him out.

"What do you mean?"

"We've got to get out of here."

I told him about the robbery and my feeling that this was a dangerous camping place. He didn't agree, and thought we would be fine setting up our tents on the field. There it was: the trustfulness of youth. I couldn't say he was wrong—we probably would have been safe camping there—but I had a powerful premonition of danger and insisted we move, and he yielded cheerfully to my strong opinion.

We carried the boats back over the rocks to the river—the mosquitoes were feasting in hordes on my exposed calves as I walked into the water—and loaded the boats again. We set out into the blackness, both of us quite tired after a long day. After paddling for a while, my flashlight beam revealed a spot where we could land. Isaac got out to investigate the terrain above the rocks. I waited in my kayak, almost nodding off. After a time he came back, got into his kayak without a word, and we paddled away.

After a time I said, "You found 70 virgins lying on velvet couches up there, but figured staying there would make us go soft, right?"

"I thought I'd keep it a secret and come back later."

A mile later, we came to another possible spot. Again Isaac went up to investigate while I remained slumped in my kayak. On the youth versus adult comparison, Isaac was clearly demonstrating the superior stamina of youth, and I was happy to take advantage of every ounce of it. This time he found a grassy spot, screened from the levee and the bike path by some trees, out of sight and out of mind of Kenner's bad guys. He lifted one end of my kayak, I took the other, and we carried it up over the rocks.

I told him, "Thanks for saving the situation."

He replied, "We did it together."

I was so tired I could hardly set up my tent. The theft of my toiletries meant that I felt no guilt about dropping into my sleeping bag without flossing and brushing. I used four of Pam's binder clips to pinch the mosquito net closed, and not one mosquito disturbed six hours of dreamless sleep.

We awoke with the sun, yawning and stretching on our last day on the river. The GPS put us 10.9 direct miles from Jackson Square; the map showed that curves made it 15 river miles. During the night, tiny brown ants had swarmed over our boats and infested our food supplies and everything tainted with food—including the sugarcane stalks Isaac was carting home. We brushed them away by the thousands.

River traffic had thinned, there being few barges this far down the river. We paddled easily, savoring the last miles of our trip, taking pictures of each other in front of bridges, skyscrapers, and the old Market Street power plant. We were keenly interested in the cranes and machinery of the docks. One crane that handled cargo containers was over 15 stories high, and was festooned with steel staircases and walkways so workers could access every part of it. I commented that getting to work would provide the crane operator with something of a workout. A man approached it as we watched, eager to see him huff and puff his way up all those flights of stairs. Instead, he walked to one side and got in an elevator. Even crane operators lead a life of ease these days.

In the last mile before Jackson Square, we faced an interesting challenge in the form of a huge fountain spraying a jet of water high in the air. This might have been a fountain of celebration or welcome, or even a municipal work of art, except that the water spraying into the sky was coal black. This grimy display was the product of a dredging operation along the waterfront where the cruise ships tie up. Machinery was extracting the toxic black mud from the bottom, pumping it to the middle of the river along a pipe suspended on floats, and spraying it back into the river. Apparently the theory was that the stronger current in the middle of the river would wash the muck away to, well, somewhere else.

The dredging was under the supervision of the U.S. Army Corps of Engineers, a bureaucracy that has received lots of well-deserved criticism for the mismanagement of levees, canals, and wetlands that led to the devastation of New Orleans in Hurricane Katrina. This fountain of filth served as a reminder to the city's beleaguered survivors that the Corps was as fat, happy, and irresponsible as ever.

It posed a problem for us, since it forced us to detour way out into the middle of the ship channel to get past the floating discharge pipe. Isaac was squeezed between the foul shower and a container ship coming up the river, but managed to ride out the ship's wake.

At 12:40, we reached the Moon Walk, the wooden steps on the levee alongside Jackson Square, where Mercedes and Janice were waving with excitement.

As I got to know Isaac's family during the rest of the day, I discovered the original coincidence of meeting him on the vast Mississippi was echoed in other unusual connections. Over 20 years earlier Isaac's mother, Janice, had worked as a secretary in the same Washington DC think tank where I was employed when I made my first kayak trip, down the Potomac. As we were driving in the truck together, I overheard Mercedes singing softly to herself just the way my daughter Rachael does. It turned out she is also a singer, studying opera at Montana State University. From the few bars of a Handel aria she sang during supper, I could see she had a fine voice and signed up to join her fan club.

Since they hadn't made arrangements for lodging, I suggested the Block-Keller House bed-and-breakfast where I was staying, and they took me up on it. This is another one of those grand old mansions run as a bed-and-breakfast, Brian and Jeff serving as the heroic owner-managers.

It was October 31, Halloween, and in New Orleans this day is celebrated as a mini-Mardi Gras. After we settled at the Block-Keller House, the four of us took a trolley car back down to the French Quarter for supper and to see the festivities. It was a pleasant, scaled-down celebration, without the vast crowds and the alcoholic and rowdy excesses of the real Mardi Gras. We saw a small parade of people dressed in costumes, including one elaborate and convincing costume of a headless man. Marchers and spectators sported the classic New Orleans bead necklaces; giggles and shrieks announced an occasional furtive flashing of breasts by young, and not so young, women, to motivate balcony dwellers to throw down necklaces—or perhaps brassieres.

The next day I said goodbye to Isaac, Janice, and Mercedes who were eager to return to the prairies of Montana. With Isaac's kayak lashed to the rack on top of their pickup truck, and the bed of the truck crammed with camping equipment, freeze-dried food, and sugarcane stalks, they swung out of the driveway into the traffic on Canal Street. I waved for as long as I could see the truck.

Though I had read about the devastation Hurricane Katrina caused in New Orleans, I was not prepared to understand how a city could be at the same time standing, yet wrecked. The area around my bed-and-breakfast, 2 miles from the French Quarter along Canal Street, was typical. To walk around, you would think at first glance that nothing was wrong. There was a chiropractor's office here, a hair styling salon there, a pizza restaurant, and so forth, and houses along the side streets. But the stores and businesses were in most cases empty and closed, and the houses unoccupied.

I asked Brian at the B&B what the problem was.

He put it simply and emphatically: "There was 14 feet of water out there on Canal Street!"

This water was dirty, salty seawater, and everything it flooded was wrecked—drywall, flooring, furniture, appliances, and electrical wiring—leaving all those seemingly normal houses and places of business uninhabitable. To bring them back to life required a complete rehab job on each one. This was being done, bit by bit, but even 14 months after the hurricane, most had yet to be touched. The Block-Keller House stands on a rise, so the house itself was spared, but the basement, which had been fitted out with four sleeping units, was ruined. Jeff and Brian had to strip it out to bare concrete, which is how they plan to leave it.

"We learned our lesson," said Brian.

A few parts of the city, notably the downtown area and French Quarter, stood above the floodwaters and were relatively unharmed. Tourists who spend their time in this central section see hotels, shops, and restaurants functioning as usual, and can easily assume that all of New Orleans is back to normal, when the truth is that about two-thirds of it is not.

The work of rebuilding the crippled city goes on. On the airplane I boarded leaving New Orleans, the majority of the passengers wore distinctive blue T-shirts with the slogan "Out of Chaos, Hope." They were volunteer workers from Presbyterian churches in Oregon, most of them of retirement age, who had spent a week gutting ruined houses in preparation for rehab work. During their stay they lived in a tent city and were fed by another group of volunteers from local churches. Some were completing their second tour of duty.

I became involved in the rebuilding campaign too. Before leaving on the kayaking trip, Judy brought an article in a gardening magazine to my attention. It described the devastation of Longue Vue Gardens, an estate donated to the community in 1968, by philanthropists Edith and Edgar Stern. It was being brought back to life with the help of volunteers from other parts of the country. Being an advocate of hands-on tourism, I went over to Longue Vue to see if the voluntary organization that runs the place still needed help.

They welcomed me with open arms. They had seen no out-of-town volunteers for many months, even though they still had much to do to rehabilitate the gardens. Head gardener Amy Graham put me right to work alongside other volunteers and staff. On my first morning, I joined a team weeding the iris beds. On other days, I helped plant pansies, watered planters and pots, and took part in a crash effort to plant 1,500 new boxwood shrubs to replace ones the seawater had killed.

Gardening with others is a highly social activity, with chatting positively encouraged, and I soon got to know other volunteers and staff. Reynard, a proud Creole living in his family's ancestral home, was a fount of opinion about local politics, culture, and history. Though I found his lectures spellbinding, his coworker Hillary had rather tired of them after so many months. "Reynard has an opinion on everything," she would gently comment, rolling her eyes as he launched into another disquisition. Reynard was also a talented artist (in a city of many talented artists, as the scores of galleries in the French Quarter demonstrate), and sported a baseball cap with the most stupendously tattered bill I have ever seen: an artifact worth real money in the right market.

Two lads from Honduras joined us as temporary laborers on the second day to plant the boxwood. They picked up the shovels and dug eagerly, but their smooth, uncalloused hands revealed they were not tillers of the soil by trade. They did not know a word of English, so Amy hadn't been able to learn their names. I became the interpreter. She would say, "Dig the trenches deeper," they would look up with a puzzled frown, and I would say "*Más profoundo, más hondo,*" and they nodded in understanding.

Volunteering and working with locals was a superb way to get to know about the city, its history, problems, restaurants, and places of interest. I felt sorry for the tourists I saw walking around the French Quarter peering tentatively into shops, so isolated from the life of the city. Here I was, only three days in town and practically a local myself. On Friday, Amy invited everybody to a bonfire party at her house. Her house stood next to the Mississippi, on the river side of the levee, but it was built on stilts so that it stood as high above the Mississippi as the top of the levee. We sat around the bonfire as the moon rose, and watched freighters glide up the waters I had paddled just a few days earlier.

The high point of my time in New Orleans will always be our arrival at Jackson Square. From a half mile away we could see two figures waving at us, and long before we could make out their features we knew it was Janice and Mercedes. On other kayak trips, I arrived at my final destination lonely and unanticipated. Here, for the first time, people who knew me, or who at least knew about me, were drawing me toward the goal with threads of enthusiasm and affection.

From all the hugging, questioning, and picture-taking of the arrival scene, two vignettes stand out.

A young woman with a guitar was seated on the great wooden steps, paying no attention to us, murmuring a song while she strummed the strings. Her body language suggested to me she might be depressed, and she seem to be wearing a "Leave me alone" sign. After we lifted the kayaks to the top of the levee, and while I was breaking down my boat for packing, Isaac went down and spoke to her. He was not rebuffed but carried on a 20-minute conversation.

I wondered how far he got with her. When he rejoined us, I asked, "Did you ask her name?"

"It's Linda."

No, we do not have a shy Isaac any more, I thought. *Ladies of Emigrant, Montana, beware the returning kayaker!*

Most people on the levee that afternoon merely glanced at us and walked on, but one man took a keen interest in our expedition. He was middle-aged, rather short with black hair, eager, and energetic. He spent an hour with us, taking pictures, helping us carry equipment to the top of the levee, and plying us with questions.

"What a wonderful adventure!" he said. "Imagine all the things you must have seen!" In all his comments, he was strictly the admiring observer: the idea of making such a trip himself had never crossed his mind.

As we were breaking up to go our separate ways, he retrieved a green electric-powered bicycle, and I asked him about it.

"Isn't it neat? I got it at Wal-Mart for $300."

"Can you pedal it, too?"

"Pedal or batteries, either or both. You see, at my age," he said, lowering his voice, "I need some extra help."

"How old are you?"

"Fifty-five," he said. "How old are you?"

I hesitated, so he supplied his own answer.

"I'd say about forty-five, right?"

I shrugged. When your age has been underestimated by 22 years, it's impolite to call attention to the error. He interpreted my shrug as agreement.

"It takes young guys like you two to make these kinds of trips," he said.

A jolt of sadness ran through me. How imprisoned was this man in oldness! He was two years younger than I was when I made my first kayak trip down the Potomac River, a decade and over a thousand kayaking miles ago. My brain struggled to find words to explain to him that age is a state of mind, that seeking adventure can't be limited by the calendar, that it's never too late to run away from home. But in those few moments atop that New Orleans levee, I couldn't see how to convey this idea in an effective way.

Then I thought, *Perhaps I could write a book that would show him.*

Afterword

LOOKING BACK ON THE ADVENTURES recounted in this book, I see a quite unexpected theme: the importance of people. One would think that solo kayak journeys are the last place to expect a human dimension. After all, isn't kayaking a purely physical activity, a contest of wooden paddles against agitated molecules of air and water? But as the journeys played out, the people I met proved to be the most memorable aspect. I began by running away from home, leaving family behind, but in the bargain I gained a much larger "family" of helpers, advisors, and comrades.

To say I am grateful to all of you who contributed to my journeys understates the case. You taught me that I could step ashore anywhere in America and enter into a relationship with helpful, interesting people. And at an even deeper level, you gave me a glimpse of the precious human interconnectedness of our planet. Some of you I have named, some I have not, and some of your names I changed for discretion, but it doesn't matter. You know who you are, and even if the kayaker you met and helped some years back wasn't me, it doesn't matter either, because struggling lonely kayakers, too, are all interconnected.

I want to acknowledge, also, the circle of friends who helped me in writing this book. The literary side of this project was an adventure in its own right, one that plunged me into a new and exciting realm. I began exploring the world of narrative writing by attending writers' conferences, and I profited immensely from their numerous panels, workshops, and discussions. I especially want to thank Jake Howe and the other volunteer organizers of the 2006 Flathead River Writers' Conference, and Mike Larsen, the prime mover of the 2007 San Francisco Writers' Conference.

I also owe a debt to fellow members of the Sandpoint chapter of the Idaho Writer's League, who patiently listened to early versions of this work and made many helpful suggestions for improvement.

Where would a writer of a kayaking book be without an editor? I can't resist answering: up the creek without a paddle. I was fortunate to have not one, but two skilled and thoughtful mentors supervising my literary strokes: Sandy Compton and Heather McElwain.

When Tom Sawyer returned from his death-defying adventures, he was welcomed back by an aunt so relieved she was willing to overlook his history of pranks. My family not only cheerfully did the overlooking, but pitched in to help produce this book. Reading and commenting on early versions were my sisters Dorothy and Clare, my daughters Ellen and Rachael, and my nephew Phil. I give an especially big hug to my wife Judy who supported the trips, and the book, at every turn, and who last summer finally came out with me on the lake in a kayak (we're still working on the camping in the rain part).

Sandpoint, Idaho
May 2008